Editor: Bill Buford
Deputy Editor: Ursula Doyle
Managing Editor: Claire Wrathall
Editorial Assistant and Picture Researcher: Cressida Leyshon
Contributing Editor: Robert McSweeney

Managing Director: Catherine Eccles
Financial Controller: Geoffrey Gordon
Marketing and Advertising: Sally Lewis
Circulation Manager: Lesley Palmer
Subscriptions: Kelly Cornwall
General Assistant: Nita Dent

Picture Editor: Alice Rose George
Executive Editor: Pete de Bolla
US Publisher: Anne Kinard, Granta, 250 West 57th Street, Suite 1316, New York, NY 10107.

Editorial and Subscription Correspondence: Granta, 2–3 Hanover Yard, Noel Road, London N1 8BE. Telephone: (071) 704 9776.
Fax: (071) 704 0474. Subscriptions: (071) 704 0470.
A one-year subscription (four issues) is £21.95 in Britain, £29.95 for the rest of Europe and £36.95 for the rest of the world.

Granta is printed in the United States of America. The paper used in this publication meets the minimum requirements of American National Standard for Information Sciences—Permanence of Paper for Printed Library Materials, ANSI Z39.48-1984 ∞

Granta is published by Granta Publications Ltd and distributed by Penguin Books Ltd, Harmondsworth, Middlesex, England; Viking Penguin, a division of Penguin Books USA Inc, 375 Hudson Street, New York, NY 10014, USA; Penguin Books Australia Ltd, Ringwood, Victoria, Australia; Penguin Books Canada Ltd, 10 Alcorn Avenue, Toronto, Ontario, Canada M4V 3B2; Penguin Books (NZ) Ltd, 182–190 Wairau Road, Auckland 10, New Zealand.

Cover by Senate. Cover photograph: Alex Webb (Magnum)

Granta 48, Autumn 1994
ISBN 0-14-014087-5

Contents

GRANTA

WILLIAM BOYD
THE DESTINY OF NATHALIE X

THE SCREEN IS BLACK

MAN'S VOICE (OVER): I once heard a theory about this town, this place where we work and wrangle, where we swindle and swive. It was told to me by this writer I knew. He said: 'It's only a dance, but then again, it's the only dance.' I'm not sure he's right, but, anyway, he's dead now . . .

FADE UP

Once upon a time—actually, not so very long ago at all, come to think of it—in east central West Africa, on one enervating May morning Aurélien No sat on the stoop of his father's house staring aimlessly at the road that led to Murkina Leto, state capital of the People's Republic of Kiq. The sun's force seemed to press upon the brown, dusty landscape with redundant intensity, Aurélien thought idly, there was surely no moisture left out there to evaporate and it seemed . . . He searched for a word for a second or two: it seemed 'stupid' that all that calorific energy should go to waste.

He called for his little brother Marius to fetch him another beer, but no reply came from inside the house. He scratched his cheek; he thought he could taste metal in his mouth—that new filling. He shifted his weight on his cane chair and wondered vaguely why cane made that curious squeaking sound. Then his eye was caught by the sight of a small, blue van that was making its way up the middle of the road with what seemed like undue celerity, tooting its horn at the occasional roadside pedestrian and browsing cow not so much to scare them out of the way as to announce the importance of this errand it was on.

To Aurélien's mild astonishment the blue van turned abruptly into his father's driveway and stopped equally abruptly before the front door. As the laterite dust thrown up by the tyres slowly dispersed, the postman emerged from the auburn cloud like a messenger from the gods carrying before him a stiff envelope blazoned with an important-looking crest.

MARIUS NO: For sure, I remember that day when he won the prize. Personally, I was glad of the distraction. He had been emmerding me all morning. 'Get this,' 'Get that,' 'Fetch me a

Photo: Susan O'Connor

beer.' I just knew it had gone quiet for ten minutes. When I came out on to the stoop, he was sitting there, looking even more vacant than normal, just staring at this paper in his hands. 'Hey, Coco,' I said to him. 'Military service, mm? Poor *salaud.* Wait till those bastard sergeants give you one up the *cul.*' He said nothing, so I took the paper from his hands and read it. It was the 100,000 francs that had shocked him, struck him dumb.

When *Le Destin de Nathalie X* (*metteur en scène* Aurélien No) won the Prix d'Or at the *concours général* in Paris of L'Ecole Supérieur des Etudes Cinématographiques (ESEC), the Kiq Minister of Culture (Aurélien's brother-in-law) laid on a reception for 200 guests at the ministry. After a long speech the Minister called Aurélien on to the podium to shake him publicly by the hand. Aurélien had gathered his small tight dreadlocks into a loose sheaf on the top of his head, and the photographs of that special evening show him startled and blinking in the silvery wash of the flash bulbs, some natural flinch causing the fronds of his dreadlock sheaf to toss simultaneously in one direction as if blown by a stiff breeze.

The Minister asked him what he planned to do with the prize money.

'Good question,' Aurélien said and thought for ten seconds or so before replying. 'It's a condition of the prize that I put the money towards another film.'

'Here in Kiq?' the Minister said, smiling knowingly.

'Of course.'

DELPHINE DRELLE: 'It's impossible,' I said when he called me. 'Completely out of the question. Are you mad? What kind of film could you make in Kiq?' He came to my apartment in Paris, he said he wanted me to be in his new film. I say I don't want to be an actress. Well, as soon as I started explaining, Aurélien saw I was making sense. That's what I like about Aurélien, by the way: he is responsive to the powers of reason. Absolutely not, I said to Aurélien, never in my life. He said he had an idea, but only I could do it. I said, look what happened the last time, do you think I'm crazy? I've only been out of the clinic one month. He just smiled at me. He said, what do you think if we go to Hollywood?'

Aurélien No turned out of the rental park at LAX and wondered which direction to take. Delphine Drelle sat beside him studying her face intently in the mirror of her compact and moaning about the dehydrating effect of international air travel. In the back seat of the car sat Bertrand Holbish, a photographer and ex-boyfriend of Delphine, squashed in the cramped space left by the two large scratched and dented aluminium boxes that held the camera and the sound equipment.

Aurélien turned left, drove 400 metres and turned left again. He saw a sign directing him to the freeway and followed it until he reached a hotel. Dollarwize Inn, he saw it was called as he pulled carefully into the forecourt. The hotel was a six-storey rectangle. The orange plastic cladding on the balconies had been bleached salmon pink by the sun.

'Here we are,' Aurélien said. 'This is perfect.'

'Where's Hollywood?' Bertrand Holbish asked.

'Can't be far away,' Aurélien said.

BERTRAND HOLBISH: Immediately, when he asked me, I said to Aurélien that I didn't know much about sound. He said you switch it on, you point the volume. No, you check the volume and you point the, ah, what's the word? . . . What? Ah, yes, 'boom'; I said: you pay my ticket? You buy me drugs? He said of course, only don't touch Delphine [laughs, coughs]. That's Aurélien for you, one crazy guy.

DELPHINE DRELLE: Did I tell you that he is a very attractive man, Aurélien? Yes? He's a real African, you know, strong face, strong African face . . . and his lips, they're like they're carved. He's tall, slim. He has this hair, it's like that tennis player, Noah, like little braids hanging down over his forehead. Sometimes he puts beads on the end of them. I don't like it so much. I want him to shave his head. Completely. He speaks real good English, Aurélien. I never knew this about him. I asked him once how he pronounced his name, and he said something like 'Ngoh'. He says it is a common name in Kiq. But everybody pronounces it differently. He doesn't mind.

When Aurélien went out the next day to scout for locations he discovered that the area they were staying in was called Westchester. He drove through the featureless streets—unusually wide, he thought, for such an inactive neighbourhood—the air charged and thunderous with landing jetliners, until he found a small cluster of shops beneath a revolving sign declaiming BROGAN'S MINI-MALL. There was a deli, a drugstore, a novelty store, a Korean grocery and a pizzeria-cum-coffee shop that had most of the features he was looking for: half a dozen tables on the sidewalk, a predominantly male staff, a licence to sell alcoholic beverages. He went inside, ordered a cappuccino and asked how long they stayed open in the evenings. Late, came the answer. For the first time since he had suggested coming to Los Angeles, Aurélien sensed a small tremor of excitement. Perhaps it would be possible after all. He looked at the expressionless tawny faces of the men behind the counter and the cheerful youths serving food and drink. He felt sure these gentlemen would allow him to film in their establishment—for a modest fee, of course.

MICHAEL SCOTT GEHN: Have you ever seen *Le Destin de Nathalie X*? Extraordinary film, extraordinary. No, I tell you, I'd put it right up there with *Un Chien Andalou*, Todd's *Last Walk*, *Chelsea Girls*, Downey's *Chafed Elbows*. That category of film. Surreal, bizarre . . . Let's not beat about the bush, sometimes downright incomprehensible, but it gets to you. Somehow, subcutaneously. You know, I spend more time thinking about certain scenes in *Nathalie X* than I do about Warner's annual slate. And it's my business, what more can I say? Do you smoke? Do you have any non-violent objections if I do? Thank you, you're very gracious. I'm not kidding, you can't be too careful here. *Nathalie X* . . . OK. It's very simple and outstandingly clever. A girl wakes up in her bed in her room . . .

Aurélien looked at his map. Delphine and Bertrand stood at his shoulder, sun-glassed, fractious.

'We have to go from here . . . to here.'

'Aurélien, when are we going to film?'

'Tomorrow. Maybe. First we walk it through.'

Delphine let her shoulders slump. 'But we have the stock. Why don't we start?'

'I don't know. I need an idea. Let's walk it through.'

He took Bertrand's elbow and guided him across the road to the other side. He made half a square with his thumbs and his forefingers and framed Delphine in it as she lounged against the exit sign of the Dollarwize Inn.

'Turn right,' Aurélien shouted across the road. 'I'll tell you which way to go.'

MICHAEL SCOTT GEHN: . . . a girl wakes up in her own bed in her own room, somewhere in Paris. She gets out of bed and puts on her make-up, very slowly, very deliberately. No score, just the noises she makes as she goes about her business. You know, paints her nails, mascara on eyelashes. She hums a bit, she starts to sing a song to herself, snatches of a song in English. Beatles song, from the *White Album*, what's it called? Oh yeah: 'Rocky Racoon'. This girl's French, right, and she's singing in English with a French accent, just quietly to herself. The song sounds totally different. Totally. Extraordinary effect. Bodywide goosebumps. This takes about twenty, thirty minutes. You are completely, but *completely*, held. You do not notice the time passing. That something so totally—let's not beat about the bush—banal, can hold you that way. Extraordinary. We're talking mundanity, here, absolute diurnal minutiae. I see, what, 250 movies a year in my business, not counting TV. I am replete with film. Sated. But I am held. No, mesmerized would be fair. [Pause.] Did I tell you the girl was naked?

'Turn left,' Aurélien called.

Delphine obliged and walked past the mirror-glass façade of an office building.

'Stop.'

Aurélien made a note on the map and turned to Bertrand.

'What could she do here, Bertrand? She needs to do something.'

'I don't know. How should I know?'

'Something makes her stop.'

'She could step in some dog shit.'

Aurélien reflected for a while. He looked around him: at the cracked, parched concrete of the street, the dusty burnish on the few parked cars. There was a bleached, fumy quality to the light that day, a softened glare that hurt the eyes. The air reverberated as another jumbo hauled itself out of LAX.

'Not a bad idea,' he said. 'Thanks, Bertrand.' He called to Delphine. 'OK, go up to the end of the road and turn left.'

MICHAEL SCOTT GEHN: I've written a lot about this movie, analysed the hell out of it, the way it's shot, the way it manipulates mood, but it only struck me the other day how it works. Essentially, basically. It's all in the title, you see. '*Le Destin*'. The Destiny of Nathalie X. Destiny. What does destiny have in store for this girl, I should say, this astoundingly attractive girl? She gets up, she puts on her make-up, she sings a song, she gets dressed. She leaves her apartment building and walks through the streets of Paris to a café. It's night-time. She sits in this café and orders a beer. We're watching her, we're waiting. She drinks more beers, she seems to be getting drunk. People come and go. We wait. We wonder: What is the destiny of Nathalie X? (It's pronounced 'eeks' in French. Not 'ecks', 'eeks'.) And then? But I don't want to spoil the movie for you.

They started filming on their sixth day in Los Angeles. It was late afternoon—almost magic hour—and the orange sun basted the city in a warm, viscous light. Aurélien shot the sequence of the walk in front of the mirror-glass building. The moving cloudscape on the mirror-glass curtain wall was disturbingly beautiful. Aurélien had a moment's regret that he was filming in black and white.

Delphine wore a short, black skirt and a loose, V-neck, taupe cashmere sweater (no bra). On her feet she wore skin-coloured kid loafers, so fine you could roll them into a ball. She had a fringed suede bag over her shoulder. Her long hair was dyed a light sandy blonde and—after much debate—was down.

Aurélien set up the camera across the road for the first take. Bertrand stood beside him and pointed his microphone in the general direction of Delphine.

Aurélien switched on the camera, chalked SCENE ONE on the clapperboard, walked into frame, clicked it and said *'Vas y, Delphine.'*

Nathalie X walked along the sidewalk. When she reached the middle of the mirror-glass wall she stopped. She took off one of her shoes and peeled a coin of chewing-gum from its sole. She stuck the gum to the glass wall, refitted her shoe and walked on.

MICHAEL SCOTT GEHN: I have to say as a gesture of contempt for Western materialism, the capitalist macrostructure that we function in, that takes some beating. And it's not in the French version. Aurélien No has been six days in Los Angeles and he comes up with something as succinct, as moodily epiphanic as that. That's what I call talent. Not raw talent, talent of the highest sophistication.

BERTRAND HOLBISH: The way Delphine cut her hair, you know, is the clue, I think. It's blonde, right? Long, and she has a fringe, OK? But not like anybody else's fringe. It's just too long. It hangs to her lower eyelash. To here [gestures], to the middle of her nose. So she shakes her head all the time to clear her vision a little. She pulls it aside—like this—with one finger when she wants to see something a little better . . . You know, many, many people look at Delphine and find this very exciting, sexually, I mean. She's a pretty girl, for sure, nice body, nice face. But I see these girls everywhere. Especially in Los Angeles. It's something about this fringe business that makes her different. People look at her all the time. When we were waiting for Aurélien we—Delphine and me—used to play backgammon. For hours. The fringe, hanging there, over her eyes. It drove me fucking crazy. I offered her 500 dollars to cut it one centimetre, just one centimetre. She refused. She knew, Delphine, she knew.

Aurélien filmed the walk to the café first. It took four days, starting late afternoon, always approaching the café at dusk.

He filmed Nathalie's *levée* in one sustained twelve-hour burst. Delphine woke, made up, sang and dressed eight times that day in a series of long takes, cuts only coming when the film ran out. The song changed: Delphine sang Bob Dylan's 'She belongs to me' with the pronoun changed to 'he'. This was Delphine's idea, and a good one, Aurélien thought. The only problem was she kept forgetting. 'He's an artist, she don't look back,' Delphine sang in her flat, breathy voice as she combed her hair. 'He never stumbles, she's got no place to fall.'

Every evening they would go to the pizzeria and eat. Aurélien insisted that Delphine get drunk, not knee-walking drunk, but as far as woozy inebriation. Of course the waiters came to know them, and conversation ensued. 'What you guys doin' here anyway? Making a movie? Great. Another beer for the lady? No problemo.'

After a week's regular visiting Aurélien asked the owner, a small nervy man called George Malinverno, if they could film at the pizzeria, outside on the 'terrace', for one night only. They agreed on a remuneration of 200 dollars.

MICHAEL SCOTT GEHN: Have you ever heard of the Topeka Film Festival? That's Topeka, Kansas? No? Neither have I. So you can understand that I was kind of pissed when my editor assigned me to cover it. It ran a week, the theme was 'Kansas in the Western 1970–1980'. It's not my subject, my last book was on Murnau, for Christ's sake, but let's not get embroiled in office politics. The point is I'm on my way to the airport and I realize I've left my razor and shaving-foam behind. I pull into this mini-mall where there's a drugstore. I'm coming out of the shop and I see there's a film crew setting up a shot at the pizzeria. Normally I see a film crew and chronic catatonia sets in. But there's something about this one: the guy holding the boom mike looks like he's stoned—even I can see that it keeps dropping into shot. So I wander over. The camera is set up behind these plants, kind of poking through a gap, like it's hidden or something. And there's this black guy behind the camera with this great hair with beads on it. I see he's DP and clapperboy and director. He calls out into the darkness and this sensational-looking girl walks into the pizzeria terrace thing. She sits down and orders a beer, and they just keep filming. After about two minutes, the sound man drops the boom, and they have to start over. I hear them talking—French. I couldn't believe it. I had this guy figured for some wannabe homeboy director out of South Central LA. But they're talking French to each other. When was the last time a French crew shot a movie in this town? I introduced myself, and that's when he told me about *Nathalie X* and the Prix d'Or. I bought them all some drinks, and he told me his story and gave me a video cassette of the movie. Fuck Topeca, I thought, I knew this was too good to miss. French underground movies shooting next door to LAX. Are you kidding me? They were all staying in some fleabag motel under the flightpath, for God's sake. I called my editor and threatened to take the feature to *American Film*. He reassigned me.

The night's shooting at the pizzeria did not go well. Bertrand proved incapable of holding the boom aloft for more than two minutes, and this was one sequence where Aurélien knew he needed sound. He spent half an hour taping a mike under Delphine's table and snaking the wires round behind the potted plants. Then this man who said he was a film critic turned up and offered to buy them a drink. While Aurélien was talking to him, Delphine drank three Margaritas and a Negroni. When they tried to restart, her reflexes had slowed to such an extent that when she remembered she had to throw the glass of beer, the waiter had turned away, and she missed completely. Aurélien wrapped it up for the night. Holbish wandered off, and Aurélien drove Delphine back to the hotel. She was sick in the parking-lot and started to cry, and that's when Aurélien thought about the gun.

KAISER PREVOST: I rarely read *film/e*. It's way too pretentious. Ditto that creep Michael Scott Gehn. Any guy with three names and I get irrationally angry. What's wrong with plain old Michael Gehn? Are there so many Michael Gehns out there that he has to distinguish himself? 'Oh, you mean Michael *Scott* Gehn, I got you now.' I'd like a Teacher's, straight up, with three ice cubes. Three. Thank you. Anyway for some reason I bought it that week—it was the issue with that great shot of Jessica, no, Lanier on the cover—and I read the piece about this French director Aurélien No and this remake *Seeing Through Nathalie* he was shooting in town. Gehn—sorry Michael Scott Gehn—is going on like this guy is sitting there holding God's hand, and I read about the Prix d'Or and this *Nathalie X* film and I think, hmmm, has Aurélien got representation? This is Haig. This is not Teacher's.

MICHAEL SCOTT GEHN: I knew, I just knew when this young guy Kaiser Prevost calls me up, things would change. 'Hi, Michael,' he says, 'Kaiser Prevost here.' I don't know jack shit about any Kaiser Prevost but I do know I hate it when someone uses my Christian name from the get-go—what's wrong with Mister Gehn? Also his tone just assumes, just oozes the assumption that I'm going to know who he is. I mean, I am a film critic of some reputation, if I may be immodest for a moment, and these young guys in the agencies . . . There's a problem of perspectives, that's what it comes down to, that's what bedevils us. I have a theory about this town: there is no overview, nobody steps back, no one stands on the mountain looking down on the valley. Imagine an army composed entirely of officers. Let me put it another way: imagine an army where everyone *thinks* they're an officer. That's Hollywood, that's the film business. No one wants to accept the hierarchy, no one will admit they are a foot soldier. And I'm sorry, a young agent in a boutique agency is just a GI Joe to me. Still, he was a persuasive fellow and he had some astute and flattering things to say about the article. I told him where Aurélien was staying.

Aurélien No met Kaiser Prevost for breakfast in the coffee shop of the Dollarwize. Prevost looked around him as if he had just emerged from some prolonged comatose sleep.

'You know, I've lived in this town for all my life and I don't think I've ever even driven through here. And as for shooting a movie . . . It's a first.'

'Well, it was right for me.'

'Oh no. I appreciate that. I think it's fresh, original. Gehn certainly thinks a lot of you.'

'Who?'

Prevost showed him the article in *film/e.* Aurélien flicked through it. 'He has written a lot.'

'Have you got a rough assembly of the new movie? Anything I could see?'

'No.'

'Any dailies? Maybe you call them rushes.'

'There are no dailies on this film. None of us see anything until it is finished.'

'The ultimate *auteur*, huh? That is impressive. More than that, it's cool.'

Aurélien chuckled. 'No, it's a question of—what do you say?—*faute de mieux.*'

'I couldn't have put it better myself. Look, Aurélien, I'd like you to meet somebody, a friend of mine at a studio. Can I fix that up? I think it would be mutually beneficial.'

'Sure. If you like.'

KAISER PREVOST: I have a theory about this town, this place, about the way it works: it operates best when people go beyond the bounds of acceptable behaviour. You reach a position, a course of action suggests itself, and you say, 'This makes me morally uncomfortable,' or 'This will constitute a betrayal of friendship.' In any other walk of life you withdraw, you rethink. But my theory goes like this: make it your working maxim. *When you find yourself in a position of normative doubt then that is the sign to commit.* My variation on this theory is that the really successful people go one step further. They find themselves in this moral grey area, they move right on into the black. Look at Vincent Bandine.

I knew I was doing the right thing with Aurélien No because I had determined not to tell my boss. Sheldon started ArtFocus after ten years at ICM. It was going well but it's clear that the foundations are giving. Two months ago we lost Larry Swiftsure. Last Saturday I get a call from Sheldon: Donata Vail has walked to CAA. His own Donata. He was weeping and was looking for consolation, which I hope I provided. Under these circumstances it seemed to me at best morally dubious that I should go behind his back and try and set up a deal for Aurélien at Alcazar. I was confident it was the only route to take.

The gun idea persisted, it nagged at Aurélien. He talked about it with Bertrand, who thought it was an amusing notion.

'A gun, why not? Pam-pam-pam-pam.'

'Could you get me one? A handgun?' Aurélien asked. 'Maybe one of those guys you know . . . '

'A prop gun? Or a real one?'

'Oh, I think it should be real. Don't tell Delphine, though.'

The next day Bertrand showed Aurélien a small, scarred automatic. It cost 500 dollars. Aurélien did not question him about its provenance.

He reshot the end of Nathalie's *levée*. Nathalie, dressed, is about to leave her room, her hand is on the doorknob. She pauses, turns and goes to a dresser, from the top drawer of which she removes the gun. She checks the clip and places it in her fringed suede shoulder bag. She leaves.

He and Delphine had a prolonged debate about whether they should reshoot the entire walk to the restaurant. Delphine thought it was pointless. How, she argued, would the audience know if the gun were in her shoulder bag or not? But *you* would know, Aurélien countered, and everything might change. Delphine maintained that she would walk the same way whether she had a gun in her bag or not; also they had been in Los Angeles for three weeks and she was growing bored; *Le Destin* had been filmed in five days. A compromise was agreed: they would reshoot only the pizzeria sequence. Aurélien went off to negotiate another night's filming.

BOB BERGER: I hate to admit it but I was grateful to Kaiser Prevost when he brought the *Nathalie X* project to me. As I told him, I had admired Aurélien No's work for some years and was excited and honoured at the possibility of setting up his first English-language film. More to the point, the last two films I exec-ed at Alcazar had done me no favours: *Disintegrator* had only grossed thirteen before they stopped tracking, and *Sophomore Nite II* had gone straight to video. I liked the idea of doing something with more art quality and with a European kind of angle. I asked Kaiser to get a script to me soonest and I raised the project at our Monday morning staff meeting. I said I thought it would be a perfect vehicle for Lanier Cross. Boy, did that make Vincent sit up. Dirty old toad (he's my uncle).

KAISER PREVOST: I'll tell you one fact about Vincent Bandine. He has the cleanest teeth and the healthiest gums in Hollywood. Every morning a dental nurse comes to his house and flosses and cleans his teeth for him. Every morning, 365 days a year. That's what I call class. Have you any idea how much that must cost?

Kaiser Prevost thought he detected an unsettled quality about Aurélien as he drove him to the meeting at Alcazar. Aurélien was frowning as he looked about him. The day was perfect, the air clear, the colours ideally bright; more than that he was going to a deal meeting at a major minor studio, or minor major depending on whom you were talking to. Usually in these cases the anticipation in the car would be heady, palpable. Aurélien just made clicking noises in his mouth and fiddled with the beads on the end of his dreadlocks. Prevost told him about Alcazar Films, its money base, its ten-picture slate, its deals or potential deals with Goldie, Franklin Dean, Joel, Demi, Carlo Sancarlo and ItalFilm. The names seemed to make no impact.

As they turned up Coldwater to go over into the valley, Prevost finally had to ask if everything was all right.

'There's a slight problem,' Aurélien admitted. 'Delphine has left.'

'That's too bad,' Prevost said, trying to keep the excitement out of his voice. 'Gone back to France?'

'I don't know. She's left with Bertrand.'

'Bitch, man.'

'We still have the whole last scene to reshoot.'

'Listen, Aurélien, relax. One thing you learn about working in this town. Everything can be fixed. Everything.'

'How can I finish without Delphine?'

'Have you ever heard of Lanier Cross?'

VINCENT BANDINE: My nephew has two sterling qualities: he's dumb and he's eager to please. He's a good-looking kid too, and that helps, no doubt about it. Sometimes, sometimes, he gets it right. Sometimes he has a sense for the popular mood. When he started talking about this *Destiny of Nathalie* film I thought he was way out of his depth until he mentioned the fact that Lanier Cross would be buck naked for the first thirty minutes. I said get the French guy in, tie him up, get him together with Lanier. She'll go for the French part. If the No fellow won't play, get the Englishman in, what's his name, Tim Pascal, he'll do it. He'll do anything I tell him.

I have a theory about this town: there's too much respect for art. That's where we make all our mistakes, all of them. But if that's a given, then I'm prepared to work with it once in a while. Especially if it'll get me Lanier Cross nekkid.

MICHAEL SCOTT GEHN: When I heard that Aurélien No was doing a deal with Vincent Bandine at Alcazar I was both suicidal and oddly proud. If you'd asked me where was the worst home possible for a remake of *Nathalie X* I'd have said Alcazar straight off. But that's what heartens me about this burg, this place we fret and fight in. I have a theory about this town: they all talk about the 'business', the 'industry', how hard-nosed and bottom-line obsessed they are, but it's not true. Or rather not the whole truth. Films of worth are made, and I respect the place for it. God, I even respected Vincent Bandine for it and I never thought those words would ever issue from my mouth. We shouldn't say: look at all the crap that gets churned out; instead we should be amazed at the good films that do emerge from time to time. There is a heart here and it's still beating, even though the pulse is kind of thready.

Aurélien was impressed with the brutal economy of Bob Berger's office. A black ebony desk sat in the middle of a charcoal grey carpet. Two large, black leather sofas were separated by a thick sheet of glass resting on three sharp cones. On one wall were two black-and-white photographs of lily trumpets, and on another was an African mask. There was no evidence of work or the tools of work apart from the long flattened telephone on his desk. Berger himself was wearing crushed banana linen, he was in his mid twenties, tall and deeply tanned.

Berger shook Aurélien's hand warmly, his left hand gripping Aurélien's forearm firmly as if Aurélien were a drowning man about to be hauled from a watery grave. He drew Aurélien to one of the leather sofas and sat him upon it. Prevost slid down beside him. A great variety of drinks were offered, though Aurélien's choice of beer caused some consternation. Berger's assistant was dispatched in search of some. Prevost and Berger's decaff espressos arrived promptly.

Prevost gestured at the mask. 'Home sweet home, eh, Aurélien?'

'Excuse me?'

'I love African art,' Berger said. 'What part of Africa are you from?'

'Kiq.'

'Right,' Berger said.

There was a short silence.

'Oh. Congratulations,' Berger said.

'Excuse me?'

'On the prize. Prix d'Or. Well deserved. Kaiser, have we got a print of *Nathalie X*?'

'We're shipping it over from Paris. It'll be here tomorrow.'

'It will?' Aurélien said, a little bemused.

'Everything can be fixed, Aurélien.'

'I want Lanier to see it. And Vincent.'

'Bob, I don't know if it's really Vincent's scene.'

'He has to see it. OK, after we sign Lanier.'

'I think that would be wise, Bob.'

'I want to see it again, I must say. Extraordinary piece.'

'You've seen it?' Aurélien said.

'Yeah. At Cannes, I think. Or possibly Berlin. Have we got a script yet, Kaiser?'

'There is no script. Extant.'

'We've got to get a synopsis. A treatment at least. Mike'll want to see something on paper. He'll never let Lanier go otherwise.'

'Shit. We need a goddamn writer, then,' Prevost said.

'Davide?' Berger said into the speaker phone. 'We need a writer. Get Matt Friedrich.' He turned to Aurélien. 'You'll like him. One of the old school. What?' He listened to the phone again and sighed. 'Aurélien, we're having some trouble tracking down your beer. What do you say to a Dr Pepper?'

BOB BERGER: I have a theory about this town, this place. You have people in powerful executive positions who are, to put it kindly, very ordinary-looking types. I'm not talking about intellect, I'm talking about looks. The problem is these ordinary-looking people control the lives of individuals with sensational genetic advantages. That's an unbelievably volatile mix, I can tell you. And it cuts both ways; it can be very uncomfortable. It's fine for me, I'm a handsome guy, I'm in good shape. But for most of my colleagues . . . It's the source of many of our problems. That's why I took up golf.

LANIER CROSS: Tolstoy said: 'Life is a *tartine de merde* that we are obliged to consume daily.'

'This is for me?' Aurélien said, looking at the house, its landscaped, multi-levelled sprawl, the wide maw of its vast garage.

'You can't stay down by the airport,' Prevost said. 'Not any more. You can shoot in Westchester but you can't live there.'

A young woman emerged from the front door. She had short chestnut hair, a wide white smile and was wearing a spandex leotard and heavy climbing boots.

'This is Nancy, your assistant.'

'Hi. Good to meet you, Aurélien. Did I say that right?'

'Aurélien.'

'Aurélien?'

'It's not important.'

'The office is in back of the tennis court. It's in good shape.'

'Look, I got to fly, Aurélien. You're meeting Lanier Cross seven-thirty a.m. at the Hamburger Haven on the Shore. Nancy'll fix everything up.'

To his surprise Kaiser Prevost then embraced him. When they broke apart Aurélien thought he saw tears in his eyes.

'We'll fucking show them, man, we'll fucking show them.

Onward and upward, way to fucking go.'

'Any news of Delphine?'

'Who? No. Nothing yet. Any problems, call me, Aurélien. Twenty-four hours a day.'

MATT FRIEDRICH: *Le Destin de Nathalie X* was not as boring as I had expected but then I was expecting terminal boredom. I was bored, sure, but it was nice to see Paris again. That's the great thing they've got going for them, French films, they carry this wonderful cargo of nostalgic francophilia for all non-French audiences. Pretty girl too, easy on the eye. I never thought I could happily watch a girl drink herself drunk on beer in a French café but I did. It was not a wasted hour and a half.

It sure freaked out Prevost and Berger, though. 'Extraordinary,' Prevost said, clearly moved, 'extraordinary piece.' Berger mused awhile before announcing, 'That girl is a fox.' 'Michael Scott Gehn thinks it's a masterpiece,' I said. They agreed, vehemently. It's one of my tricks: when you don't know what to say, when you hated it or you're really stuck and anything qualified won't pass muster, use someone else's praise. Make it up if you have to. It's infallible, I promise.

I asked them how long they wanted the synopsis to be: sentence length or half a page. Berger said it had to be over forty pages, closely spaced, so people would be reluctant to read it. 'We already have coverage,' he said, 'but we need a document.' 'Make it as surreal and weird as you like,' Prevost said, handing me the video cassette, 'that's the whole point.'

We walked out into the Alcazar lot and went in search of our automobiles. 'When's he meeting Lanier?' Berger said. 'Tomorrow morning. She'll love him, Bob,' Prevost said. 'It's a done deal.' Berger gestured at the heavens. 'Bountiful Jehovah,' he said, 'get me Lanier.'

I looked at these two guys, young enough to be my sons, as they crouched into their sleek, haunchy cars under a tallow moon, fantasizing loudly, belligerently, about this notional film, the deals, the stars, and I felt enormous pity for them. I have a theory about this town: our trouble is we are at once the most confident and the most insecure people in the world. We seem bulging with self-assurance, full of loud-voiced swagger, but in reality we're terrified, or we hate ourselves, or we're all taking happy pills of some order or another, or seeing shrinks, or getting counselled by fakirs and shamans, or fleeced by a whole gallimaufry of frauds and mountebanks. This is the Faustian pact—or should I say this is the Faust deal—you have to make in order to live and work here: you get it all, sure, but you get royally fucked up in the process. That's the price you pay. It's in the contract.

Aurélien No was directed to Lanier Cross's table in the dark rear angles of the Hamburger Haven. Another man and a woman were sitting with her. Aurélien shook her thin hand. She was beautiful, he saw, but so small, a child-woman, the musculature of a twelve-year-old with the sexual features of an adult. He found it hard not to stare at her breasts.

She introduced the others, an amiable, grinning, broad-shouldered youngster and a lean, crop-haired woman in her forties with a fierce, strong face.

'This is my husband,' she said. 'Kit Vermeer. And this is Naomi Tashourian. She's a writer we work with.'

'We love your work,' Kit said.

'Beautiful film,' echoed Lanier.

'You've seen it?' Aurélien said.

'We saw it two hours ago,' Lanier said.

Aurélien looked at his watch: Nancy had made sure he was punctual—7.30 a.m.

'I called Berger, said I had to see it before we met.'

'We tend to sleep in the day,' Kit said. 'Like bats.'

'Like lemurs,' Lanier said. 'I don't like bats.'

'—like lemurs.'

'It's a beautiful film,' Lanier said. 'That's why we wanted to meet with you.' She reached up and unfastened a large plastic bulldog clip on the top of her head and uncoiled a great dark glossy hank of hair a yard long. She pulled and tightened it, screwing it up, winding it around her right hand, piling it back on the top of her head before she refastened it in position with the clip. Everyone remained silent during this operation.

'That's why we wanted you to meet Naomi.'

'This is a remake, right?' Naomi said.

'Yes. I think so.'

'Excellent,' Lanier said. 'I know Kit wants to put something to you. Kit?'

Kit leaned across the table. 'I want to play the waiter,' he said.

Aurélien thought before answering. 'The waiter is only in the film for about two minutes, right at the end.'

'Which is why we thought you should meet Naomi.'

'The way I see it,' Naomi said, 'is that Nathalie has been in a relationship with the waiter. That's why she goes to the restaurant. And we could see, in flashback, you know, their relationship.'

'I think it could be extraordinary, Aurélien,' Lanier said.

'And I know that because of our situation, I and Lanier, our marital situation,' Kit added, 'we could bring something extraordinary to that relationship. And beautiful.'

Lanier and Kit kissed each other, briefly but with some passion, before resuming the argument in favour of the flashback. Aurélien ordered a beer and some steak and french fries as they fleshed out the relationship between Nathalie X and her waiter-lover.

'And Naomi would write this?' Aurélien asked.

'Yes,' Lanier said. 'I'm not ready to work with another writer just yet.'

'I think Bob Berger has another writer—Matt Friedrich.'

'What's he done?' Kit said.

'We have to let Matt go, Aurélien,' Lanier said. 'You shouldn't drink beer this early in the morning.'

'Why not?'

'I'm an alcoholic,' Kit said. 'It's the thin end of the wedge, believe me.'

'Could you guys leave me alone with Aurélien?' Lanier said.

They left.

LANIER CROSS: I have a theory about this town: the money doesn't matter. THE MONEY DOESN'T MATTER. Everybody thinks it's about the money but they're wrong. They think it's only because of the money that people put up with the godawful shit that's dumped on them. That there can be only one possible reason why people are prepared to be so desperately unhappy. Money. Not so. Consider this: everybody who matters in this town has more than enough money. They don't need any more money. And I'm not talking about the studio heads, the top directors, the big stars, the people with obscene amounts. There are thousands of people in this town, possibly tens of thousands, who are involved in movies who have more money than is reasonably acceptable. So it's not about money, it can't be, it's about something else. It's about being at the centre of the world.

'She loved you,' Kaiser Prevost said. 'She's all over you like a rash.'

'Any news of Delphine?'

'Who? Ah, no. What did you say to her, to Lanier? Bob called, she'll do it for nothing. Well, half her normal fee. Sensational idea about Kit Vermeer. Excellent. Why didn't I think of that? Maybe that's what swung it.'

'No, it was her idea. How are we going to finish the film without Delphine?'

'Aurélien. Please. Forget Delphine Drelle. We have Lanier Cross. We fired Friedrich, we got Tashourian writing the flashback. We're in business, my son, in business.'

NAOMI TASHOURIAN: I have a theory about this town, this place. Don't be a woman.

Aurélien sat in the cutting-room with Barker Lear, an editor, as they ran what existed of *Seeing Through Nathalie* on the Moviola.

Barker, a hefty man with a grizzled ginger goatee, watched Delphine sit down at the pizzeria and order a beer. She drank it down and ordered another, then the sound boom which had been bobbing erratically in and out of frame for the past few minutes fell fully into view and the screen went black.

Barker turned and looked at Aurélien who was frowning and tapping his teeth with the end of a pencil.

'That's some film,' Barker said. 'Who's the girl? She's extraordinary.'

'Delphine Drelle.'

'She a big star in France?'

'No.'

'Sorta hypnotic effect, she has . . . ' He shrugged. 'Shame about the boom.'

'Oh, I don't worry about that sort of thing,' Aurélien said. 'It adds to the verisimilitude.'

'I don't follow.'

'You're meant to know it's a film. That's why the end works so well.'

'So what happens in the end? You've still got to shoot it, right?'

'Yes. I don't know what happens. Neither does Delphine.'

'You don't say?'

'She gets drunk you see. We watch her getting drunk. We don't cut away. We don't know what she might do. That's what makes it so exciting—that's the "Destiny of Nathalie X".'

'I see . . . So, ah, what happened at the end of the first film?'

'She goes to the café, she drinks six or seven beers very quickly and I can see she's quite drunk. She orders another drink, and when the waiter brings it, she throws it in his face.'

'You don't say? Then what?'

'They have a fight. Delphine and the waiter. They really hit each other. It's fantastic. Delphine, she's had this training, self-defence. She knees this guy in the *couilles*. Boff!'

'Fascinating.'

'He falls over. She collapses, crying, she turns to me, swears at me. Runs off into the night. The end. It's amazing.'

Barker rubbed his beard, thinking. He glanced at Aurélien covertly.

'Going to do the same thing here?'

'No, no. It's got to be different for the USA, for Hollywood. That's why I gave her the gun.'

'Is it a real gun?'

'Oh yes. Otherwise what would be the point?'

BARKER LEAR: I definitely had him for a wacko at first, but after I spent an afternoon with him, talking to him, it seemed to me he really knew what he was doing. He was a real calm guy, Aurélien. He had his own vision, didn't worry about other people, what other people might think about him. And it was the easiest editing job I ever did. Long, long takes. Lot of hand-held stuff. The walk had a few reverses, few mid-shots, dolly shots. And the film was kind of exciting, I have to admit, and I was really quite disappointed that he still hadn't shot the end. This girl Delphine, with this crazy blonde fringe over her eyes, there was definitely something wild about her. I mean, who knows, once she got loaded, what she might have done. Maybe Aurélien wasn't a wacko, but she definitely was.

You know, I have a theory about this town, this place. I've been working here for twenty-five years and I've seen them all. In this town you have very, very clever people and very, very wacko people, and the problem is—and that's what makes this place different—the very clever people *have* to work with the very wacko people. They have to, they can't help it, it's the nature of the job. That doesn't happen other places for one simple reason—clever and wacko don't mix.

Aurélien stood by the pool with Nancy, enjoying the subdued play of morning light on the water. Today Nancy's hair was white blonde, and she wore a tutu over her leotard, and cowboy boots with spurs. She handed him a pair of car keys and an envelope with 1,000 dollars in it.

'That's the new rental car. Celica OK? And there's your per diem. And you've got dinner at Lanier Cross's at six-thirty.'

'Six-thirty p.m.?'

'Ah, yeah . . . She can make it six if you prefer. She asked me to tell you it will be vegetarian.'

'What are all those men doing? Is it some kind of military exercise?'

'Those are the gardeners. Shall I make them go away?'

'No, it's fine.'

'And Tim Pascal called.'

'Who's he?'

'He's an English film director. He has several projects in

development at Alcazar. He wanted to know if you wanted to lunch or drink or whatever.'

The doorbell rang. Aurélien strode across the several levels of his cool, white living-room to answer it; as he did so, the bell rang twice again. It was Delphine.

KAISER PREVOST: I have a theory about this town: it doesn't represent the fulfilment of the American dream, it represents the fulfilment of an American reality. It rewards relentless persistence, massive stamina, ruthlessness and the ability to live with grotesque failure. Look at me: I am a smallish guy, a hundred and thirty-eight pounds, with pretty severe myopia, and near average academic qualifications. But I have a personable manner and an excellent memory and a good head of hair. I will work hard and I will take hard decisions and I have developed the thickest of thick skins. With these attributes in this town nothing can stop me. Or those like me. We are legion. We know what they call us but we don't care. We don't need contacts, we don't need influence, we don't need talent, we don't need cosmetic surgery. That's why I love this place. It allows us to thrive. That's why when I heard Aurélien had never showed for dinner with Lanier Cross I didn't panic. People like me take that kind of awful crisis in their stride.

Aurélien turned over and gently kissed Delphine's right breast. She stubbed out her cigarette and hunched into him.

'This house is incredible, Aurélien. I like it here.'

'Where's Holbish?'

'You promised you wouldn't mention him again. I'm sorry Aurélien, I don't know what made me do it.'

'No, I'm just curious.'

'He's gone to Seattle.'

'Well, we can manage without him. Are you ready?'

'Of course, it's the least I can do. What about the pizzeria?'

'I was given 1,000 dollars cash today. I knew it would come in useful.'

MATT FRIEDRICH: I have to admit I was hoping for the *Seeing Through Nathalie* rewrite. When Bob Berger fired me and said that Naomi Tashourian was the new writer, it hurt for a while. It always does no matter how successful you are. But in my case I was due a break and I thought *Nathalie* was it. I've missed out on my last three Guild arbitrations, and a Lanier Cross film would have helped, however half-baked, however art-house. Berger said they would honour the fee for the synopsis I did (obfuscation takes on new meaning), but I guess the cheque is still in the post. But, I do not repine, as a great English novelist once said, I just get on with the job.

I have a theory about this town, this *Spielraum* where we dream and dawdle: one of our problems—perhaps it's *the* problem—is that here ego always outstrips ability. Always. That applies to everyone: writers, directors, actors, heads of production, d-boys and unit runners. It's our disease, our mark of Cain. When you have success here you think you can do anything and that's the great error. The success diet is too rich for our digestive systems: it poisons us, addles the brain. It makes us blind. We lose our self-knowledge. My advice to all those who make it is this: *take the job you would have done if the film had been a flop.* Don't go for the big one, don't let those horizons recede. Do the commercial, the TV pilot, the documentary, the three-week rewrite, the character role or whatever it was you had lined up first. Do that job and then maybe you can reach for the forbidden fruit, but at least you'll have your feet on the ground.

'Kaiser?'

'Bob?'

'He's not in the house, Kaiser.'

'Shit.'

'He's got to phone her. He's got to apologize.'

'No. He's got to lie.'

'She called Vincent.'

'Fuck. The bitch.'

'That's how bad she wants to do it. I think it's a good sign.'

'Where is that African bastard? I'll kill him.'

'Nancy says the French babe showed.'

'Oh, no. No fuckin' no!'

'It gets worse, Kaiser. Vincent told me to call Tim Pascal.'

'Who the fuck's he?'
'Some English director. Lanier wants to meet with him.'
'Who's his agent?'
'Sheldon . . . Hello? Kaiser?'

GEORGE MALINVERNO: I got a theory about his town, this place: everybody likes pizza. Even the French. We got to know them real well, I guess. They came back every night, the French. The tall black guy, the ratty one, the blonde girl. Real pretty girl. Every night they come. Every night they eat pizza. Every night she ties one on. Everybody likes pizza [bitter laugh]. Everybody. Too bad I didn't think of it first, huh?

They film, one night. And the girl, she's steaming. Then, I don't know, something goes wrong and we don't see them for a while. Then he comes back. Just the black guy, Aurélien, and the girl. He says can they film, one night, 1,000 bucks. I say for sure. So he sets up the sound and he sets up the camera behind the bushes. You know it's not a disturbance, exactly. I never see anybody make a film like this before. A thousand bucks, it's very generous. So the girl she walks up, she takes a seat, she orders beer and keeps on drinking. Soon she's pretty stewed. Aurélien sits behind the bushes, just keeps filming. Some guy tries to pick her up, puts his hand on the table, like, leans over, she takes a book of matches, like that one, and does something to the back of his hand with the corner. I couldn't see what she did, but the guy gasps with pain, shudders like this, just backs off.

Then we get a big party in, birthday party, they'd already booked, fourteen people. She sits there drinking and smoking, Aurélien's filming. Then we bring the cake out of the kitchen, candles all lit. Whenever there's a birthday we get Chico to sing. Chico, the little waiter, tubby guy, wanted to be an opera singer. Got a fine, strong voice. He's singing 'Happy Birthday to You'—he's got a kind of drawn-out, elaborate way of singing it. Top of his voice, *molto vibrato*, you know. Next thing I know, the girl's on her feet with a fuckin' gun in her hand, screaming in French. Nobody can hear because Chico's singing his balls off. I tear out from behind the bar, but I'm too late. POW. First shot blows the cake away. BAM. Second one gets Chico in the thigh.

Flesh wound, thanks God. I charge her to the ground, Roberto jumps on top. We wrestle the gun away. She put up quite a fight for a little thing. Did something to my shoulder too, she twisted it in some way, never been the same since. Aurélien got the whole thing on film. I hear it looks great.

Aurélien sat outside the Alcazar screening-room with Kaiser Prevost and Bob Berger. Berger combed and recombed his hair, he kept smelling his comb, smelling his fingertips. He asked Prevost to smell his hair. Prevost said it smelt of shampoo. Prevost went to the lavatory for the fourth time.

'Relax,' Aurélien said to them both. 'I'm really pleased with the film. I couldn't be more pleased.'

Berger groaned. 'Don't say that, don't say that.'

'If he likes it,' Kaiser said, 'we're in business. Lanier will like it, for sure, and Aurélien will apologize. Won't you, Aurélien? Of course you will. No problem. Lanier loved him. Lanier loved you, didn't she, Aurélien?'

'Why are we worried about Lanier?' Aurélien said. 'Delphine came back. We finished the film.'

'Jesus Christ,' said Bob Berger.

'Don't worry, Bob,' Kaiser said. 'Everything can be fixed.'

Vincent Bandine emerged from the screening-room.

Aurélien stood up. 'What do you think?'

VINCENT BANDINE: I believe in candour. I have a theory about this town, this place: we don't put enough stock in candour. I am into candour in a big way. So I take Aurélien aside, gently, and I say, 'Aurélien, or whatever your name is, I think your film is goatshit. I think it's a disgusting boring piece of grade-A manure. I wouldn't give the sweat off my balls for your goatshit film.' That's what I said, verbatim. And I have to give it to the kid, he just stood there and looked at me, sort of slight smile on his face. Usually when I'm this candid they're in deep shock or weeping or vomiting by now. And he looks at me and says, 'I can't blame you for thinking like this. You're not a man of culture, so I can't blame you for thinking like this.' And he walks. He walks out jauntily. I should have had his fucking legs broken. I've got the biggest collection of Vuillard paintings on the west coast of America. I should have had his fucking legs broken. We had to pay the waiter fifty grand not to press charges, keep the Alcazar name out of things. The girl went to a clinic for three weeks to dry out . . . Aurélien No. Not a man of culture, eh?

KIT VERMEER: Ah, Lanier took it badly. Do you mind? Thank you. Bats and lemurs, man, wow, they didn't get a look in. Bats and lemurs. Story of my life. *Weltanschauung*, that's what I'm up for. No, *Weltschmerz*. That's my bag. Bats and lemurs. Why not owls and armadillos? No, I'm not looking at you, sir, or talking to you. Forsooth. Fuckin' nerd. Wank in a bath, that's what an English friend of mine calls them. What a wank in a bath. Owls and armadillos.

MATT FRIEDRICH: Aurélien came to see me before he left, which was gracious of him, I thought, especially for a film director, and he told me what had happened. I commiserated and told him other sorry stories about this town, this place. But he needed no consoling. 'I enjoyed my visit,' he said. 'No, I did. And I made the film. It was a curious but interesting experience.'

'It's just a dance,' I think I remember saying to him. 'It's just a dance we have to do.'

He laughed. He found that funny.

END ROLLER

BOB BERGER

is working from home where he is writing several screenplays

DELPHINE DRELLE

plays the character Suzi de la Tour in NBC's *Till Darkness Falls*

KAISER PREVOST

works for the investment bank Harbinger Cohen in New York City

BERTRAND HOLBISH

manages the Seattle band Morbid Anatomy

MARIUS NO
is in his first year at L'Ecole Supérieur des Etudes Cinématographiques

NAOMI TASHOURIAN
has written her first novel *Credits Not Contractual*

MICHAEL SCOTT GEHN
is chief executive critic and on the editorial board of *film/e*

KIT VERMEER
is a practising Sikh and wishes to be known as Khalsa Hari Atmar

LANIER CROSS
is scheduled to star in Lucy Wang's film *Charles Baudelaire's Les Fleurs du Mal*

VINCENT BANDINE
has announced Alcazar Films' eighteen-picture slate for the coming year

GEORGE MALINVERNO
has opened a third pizzeria in Pacific Palisades

BARKER LEAR
lives in San Luis Obispo

MATT FRIEDRICH
has taken his own life

'NATHALIE X AUX ETATS UNIS'
has been nominated for an Academy Award in the Best Foreign Film category

AURÉLIEN NO
is not returning your calls

GRANTA

Lynda Schuster
The Final Days of Dr Doe

In the summer of 1990, tens of thousands of Liberians died in a civil war of remarkable brutality. Many more starved to death. I know this because I was living there, a journalist married to an American diplomat. Two rival rebel groups hacked their way through the country, bent on overthrowing the dictatorial president, Samuel Kanyon Doe.

A civil war might begin with a rumour: something is happening up-country. The rumour swells: the fighting is moving towards the large cities; it is moving towards the capital. Refugees appear with horror stories. But because the war is happening out *there*, out in the bush where the government press doesn't go, we in the capital can deny its gravity. Something will stop the conflict before it reaches us; the rebels will give up; the government will cave in; the President will bow out.

This is war as it happens in Africa, Asia, Latin America: out of sight of the television cameras, transforming a place into one where the clocks strike thirteen and twelve-year-olds flaunt AK-47s. After a while, the original aim of the conflict—the ousting of the president, the defence of the government, the primacy of the tribe—ceases to matter; only the killing counts. The killing becomes a sickness, a rottenness infecting everyone, destroying the stuff that holds a people together.

Because of this war, Liberia, a country that was founded by freed American slaves, that prided itself on being Africa's first republic, will never the be the same. Nor will I.

Dennis Jett is my husband. I met him several years before when my newspaper, the *Wall Street Journal*, transferred me to South America from the Middle East, and I stopped off in Washington to interview the experts in my new field. He was the State Department's Argentina desk officer: tall, lanky, nice smile. Terrible interview. I closed my notebook after five minutes.

But it was the start of something. Dennis changed posts, and I changed beats, and despite the miles and time-zones and border-crossings that separated us, we fell in love. But when he was then assigned to be deputy ambassador to Liberia, it became impossible to spend any time together. I was working in South

Opposite: Dennis Jett and Lynda Schuster.

Africa, and it took days to fly from Johannesburg to Monrovia. And so, in the summer of 1989, Dennis proposed that we get married—in Liberia.

I quit my newspaper job, shipped my books and Blanche, my black Labrador retriever, to Liberia and began researching a book in Monrovia. We decided we'd marry on New Year's Eve in a civil ceremony with a few friends as witnesses and four relatives who would be visiting us then: my father, his Dutch wife, one of my sisters and Dennis's daughter.

But before the wedding, Dennis and I took our visiting family members to see the country. There weren't many paved roads outside Monrovia; we chose the one that ran about 150 miles north-east into Nimba County, close to the borders with Guinea and Ivory Coast. Our guests were disappointed: mile after mile of the same fetid rain forest, the same thick bush, the same rice fields. Liberia is lush, fecund, almost overpowering in its damp abundance, but not beautiful.

Our days consisted of hours of driving through increasingly deadening humidity. Women walked along the roadside, their skirts an undulating rainbow in the shimmery heat. Bone-thin dogs lay on their bellies in the middle of the road. Then the terrain changed, and the climb to Yekepa began. Suddenly, out of the bush appeared air-conditioned ranch houses with lawns and swimming-pools. There was a Chinese restaurant and an eighteen-hole green golf course: a Floridian retirement community transplanted to Africa.

These were the grounds of a Swedish mining firm, now run by Americans and Liberians. Dennis, who already had been around the country, explained that such bizarre bits of Scandinavia or Germany or the United States were scattered throughout Liberia; entire foreign enclaves hacked out of the jungle, tapping rubber, cutting down trees and digging huge holes in the earth. Unlike the foreign enclaves I had seen in other parts of Africa—legacies of a colonial rule, or church missions, or compounds of foreign companies—these places here were wholly extrinsic and complete. That night we ate Cantonese food, overlooking the slightly mossy waters of a Swedish swimming-pool in the middle of the West African bush.

When we returned home to Monrovia, all the children on the streets were wearing plastic sun-glasses; an enterprising merchant must have brought in a shipment for Christmas. My favourite had pinwheels that twirled in the breeze. I joked with Dennis that the sun-glasses were a signal to a KGB or Mossad agent; later I would come to think of them as portents. The sun-glasses themselves had nothing to do with the outbreak of war, but they became fixed in my memory as a symbol of how quickly life is transformed: you leave town for a few days, and everyone is wearing plastic sun-glasses when you return. A rebellion begins suddenly, and a country is never the same again.

The next day, Dennis got a call telling him that a hundred rebels had crossed over the border from Ivory Coast into Nimba County. Some customs officials had been killed. I was uneasy; we had just been there: guerrillas lurking on the frontier while we were sightseeing?

When Dennis returned from the embassy that evening, he told us that a second rebel force had entered Monrovia itself. These conspirators—in new blue sneakers to identify themselves—had arranged to meet at the market across from the army barracks downtown. There, disaffected officers were to give them guns and ammunition to use in an attack on the Executive Mansion, home of President Samuel Doe. A potential defector must have told his superior of the plan, because loyal soldiers were waiting in the market at the appointed time and picked up twenty men in blue sneakers.

We were quiet for a moment. 'Well, is this serious?' I asked Dennis.

'I don't know,' he replied.

'What do you mean, you don't know?'

'I don't know.'

A couple of days later, while my father and I were reading in the library, the two-way radio started squawking. The radio was a feature of Liberian life: the phones rarely worked. I kept the receiver turned off on the assumption that the embassy's Marine guard would trigger the signal that automatically turned on all receivers in an emergency. It was a high-pitched, two-toned blast that never failed to make me jump. This time it was accompanied by the terse advisory to say indoors: 'There is machine-gun fire near Rally Time Market. Remain in your homes. Do not go downtown. Do not go outside.' I worried for the members of my family; I feared a *coup d'état.*

The advisory was repeated every fifteen minutes. It was maddening not to know what was happening. If I were on a story, I would have been in a taxi by now, on my way to the market, but I had no editor, no deadline, no column inches. I had become an 'official' American. Getting Dennis on the telephone at the embassy—after numerous attempts—didn't make me feel any better: government soldiers were running amok in the market, Dennis said, probably trying to round up more blue tennis shoes. And Lynda, he added before hanging up, stay inside. Please.

After several hours, the advisory was finally lifted. I watched the television news and listened to the radio, hoping for an official explanation. There was none. The government hadn't yet acknowledged the incursion from Ivory Coast. Nevertheless, checkpoints had appeared at every entrance into the city, and a dusk-to-dawn curfew seemed now to be in force. Soldiers had blocked off the road in front of the Executive Mansion, cutting the city in half. You could get to the other side, but only by taking a long detour. The capital effectively was sealed off from the rest of the country, and the President sealed off from the capital—all without a word.

The next night, the eve of our wedding, President Doe made a speech on television about the rebel attack. He looked calm and assured, a pudgy face in outsized designer glasses, a pudgy body in a terrific double-breasted suit. 'Liberian dissidents tried to invade the country and overthrow my government,' he said. 'Two people were killed. One soldier and one customs officer. But everything is under control. There is no need to panic. Everybody should go out and celebrate the New Year.'

Why all the checkpoints if it wasn't anything serious?

I slept late the morning after our wedding, New Year's morning, and was woken by a mention of Liberia on the World Service news. A man named Charles Taylor had called the BBC to say that he had started a rebellion to overthrow the Doe government, and that his men had both breached the Ivory Coast border and penetrated Monrovia. He had, he declared, no designs on the presidency himself. His goal was to turn power over to the people, and he urged the masses to take up arms.

To me, half-awake, the interview sounded like a hoax. What kind of guerrilla proclaims an insurrection in the manner of a birth or engagement announcement?

Later that morning, I phoned a Liberian friend to find out about Charles Taylor. 'Bossy?' she scoffed. 'I've known Bossy since he was seven years old. He was a bully at school, someone who always knew better than anyone else.' My friend also said that Taylor had once held a prestigious position in Doe's government, but after being charged with embezzling one million dollars, he fled to the United States where he was arrested. While awaiting extradition back to Liberia he managed to escape and then he disappeared.

Like my friend, I couldn't take Taylor seriously. The whole business—this new war—seemed like a minor thing, if only because there was so little information. Nimba County, where Taylor had breached the Liberian border, was extremely isolated. From Monrovia, I could reach a relative or friend with ease anywhere in the world, but it was difficult to reach anyone in the rest of Liberia.

2

Liberia was established in 1822 by a group of freed US slaves sponsored by an organization called the American Colonization Society—President James Monroe, Daniel Webster, General Andrew Jackson and Francis Scott Key were among its members. The society's aim was to resettle 'free persons of color' back in Africa, its all-white membership believing that resettlement was a way to right slavery's wrongs. Many members were also worried about the 'adverse' effect of suddenly letting loose a lot of former slaves: shipping them off to Africa provided a seemingly humanitarian solution.

In 1819, Congress allocated 100,000 dollars for the rather ill-defined purpose of transporting freed slaves, and President James

Monroe decided the money could be used to build a holding camp in Africa to house them before they were repatriated to their homelands. The American Colonial Society was awarded the funds, and the project provided an opening to start a colony in Africa.

A boat was hired, the brig *Elizabeth*, and eighty-six free blacks signed on, ostensibly as artisans and carpenters. More than half of the emigrants were illiterate; twenty-six were children under ten. All were supposedly guaranteed passage back to the United States upon completing their task of building a holding camp, but after the *Elizabeth* sailed out of New York harbour in early 1820, all pretence of the passengers being anything but pioneers was dropped: they and the accompanying agents from the American Colonial Society drafted a document stating the group's intention to start a settlement and the laws that would govern it.

The *Elizabeth* moved southward. Within weeks of its landing, fever struck; all of the white agents and one-quarter of the would-be settlers perished. The survivors straggled back to Sierra Leone to await the arrival later that year of another ship—many of whose voyagers also died soon after reaching the malaria-infested West African coast.

A third boat sponsored by the Society brought a fresh group of settlers in 1821, picked up the remnants of the previous two expeditions and, accompanied by a US naval vessel, continued down the coast from Sierra Leone to a site that had been scouted out years earlier by the American Colonial Society's agents. There, after lengthy negotiations, the Society bought a sixty-mile stretch of land from six Bassa chieftains. Thus was born, in April 1822, the first black American settlement, near what would become Monrovia, its capital.

The site chosen by the agents proved to be one of the most forbidding and disease-ridden parts of the continent. The freemen—many of whose families had been in the United States for generations—had never set foot in Africa, let alone a jungle. There was no potable water or arable land, and for six months of the year the place disappeared under 200 inches of rain. Many died from malaria; others died violently during the regular raids on the settlements led by neighbouring tribes.

Still, the Society kept sending out more free blacks, until a small colony of 1,200 settlers was established under the authority of one particularly enthusiastic Society agent, Jehudi Ashmun. He designed the capital and built a string of new settlements inland along a twenty-mile strip of the St Paul River.

It didn't take long before the settlers tired of their indeterminate political status: the United States refused to recognize them as members of an official colony, while the British—who, like the French, were busily swallowing up huge chunks of the region—refused to recognize their sovereignty. Undeterred and defiant the delegates from the different settlements met on 26 July 1947, ratified a constitution prepared by a Harvard professor and issued the Liberian Declaration of Independence—thus creating Africa's first independent republic.

The erstwhile slaves then set about recreating the only life they had known: that of the ante-bellum South. They built clapboard houses with shuttered windows and gabled roofs. They wore top-hats and morning coats, 'introduced' their daughters at débutante balls, danced the Virginia reel and quadrille. They adopted a red, white and blue flag, with eleven stripes to represent the number of signatories to the Declaration of Independence and one star to signify Africa's sole republic. They set up a government that included a president and vice-president, a Senate and House of Representatives. They called their capital Monrovia after President Monroe, who had championed the cause of a 'little America destined to shine gem-like in the darkness of vast Africa.'

And in a final flourish of authenticity, the Americo-Liberians—as they now called themselves—denied full franchise to the members of the indigenous population and turned its sixteen tribes into an under-privileged majority (who, until the fifties, were known as 'aborigines'). The Americo-Liberians established tribal land units restricting the movement of each ethnic group—long before similar 'homelands' were created by the white-minority government in South Africa. Indigenous people were seen as members of tribes, not citizens of Liberia.

The country's 'true' citizens, meanwhile, lived in the coastal areas, governed by an élite of educated, wealthy, light-skinned immigrants from Virginia and Maryland, supplemented by a wave of West Indian arrivals in the mid-1800s. This élite spurned farming, associating it with their former bondage, and became absentee landlords instead, leaving the lower-class settlers to cultivate their rice, sugarcane and coffee. The Americo-Liberians formed their own political party, the True Whig Party, which held power for more than a century. A coterie of party and government officials hand-picked the presidential candidates behind closed doors, determined national policy and controlled the lucrative government contracts. True Whig leaders countenanced neither criticism nor opposition and turned Liberia, ostensibly a multi-party democracy, into a virtual one-party state.

Americo-Liberian attitudes only began to change in 1944 when William Tubman became president. He enacted a set of reforms aimed at bringing Liberia's indigenous population into the mainstream. He revised property requirements for voting, granted the tribal districts representation in Congress and created government jobs for educated indigenous youths. He even travelled up-country, a journey rarely undertaken by any other president, to explain his Unification Policy to local chiefs.

Tubman's Unification Policy called for the construction of roads, schools and clinics in the interior, and the opening up of Liberia to foreign investment in mining and agriculture. And at his behest, the foreign firms came, building enclaves in the bush, digging iron ore, tapping the rubber trees. They, along with the missionaries whom Tubman also allowed into the interior, helped to establish some very basic medical facilities and built some roads and houses. But although President William Tolbert, who assumed power in 1971, continued many of Tubman's social programmes, the essential gulf between descendants of the settlers and the original population remained. After decades of ostensible reforms, four per cent of the population still controlled sixty per cent of Liberia's wealth. Tolbert's friends and family held important positions in the government, in the True Whig Party, on the boards of international firms and in the companies that ran the country's transportation, its fishing industry and food production.

Indigenous people were still regarded as 'backward'. But the younger generation had little tolerance for the continued inequalities. Tensions rose throughout the seventies, as student

Photo: Catherine Leroy (Gamma/Frank Spooner)

Above: Samuel Doe in 1981, the year after he took power.

organizations, opposition groups and political dissidents struggled to achieve real reforms, until Liberia was set to explode. Which it did, first on 14 April 1979, when hundreds of students and unemployed youths who had drifted to Monrovia in search of work rioted following a fifty per cent hike in rice prices. And many were killed. Then, almost one year later, Master Sergeant Samuel Doe and sixteen colleagues ended almost 140 years of Americo-Liberian domination by jumping the fence of the Executive Mansion late one night, disembowelling Tolbert in his bed and declaring themselves the country's new rulers.

It seems in retrospect as if Liberia's history stopped us from grasping the importance of Charles Taylor's invasion. Monrovia was still too removed from the rest of the country—even after ten years of Doe's rule. Our view was distorted. We didn't know what was coming. Most of us in the capital couldn't have known that a war had begun. We just got on with our normal lives.

3

In March 1990, everything changed. For me, the transformation occurred on a morning run with a friend. We started off early, before sunrise, before the heat and humidity and stench from the garbage piles decomposing on Monrovia's streets became unbearable. We followed the shoreline towards the Executive Mansion. People were emerging from their houses, sleepily making their way down to the sand to relieve themselves. Some squatted in the gutters, brushing their teeth. We passed Redemption Beach, where officials from the last government were executed after Doe's *coup d'état*, with representatives of the international press there to watch the spectacle: thirteen members of President Tolbert's cabinet, dressed only in underpants, were lashed to telephone poles. Their executioners were drunk, and it was a long time before all the cabinet members were killed.

We ran past Faz 2 Bar, then a video shop, and then turned at the army barracks back towards the sea. And that's where I heard the sound of a machine-gun being locked and loaded. I know the sound from El Salvador. I stopped dead. A voice came out of the half-light: 'Halt! You can't go there.' My friend slowed a bit. 'You can't go there. That's the way to the Mansion,' the voice insisted, this time louder and firmer. My friend was about to argue with the soldier, someone she recognized from the same gaggle of congenial fellows who greeted us every morning as we jogged by. I gripped my friend's arm. 'Let's go home,' I said. 'These guys are serious.'

After months of vague reports from Nimba County, the war had now erupted. In a number of surprise attacks, the rebels had captured several important towns in Nimba, including Tappita, which meant that they now controlled the coastal road. Within days, Charles Taylor's men had cut off the southern coast from the rest of Liberia and were within 300 miles of Monrovia. The

US embassy considered these very serious developments: it advised all US citizens to leave Nimba immediately.

For a while, things happened very quickly. There were gun-toting soldiers everywhere, and the area around the Mansion had become a kind of no man's land. And then: nothing. This was to be the cadence of the war: the rebels advanced, suddenly, towards Monrovia, gobbling up stretches of territory, overtaking government soldiers—and then: nothing. Taylor's people stopped and waited, for weeks on end. And we would be left—wondering, ignorant, suspended between conflict and calm.

But for the moment the war was everything. Our days consisted of hourly news bulletins: the World Service had discovered the war, and we became addicted to its broadcasts.

Taylor did much to encourage the coverage by calling London frequently; his New Year's Day announcement of the rebellion's start, it seemed, was part of a more extensive publicity strategy. He took to telephoning in the latest developments as though they were football scores. One day, he called to apologize for killing an American missionary and his British wife. The couple, who had lived in northern Nimba County for fifty years and spoke Gio fluently, had been on leave in Monrovia when the fighting began, but attempted to return home at the first opportunity. They were about a mile outside Bahn, their town, travelling with a convoy of Doe's soldiers, when Taylor's forces attacked, catching the missionaries in the crossfire. It was a mistake, Taylor told the BBC; the missionaries had been good friends to the Gio people. His troops would observe a twenty-four hour ceasefire and fly their flags at half-mast as a sign of respect. Even so, it was impossible to retrieve the bodies, and they were left to rot in the heat.

Taylor telephoned the BBC again: the train hauling iron ore from Nimba to the port at Buchanan would have to stop, because, he explained, the exported ore was enriching Doe's government. If it did not stop, he would fire on the train. The train continued to run, and in April Taylor attacked it. The driver and engineer escaped into the bush, but a British journalist and his Liberian guide were captured, taken to Taylor's base on the Ivory Coast border and held for five days. When the journalist was freed, he revealed something new about Taylor: contrary to his earlier claim, Taylor now admitted that he would like to be president once Doe had resigned or had fled. Taylor would then remain president for at least five years. After that, he might hold elections. He wasn't sure.

I was starting to piece together a vague picture of Taylor, mainly from his acquaintances: he was an Americo-Liberian, obsessed with money and power; he grew up poor; while studying in the United States, he was leader of a group of dissident Liberians and had a reputation as a firebrand; during the 1979 rice riots in Monrovia, Taylor was among those who broke into Liberia's United Nations office in New York and demanded that the ambassador cable President Tolbert ordering his resignation. Later, at a breakfast meeting of fellow Liberian students, Taylor was remembered as saying, 'You guys are the professors. I'm not interested in ideology. I just want money and I want to be on top.'

4

President Samuel Doe was the quintessential country boy, from the Krahn tribe, among the most isolated and least educated in Liberia, the son of an illiterate army private. At the time of the 1980 coup, he was a twenty-eight-year-old sergeant, skinny and shy. He inherited a corrupt political system, and lacked the experience or education to transcend it.

April 1990 marked the tenth anniversary of Doe's *coup d'état*. To celebrate the occasion, the government had planned three days of banquets, balls and receptions, but because of the war, the programme was reduced to two events on one day. The first was held in the morning, outdoors, and about 300 people attended. About a hundred were grim-faced soldiers and security agents; the rest were diplomats, civil servants and businessmen. Doe didn't bus in citizens from the countryside as he had originally planned; he didn't trust them. People from the Foreign Ministry passed around anniversary packages (each contained a tenth-anniversary beer mug; a tenth-anniversary plastic coffee cup that could be affixed to a car dashboard; and a tenth-anniversary key chain). The vice-president opened the ceremony with a speech on loyalty:

'God chooses the leader,' he proclaimed, 'so God is the only one who can tell the leader when his time is up.' Doe appeared, read a short statement about the importance of Nimba County and its people, and the soldiers formed the guard of honour for a twenty-one gun salute; there were thirteen shots. The chief of protocol announced that the President would now inspect the new road, and Doe's entire motorcade roared away; it returned about a minute later: the road turned out to be a dead end.

In the afternoon, the president hosted a luncheon in the fifth-floor ballroom of his mansion. By the time Dennis and I arrived, the room—festooned with red, white and blue crêpe paper—was already jammed with people. The waiters wore T-shirts printed with a picture of Dr Doe and TENTH ANNIVERSARY on the front, and HOTEL AFRICA on the back.

I was seated next to the vice-president's sister, who was compulsively cleaning the forks, knives and spoons with a piece of the tablecloth, when the chief of protocol suddenly shouted, 'The President of Liberia!' We all stood, a band played a march and Doe strode into the room, a dark suit flanked by men wearing reflector sun-glasses. About a dozen soldiers with M-16s held up against their chests took up positions around the room, while photographers rushed forward to snap Doe's picture before he began to speak.

I had hoped Doe would say something about the war—the reports from Nimba were becoming graver by the day—but he talked only of his anniversary, his achievements, his works-in-progress, his ideas for the future. Only once did Doe admit that something was amiss when he mentioned, as an aside, that because of the war, he had suspended his birthday celebration in Zwedru, in the county of Grand Gedeh, his home. 'I feel it would be insensitive of me,' he said.

In fact, the birthday party was cancelled because the rebels had captured the main road to the interior, effectively cutting off Zwedru from Monrovia.

The country was now divided not only physically, but politically, for the fighting had taken a decidedly tribal turn. Despite Taylor's Americo-Liberian background, most of his troops were from the Gio or Mano tribes—the main inhabitants of Nimba County and the traditional rivals of Doe's Krahns.

Doe finished his speech to polite applause, and the chief of protocol grabbed the microphone. 'C'mon,' he urged, 'I think the President deserves better than that,' and, in the manner of a high-school cheerleader, he led another round of slightly more enthusiastic clapping. Doe responded with a nod and sat down at the top table.

His wife, Nancy, was conspicuously absent. She and the President were not getting on. Nancy had her own house in town and frequently flew off to England to shop and visit their four children who attended school there. Like her husband, Nancy had had a hard time adjusting to her new station. One day she was the illiterate wife of an army sergeant, selling dried fish, peppers and bananas in the market; the next, she was the First Lady. It was a difficult transition, but she made an effort. She once invited the wives of foreign ambassadors to afternoon tea. They arrived at the Mansion elegantly dressed and coiffed and were ushered into the sixth-floor living-room, empty except for a few sofas where Nancy and her ladies-in-waiting sat. A rock band made up of six soldiers wearing khakis and sun-glasses played loud music in the hallway, making conversation impossible. The wives were offered a choice of whisky or brandy; Nancy and her entourage drank theirs neat. One by one, the wives were introduced to the First Lady; they shook her hand, were allowed to admire the view from the terrace and were seated again. Then Nancy stood. 'And now ladies,' she announced, 'we're gonna shake our bodies.' The bewildered wives were led into the hallway, where the band struck up a reggae tune, and Nancy and her friends began to dance. The wives, looking horrified, tried their best. After a couple of songs, the wives were asked to go. Nancy never invited them to the Mansion again.

Her absence from the anniversary luncheon heightened the strangeness of the occasion. Doe sat alone at the head table with several empty chairs separating him from his closest neighbour, toothpick dangling from the side of his mouth, eyes darting here and there, as armed soldiers patrolled amid diplomats, judges, legislators, professors, businessmen supping their pepper soup.

Halfway through the meal, the anniversary celebrants were called upon to present gifts. Then Doe was served dessert. He stared at it, suddenly bored, then abruptly rose, swept up in a cloud of security guards, and departed. Lunch was over; everyone filed out of the ballroom, leaving the befuddled waiters balancing their trays of un-offered cake. Afterwards, when all the diplomats and their wives were standing on the Mansion's steps waiting for the cars to be brought around, I saw Michael Gore, the British ambassador. 'In all my three years here, I've never once got dessert,' he said.

Later that afternoon Michael, after talking with Dennis, held a meeting with the other European ambassadors. Liberians had been killed by the military: if the army could turn on its own civilians, what was to stop them from venting their frustrations on foreigners? The envoys feared that their nationals would not only be caught in random acts of violence—an American, inadvertently driving through the barricades surrounding the Executive Mansion, had recently been shot—but also become specific targets. No one was immune, not even diplomats. A few days earlier, the Japanese embassy's third secretary had accidentally cut in front of the vice-president's motorcade; Liberian secret service men chased the diplomat back to the Japanese compound, pulled him out of his car and knocked him to the ground. Fearing the military might become even less restrained as the war moved closer to Monrovia, Dennis, Michael and the European ambassadors issued statements recommending that all dependents and non-essential personnel leave the country immediately.

I was stunned when Dennis told me later. 'What does it mean?' I demanded.

'What does it mean? It means we think the army is out of control, and that if it can attack diplomats with impunity, then nobody is safe.'

'Does this mean I have to go?' I asked incredulously.

'That depends.'

'On what?'

'On whether things get any worse. If they get worse, you may have to.'

'Well, I'm not going.'

'Why worry about this now?'

'I just want it on the record that I'm not leaving.'

Dennis rolled his eyes. 'Lynda, we'll burn that bridge when we get to it.'

'Funny, Dennis, very funny,' I retorted, stomping off to sulk and ponder my possible fate.

The diplomats' announcement that non-essential foreigners leave Liberia was a serious matter, a highly public judgement that reflected badly on the government. People started hoarding supplies and the shops ran out of some foods. In the days that followed, I expected to hear a response from Doe. But from the Mansion there was only silence.

The ambassadors' edict had the effect of validating everyone's worst fears. As the rebels continued their progress towards Monrovia, panic replaced the normal rhythm of life, and rumour became the stuff that sustained it. Leaving became the preoccupation of everyone—Liberians and foreigners, and especially women. When they gathered at parties, their talk was no longer of children or mail-order catalogues. I had always considered my Monday night women's group a refuge from the outside world, an eclectic, polyglot collection of women brought together by natural empathy and solidarity. But now, as soon as I arrived, I was showered with questions: should they pull their children out of school, leave now and risk losing the entire term? And if so, where should they go? For how long? How would they afford it? What was the likelihood that Doe might pack up his things and vanish one night? What if he didn't?

Many did not wait. An American acquaintance, married to a Lebanese, stopped by our house to store boxes in our basement: 'I've lived here for nine years and I'm not going to sit around to see what happens,' she said. 'I know these Liberians. I've seen what they can do to one another. This is not going to be pretty once the fighting reaches Monrovia.'

And then, unexpectedly, Doe spoke. He held a press conference that was broadcast throughout the country. He was in a foul mood, frowning, wagging his finger, shouting into the cameras, accusing journalists of rumour-mongering and warning that if their reports about rebel activity turned out to be untrue, they would be arrested as subversives. Then Doe had this message for the residents of Nimba County: 'I'm giving the rebels two weeks to surrender. After that I'm gonna blow them away. So I'm appealing to innocent people to leave Nimba. Or your children will never be seen again.'

Rumours: the army was going to use napalm up-country; it was starting a scorched-earth policy.

The international airport, always chaotic, was now a madhouse. Flight reservations became meaningless, with pre-paid tickets being re-sold to the highest bidder.

I too had yielded to the hysteria. I got the gardeners to drag two enormous garbage pails up to the house and into one of the bathrooms, where we filled them with water—in case the supply was cut. I scoured the city for cases of long-life milk, bottled water, pasta, canned tuna, rice. This was no easy task: Monrovia's supply of flour had already been exhausted, and when you could find rice—the main staple—it sold for a dollar a cup. The week before, it had been thirty cents.

Then suddenly, the debate was settled—at least for the 'official' Americans. Taylor's rebels captured a large agricultural company a few miles from Buchanan, Liberia's second biggest city. Buchanan was only an hour's drive from the international airport, which itself was only an hour from Monrovia. On 26 April 1990, the US embassy, fearing the commercial airlines would soon stop flying into the airport, decided to evacuate all dependents and non-essential personnel from the capital. Dennis disappeared into the depths of the chancellery for days on end, figuring out who should go. Although the embassy had stopped short of ordering its people out of the country—it was a 'voluntary evacuation'—Dennis was determined to get anyone with children to leave. One evening I found him perched on the edge of our bed, reading a computer print-out listing embassy families. 'You're not going to make me go?' I asked.

'No, no,' he said irritably, not looking up. 'You have dogs, not kids.'

A couple of nights later, the first convoy of 136 Americans left. Families gathered at midnight under the streetlights in front of the embassy compound, waiting to board four yellow buses. As they drove off, an armour-plated vehicle led the way. Our car and a truck carrying parts in case any bus broke down followed the convoy, with another armoured vehicle bringing up the rear. Although the embassy had been assured that the evacuees would be allowed safe passage through the city, everyone was worried about the soldiers, now almost always drunk, who manned the checkpoints. The convoy snaked slowly through the deserted streets, hazard lights flashing.

The convoys continued all week. The US Peace Corps programme closed, sending the 150 volunteers home. The development experts left. The middle managers, the young mothers, the administrators, the agronomists, the chemists, the computer analysts, the doctors, the economists, the lawyers, the medical technicians, the nurses, the professors, the secretaries: they all packed hurriedly and were gone, not knowing if they would return, not having had the chance to bid their Liberian colleagues farewell.

I accompanied Dennis on the convoys out to the airport every night and slept during the mornings. I stumbled through the days feeling woolly-headed and unsure. I couldn't concentrate on writing, and any sort of entertainment seemed silly and pointless. Within one week, the official American community in Liberia had been reduced from 621 to 143, and exodus fever had spread: the evacuation had prompted hundreds of Liberians to leave too. Those with money for an airplane ticket besieged the consular offices of the American, British, French, German, Italian, Spanish and Swiss embassies for visas; every day the applicants swarmed about the gates of the foreign compounds in shapeless crowds that formed and re-formed like colossal amoebas. If they obtained a visa, the travellers had a long wait at the airport, sometimes lasting for days, while they tried to bribe someone, anyone, for a seat on a plane. The airport was always packed with people, surrounded by piles of their possessions, suitcases, bags, baskets, backpacks, boxes, cartons, crates. They were hot and dirty and tired from waiting. There were Nigerian women and children trying to get to Lagos, Ghanaians to Accra, Lebanese to Cyprus, or even Beirut.

Monrovia, thus, was turned into a city of men. Despair enveloped the capital, which Doe did little to dispel, except to dispatch a delegation to Washington, where the US Congress had recently condemned the Liberian Army's human rights abuses in Nimba County. The people in Monrovia held out little hope for the delegation: neither, it appeared, did the US embassy. I returned home after one of my shopping quests to find Washington security experts in the house: photographing rooms, measuring doors and sketching windows. A man spread architectural blueprints across the dining-room table with a proprietorial air.

'I hope you don't mind, ma'am,' he explained with remarkable diffidence. 'But in case you get held hostage, we have to know the best way to rescue you.'

Suddenly Doe disappeared. The talk was that he had fled to Lome, the Togolese capital. Then it was that he had sought asylum in Lagos, Nigeria. He had departed, it was said, with his wife and children. No: he had left his family and had departed with his mistress. No: he had departed with only his clothes. No: only his cheque-book. But then, as suddenly, he returned. 'I have been in Nigeria,' Doe explained solemnly at a press conference, 'consoling President Ibrahim Babangida on the recent *coup d'état* attempt against him.'

At the same press conference, Doe extended indefinitely his amnesty offer to the rebels: they could, he said, give themselves up at Tappita—difficult, as the place had been in guerrilla hands since March.

Several days later, with reports circulating of more battles near the cities of Buchanan and Gbarnga, Doe called for a meeting of 300 tribal chiefs, who rapidly converged on the capital from all over the country. The invitation was seen as unusually astute.

The chiefs had strongly supported Doe when he ran for the presidency in 1985 and expected to be consulted on important matters. They would know how to deal with rebels. After all, the chiefs knew everything that went on in their villages. What better way to win a bush war than to turn the fighting over to them? But Doe surprised the chiefs. He strode into the meeting, not attired in native dress as one of them, but crisp and efficient in his general's fatigues. I called you to Monrovia not to get your advice, he said, but to give you instructions.

He then issued an appeal to patriotic, freedom-loving Liberians to take up arms: 'Ex-solders, retired officers, pensioners! Pick up your cutlasses! Your shotguns! Go jump into the bush after the rebels! Don't listen to the BBC, listen to me. For if one rebel enters Monrovia, it will be all over for him!'

The chiefs were outraged. This was an insult, to talk down to elderly dignitaries, an affront to village traditions. The chiefs left, angry and hurt.

The unreality swelled. For several nights, television news reported that Charles Taylor had been shot and seriously wounded. To prove his continued existence, Taylor held a press conference at his latest base, the Mid-Lutheran Baptist Church in Tappita. He lifted up his shirt to show the reporters there were no wounds, no scars. He was bold, confident, almost swaggering. His rebels, he said, were planning a two-pronged attack on Monrovia: one group of 1,000 men would march down the coast from Buchanan—once it was taken—while another would come down the highway from Gbarnga, in the interior. 'We are not opposed to solving this problem peacefully,' he declared. 'But Doe must go. There is absolutely nothing else but Doe must go.'

Liberian television continued to insist that Taylor was gravely injured.

Nancy Doe, the President's wife, and an entourage of her ladies-in-waiting flew to London on the presidential jet. The British airport authorities X-rayed Nancy's bags upon arrival and found them stuffed with money and jewels. After safely depositing the First Lady and her friends in England, the plane's British and Canadian flight crew quit; they refused to return to Monrovia, they said, because it was too dangerous. As no Liberians were qualified to fly the airplane, it was now stranded and furthermore had been impounded by one of Doe's creditors.

I could see the inevitable: I knew the order could come at any moment from Washington for me and the few other remaining official American spouses in Monrovia to depart. I went mad trying to make myself 'essential', so the authorities in the United States would see that the embassy couldn't function without me. I helped out in the public affairs office and I organized social

Photo: Frederic Neema (Popperfoto/Reuter)

Opposite: Charles Taylor.

events—cocktail parties, Sunday morning brunches—intended to keep up the morale of the embassy's remaining personnel.

It was during one such event, a barbecue on the beach, that we learned of the rebels' most threatening success. The embassy's greatly reduced staff—military pilots, communications technicians, security men built like bulldozers—had turned out in force for the party. We swam and sunbathed and listened to old rock hits, drank beer, played Frisbee. And then a Marine guard, who had come directly from the embassy, arrived with the news that Buchanan had fallen to the rebels. The singing stopped. The Marine explained that the army had planned a massive attack on Taylor in Buchanan. They had the soldiers, even the reinforcements, plus all the vehicles they needed; what they didn't have were arms and ammunition, which remained locked up at the Executive Mansion, from where the President was refusing to release them. He was preparing for the last stand in Monrovia.

A few days later, three heads were found on the outskirts of the city. The torsos were in a nearby field, the hands tied behind the backs. The heads were taken to the morgue of John F. Kennedy Hospital, where they were put on display 'to enable curious friends to identify the victims.' It was a macabre thing, to put these heads on view as though they were unclaimed items from the lost-and-found, but hundreds of people flocked to the hospital to see them.

By day's end, the victims had been identified: they were soldiers, one from the Mano tribe, the other two Gios. The next morning, four more soldiers were found outside the town with their throats slashed. They too were Gio and Mano. Then another six bodies turned up, some with their penises severed: more Gio and Mano soldiers. It became clear what was happening, that the army was turning on its own: soldiers from Doe's Krahn tribe were taking the tribal war to the barracks.

Two days later, the chief of police came to visit. He was tense, grim, ashen-faced. He paced the length of the living-room dressed in a uniform modelled on the summer outfits Chicago cops wore in the early sixties. Then he stopped to stare out at the sea. A Fanti fishing boat was making its way across the swells, and the chief watched its progress. 'I'm a professional and I'm a Christian and I just can't live with what's happening,' he said finally. 'They're locking up Gio and Mano soldiers in the stockades, then dragging them out to be executed. That's what they did two nights ago. They got five Gio boys out of the stockades, dragged them across the road and butchered them. There've been at least eighteen murders—and that's just the ones we know about.

'How can I do my job? I can't protect the public. If I start investigating, I'm told to leave it alone. Anyway, we all know it's sanctioned from the top. If they wanted to stop it, they could.' The chief turned his back to the window. 'I could resign so that I could live with my conscience, but then I'd have to tell Doe why I was resigning. How long then would I have to live? I'd have to get on a plane and mail him a letter. And if I don't resign, I'm a dead man when the rebels take over. How could I justify my actions, as chief of police, to them?'

I felt very sorry for the man, because there were no good answers to his questions. But I knew he was right about the soldiers. There was a madness about them, a potential for rage and brutality. Something had broken—a sense of order, of restraint. One morning, Miamah, a Liberian friend, heard an uproar outside her office and dashed outside to see the soldiers arresting one of her employees who had just arrived at work in a taxi. His offence? He read something in a newspaper that made him laugh, then shook hands with the taxi-driver. Miamah managed to extricate him, but not before glimpsing a list the soldiers had drawn up with the names of her other Gio employees. Written next to each one: 'Saboteur'.

The next week 150 Gio soldiers—previously all of good standing—were arrested and held in the open air, in the reviewing stands above the barracks' parade ground. Every day, on my way to town, I saw them, slumped on the bleachers, huddled in little groups, exhausted. What was it like to sit there day after day, not knowing if it would be your turn next to be executed?

The day after I first spotted the Gio soldiers, the taxis disappeared. Taxis had become essential—no one wanted to be out in Monrovia at night—but one day the drivers, all Mandingos, fearing death at the hands of the rebels, left for Guinea.

But for many, there was no place to hide. About 1,000 Gios and Manos had started crowding outside the United Nations compound, pleading for refuge. Someone must have then suggested that the embassies were safe, and so people descended upon the foreign missions. One afternoon, I saw packs of twenty, thirty people, hurrying along the roadside. The women carried babies tied to their backs, bundles of belongings on their heads and cooking pots in their hands; small children tried to keep pace, behind them their fathers, loaded with everything else: sleeping mats, coal, 100-pound bags of rice, blankets. They hurried from embassy to embassy, begging for a place to stay.

A delegation of ambassadors went to the Foreign Ministry to protest about the plight of the Gios and Manos. They told the government official who received them it was an outrage that these people felt so frightened that they had to seek a safe haven with foreigners; the UN envoy requested a central site in which to house and feed the refugees. The official refused, so that night the Moroccans hosted about a hundred people in their compound. The other embassies followed: the Spanish sixty; the Germans, fifty; the French, thirty-five.

That night, a friend brought me the news that the police chief was gone. He had left on a British Airways flight a few days earlier, then faxed his resignation to Doe from London. So now there was no one to police the police.

As it turned out, there was no safe haven for the Gios and the Manos—even among foreigners. On 30 May, Dennis got a call at home: the army had gone on the rampage the previous night. Soldiers appeared at the UN compound at around three-thirty in the morning and ordered the guards to open the gates; rebels were hiding in there, they said. When the guards refused, the troops stabbed one in the back, shot a second and killed a third, then broke into the compound, firing machine-guns into the air and at the 1,500 terrified Gios and Manos who had finally been allowed to sleep there. People were running, falling down, trampling one another, clawing at the fence to get away from the shooting. The soldiers grabbed about thirty men and boys, threw them into Jeeps and roared off.

The last illusion of safety had been destroyed. Pieces of people turned up all morning; three fingers were found in a pool of blood on the St Paul River bridge. A friend of mine, driving to the airport, saw four corpses dumped by the roadside, arranged with their heads resting on their crooked arms, as though looking at the traffic.

The uproar that followed prompted a conciliatory Doe to visit the UN compound to talk with the diplomats who had gathered there. Instead, he ended up addressing the numerous Gios and Manos who were still milling about; twenty army solders brandishing machine guns, one with a rocket launcher, stood between the President and his people. 'I want you to know that those who do this kind of thing are doing it on their own,' he said forcefully. 'I'm gonna deal with them drastically. If you're not happy, I'm not happy.' A low rumble started from within the crowd, but Doe ignored it. 'We're gonna provide you with security,' he continued. At that moment, a woman pushed towards him screaming 'Where is my husband?' It was as if an electric current had surged through the group, energizing and emboldening it: people who only moments before had been standing around listless and sullen had suddenly embarked on the unthinkable: they were booing the President, hissing at him, pressing forward, everyone crushed together, and in full view of the troops. Doe looked around bewildered. Spotting some diplomats, he mechanically began shaking hands. The soldiers were clearly agitated and confused. Doe could no longer make himself heard. The people were chanting—'Who's gonna believe you? Who's gonna believe you?'—when he was seized by security men, pushed into his black Mercedes limousine and driven away.

That night, the television news presenter stared into the camera and said gravely, 'The government of Liberia is conducting a massive search tonight for men dressed in army uniforms who yesterday attacked the United Nations compound. The government reiterates that it is illegal for non-combatants to dress up in army uniforms.' The government was on the lookout for killers masquerading as soldiers. I howled at the television.

A few days later, Doe held a press conference, which, along with the many journalists newly arrived in Monrovia, I attended. We were all seated in delicately wrought, peeling gilt chairs. The carpet was red, patterned with flowers, and had a big official seal of Liberia in the middle, dating from the days of Americo-Liberian rule, depicting an immigrant's ship and a settler's plough with the motto THE LOVE OF LIBERTY BROUGHT US HERE.

The President appeared to announce that he would not seek re-election next year. In a rambling, incoherent discourse, he explained: 'Between 1980 and 1990, there have been thirty-six coup attempts against me. Imagine all the political harassment! Let someone else be harassed. I'm a human being too. I'm supposed to relax, I have to think about my children. I want to do a Ph.D. I am, still, the youngest president in the world. Whoever comes after me must know the importance of being president; the process I started ten years ago must be continued. I will see to it the election is held and international observers are here so everyone will have peace of mind.'

What was he talking about?

I had heard from Liberian friends that people were trying to convince Doe of his place in history, hoping that it would allow him to accept the prospect of resigning. 'Think of yourself as the youngest president ever to take office,' it had been suggested, 'or as one of the few in Africa to step down voluntarily.' The advisers knew Doe desperately needed to believe he had done something noble. And so the President now presented himself as the learned statesman, the sagacious leader, the committed democrat; perhaps he had been persuaded and was groping for a way out.

But it was too late. The rebels were almost in Monrovia and were resolved to accept nothing less than the President's immediate departure. That very day Charles Taylor telephoned the BBC from Buchanan to boast that he now commanded 10,000 armed men. 'I myself, at this very moment, am carrying a grenade launcher and three hand-grenades,' Taylor said. 'I'm for peace, but only for peace that doesn't involve Samuel Doe. So we won't stop our assault on Monrovia for any government except our National Patriotic Front government.' Everyone and no one was for peace; I was beginning to hate them all. With the negotiations between the rebels and Doe's officials in Washington dead, and Doe insisting he would stay in office until the 1991 election, it seemed the conflict wouldn't be decided without a massive battle for Monrovia. The capital was built on a narrow peninsula, wedged between a mangrove swamp and the sea; a couple of well-aimed rockets, a few shells, several grenades—and the place could be in ruins.

The city waited. Shops—the few that still had goods—closed by noon. A telephone line went dead and couldn't be fixed: the technicians at the telephone exchange had left. Ghana Airways made its last run into Monrovia. Air Afrique cancelled all future flights. Notices appeared in the newspapers: 'This is to advise customers having vehicles under repair at Gateway Motors to take immediate delivery of such vehicles. Management will not be responsible for any vehicles that remain on its premises from today.' There was a listlessness about the city. Acquaintances would see you on the street, start a conversation, then wander off in mid-sentence. It was hot, oppressively hot; breathing was difficult. I found myself sitting in a chair, but then changed to a sofa because it looked more comfortable, then changed to another chair because it might be cooler, gave up and went outside for a walk. Outside was no better.

I awoke one morning not to the rebels, but to six US Navy warships, with 2,500 Marines aboard, heading towards Liberia in case the remaining Americans had to be evacuated. Dennis hadn't told me about the decision, but he was in no mood to be questioned. 'The situation here is very unpredictable,' he said crisply. 'We don't know how quickly the fighting will reach Monrovia, we don't know how the government will react to the foreigners still here when that happens, we don't know how much longer the airports will remain open. We need a way to get people out of here quickly, if that becomes necessary. These boats are going to be standing by.'

'Thanks for the official line,' I retorted.

He then fielded phone calls from all the other envoys in Monrovia and from officials in Washington about the make-up of a master list for full evacuation. It seemed we would take not only the 2,000 American citizens still in Liberia, but our friends as well. Consider the Senegalese, one call urged; the Ghanaians, said another, the Israelis and Belgians, too. The list lengthened: all diplomats resident in Monrovia were to be included, in addition to the Liberian children born in the United States who were entitled to American citizenship. Little girls dressed in pinafores and ankle socks, their hair done in neat cornrows, started appearing at the consulate with their US passports. They had come to register for the evacuation, they said, clutching lists of Liberian aunts, uncles, cousins, grandparents, sisters, brothers who needed to accompany them. Overwhelmed by the extended family members, officials in Washington decreed that one Liberian adult could escort each American child, but there were still about 2,400 people in that category alone. I began to think we would evacuate all of Monrovia, leaving only Doe's forces on the streets when Taylor marched into town.

Michael Gore, the British ambassador, turned up at our house with the news that his government was sending two warships and three helicopters to link up with the American fleet. This was becoming too fantastic to fathom. Dennis, Michael and I sat in the living-room, stunned, contemplating the improbability of all those vessels sailing around in circles off the Liberian coast.

The Liberians, on the other hand, were ecstatic. The Marines, it was said, were coming to shore up Doe. They were coming, it was said, to topple Doe. They were coming to aid Taylor. They were coming to wipe out Taylor. There was something for everyone, except that everyone had got it wrong. The Americans were coming not to intervene, but to pluck their own people from the midst of the impending tribal butchery and leave the country to its fate. And that included me: late that afternoon, Dennis said he had received a cable from Washington ordering me out of the country. I was to leave the next day, Marines or no Marines.

I was shocked: what of the cocktail parties, beach parties, barbecues? Hadn't I proved my worth, my essentialness? I appealed to Dennis: 'I'm the only person here who has actually been in a war. I was in Beirut, El Salvador. I know what it's like. I can be of assistance, I can keep morale up . . . '

Dennis interrupted: 'It can't be helped. Washington wants to get the numbers down here as low as possible, in case we really do have to evacuate by ship.'

'I'm not a number,' I shouted, working myself into a melodramatic, incoherent rage. 'I didn't marry the State

Department, I married you. But this is too high a price to pay, my loss of freedom. All these journalists get to stay, why can't I? Just because we're married? Fine, then I want a divorce! An annulment! I'll buy a wig and dark glasses, fly to Ivory Coast, hook up with Charles Taylor as a journalist. I'll march on the Executive Mansion with him, you can wave at me as I go by. Then I'll check into the Ducor Palace Hotel and watch the war from there.' The Labrador retrievers, disturbed by the yelling, came bounding over to lick my legs and arms, which only added another grievance to my hysterical litany. 'The dogs! I don't want to leave the dogs!'

Dennis said nothing. After all, what could he do?

Eventually, he went back to the embassy, and I stomped around the house, pulling pictures off the walls and rolling up rugs, securing the things I assumed he wouldn't have time to worry about after I left: wooden masks from Mali, carpets from Zululand, carved Ngoni warriors from Malawi, oil paintings from El Salvador and Brazil. It was hard to imagine what a crowd of crazed soldiers who broke into our house might fancy. My Italian sandals? A favourite recording of *Madam Butterfly*? Dennis's collapsible kayak that turned into a rowing machine? I locked everything up in the basement room where our friends had stored their valuables.

The telephone rang at one o'clock in the morning. There was heavy fighting near the international airport; as usual, the government soldiers had fled at the sound of gunfire. KLM was diverting its Monrovia plane to Freetown, Sierra Leone, and British Airways had cancelled its flight. They were the last scheduled airlines still flying to the country, which meant the airport was now effectively closed.

All over the country the army was deserting Doe: even some of his top generals had made discreet enquiries about seeking asylum elsewhere, one of my diplomatic friends had said.

I drove through Monrovia, looking for images of a frightened city awaiting its fate. I wanted to remember them: the forlorn Gio and Mano soldiers, still stuck on the stands of the army barracks; St Peter's Lutheran Church, now jammed with 1,500 refugees flying a huge Red Cross flag for protection; these AWOL soldiers—most easily recognized by their shaved heads—

arrested by the military and now lined up outside Antoinette Tubman Stadium when I passed on the way to buy batteries a few hours before I was to leave: a miserable lot, downcast and silent.

I had decided I wouldn't go with the other official Americans to the United States, but would pay for my own ticket and disembark in Sierra Leone. I asked our cook to bake Dennis a chocolate cake for his birthday in three weeks if I hadn't returned, and showed him Dennis's present, hidden in the basement. He and the dogs walked me to the car where a driver was waiting to take me to meet Dennis at Monrovia's small city airport. I faltered, unable to say anything.

The airstrip was chaos, with honking cars trying to unload their passengers, soldiers shouting at them to move on, husbands shouting at wives, wives shouting at children and children howling. Most Liberians huddled on one side of the waiting area, Americans on the other. The Liberian half had a heavy, desperate air about it: these were the families of the Krahn soldiers, hundreds of them, all vying to get on to a green Caribou transport to take them to what they presumed was the safety of the Grand Gedeh County, Doe's home, and out of Charles Taylor's way. On the American side, a carnival was in progress. Local boys worked the crowd, selling beach towels, mangos, ice-cream, sun-glasses, hairbrushes, headbands, chewing gum. One small boy wandered around trying to polish the men's shoes, but most were wearing sneakers. The Americans stood under a corrugated tin awning, out of the sun.

Dennis finally arrived, after having been called to the Foreign Ministry to explain once again that the United States did not believe there could be a military solution to the conflict and that a political solution was necessary. We retired to the air-conditioning of his car to eat tuna sandwiches. I felt oddly distant and detached, as though I were a spectator, watching the scene unfold through a long-range lens. It is, I think, a common response to tragedy or pain, a way of rendering yourself dumb. If I had been able to think about what I was doing—leaving Dennis to likely disaster—I would have lain down, stiff-limbed and screaming on the sizzling tarmac, and refused to go. Instead, I was able, in a misty sort of way, to observe Dennis chew and swallow, drink a soda, escort me out of the car when his driver came to tell us the plane had landed: an Air Guinea 737.

Passengers rushed to the plane, where another great divide occurred: since the flight had been chartered for the foreigners, the Americans and Europeans boarded first, leaving the mass of Liberians, who had abruptly appeared, to wait. I stood off to the side, letting Dennis say goodbye to the evacuees. Then, with most of the Americans on board, I watched myself kiss Dennis and start up the steps to board the plane, but I was too late. A great wave of Liberians had rolled forward, pushing their way up the steps: I was suddenly crushed. Those at the top were attempting to hoist up their loved ones from the bottom, and I was about to be pushed off—the steps had no rail—when one of the Americans reached down from the plane's doorway and virtually lifted me over the Liberians.

The aircraft was full, and the flight crew needed to dislodge the people clinging stubbornly to the steps. About seventy-five frightened Liberians stood there, shouting to be let on, a heart-rending sight: they were watching some of the last planes leave without them. It took a while to clear the tarmac, and I was shaking as we taxied to the end of the airstrip. The British deputy ambassador's wife, seated in the next row, was crying. The plane stopped, then raced down the runway and rose past hundreds of upturned faces. We banked hard right, flew low over palm trees and sand, then out over the sea. And Monrovia became a small, still spot, glistening in the sun.

5

Sierra Leone, only an hour's airplane journey from Liberia, could just as well have been on another planet. I stepped out of the jet into a world of tranquillity and great beauty. There were no crowds at the airport, only a few well-wishers waving from its observation deck, and a flight of egrets turning elegant loops across the sky.

I was right to remain in West Africa, if only for the news. As long as the conflict continued, and Dennis faced real danger, and I remained separated from my home, and my friends suffered unknown fates, I hungered for news. In the United States, Africa hardly counted even in its most tragic moments. In Sierra Leone, however, there were hourly bulletins. The BBC, Voice of America, American Armed Forces Radio, the English services of the French, German and Dutch broadcasting companies—all beamed at Africa, all focused on the war in Liberia. That night, the BBC reported that the rebels had taken the Firestone rubber plantation and were now flying their flag over the plantation.

At a coastal resort catering to French tourists I settled into a routine of waking early and running along the beach. Afterwards I swam, then sat in the sun. I watched fabulous, orange-headed male lizards court dull, dun-coloured female lizards with exaggerated bobs and dips that the females pretended not to notice. I watched unattached French men court unattached French women, usually with more success than their reptilian counterparts. I watched the tourists arrive and depart with a kind of tidal regularity, and the beach boys, as they called themselves, from the nearby fishing village, who had turned into tour guides. They all had wonderfully biblical names such as Moses and Samuel, except for one who was called Alfa Romeo, and they swarmed around the thatched umbrellas, offering to act as escorts to the waterfall, the rivers, the village.

In the afternoon, immense clouds gathered, and I would move indoors and watch the heavy rains. Sometimes, if the rain slackened in the evening, I would dash up the beach to the main hotel building and sit at the bar, hoping Dennis would call (the telephone was at the front desk): but he didn't; he couldn't.

But all these activities were subordinate to the day's main event: listening to the news. Greedily and impatiently, I listened.

> *5 June 1990, Agence France-Presse, Buchanan, Liberia.* Rebels of the National Patriotic Front fighting to unseat the Liberian president, Samuel Doe, have summarily executed hundreds of ethnic rivals near this key iron ore port, eyewitnesses said. The witnesses said the victims were primarily members of Mr Doe's native Krahn tribe and Mandingos, a group of Muslim traders accused of supporting the government.

6 June 1990, BBC. Latest reports from Liberia say rebel forces remain in control of the Firestone rubber plantation, a mainstay of the economy, thirty miles from the capital, Monrovia. Local people contacted by telephone say there is no sign of the government's counter-offensive. Fighting has been reported in Bong County, but these clashes are believed to involve rival rebel factions.

6 June 1990, Monrovia Radio ELWA. President Doe has sent a message of congratulation to the president, government and people of Italy on the occasion of that country's national day.

8 June 1990, Agence France-Presse, Lagos, Nigeria. The Nigerian government would welcome Liberia's president, Samuel Doe, if he wishes to settle in the country, a source close to the federal government said. 'There is nothing wrong in Nigeria receiving or granting asylum to President Doe, and he does not even need to be granted asylum to come here,' the source said.

9 June 1990, Monrovia Radio ELWA. The government of Liberia and the National Patriotic Front of Liberia have agreed to meet at a round-table conference to negotiate a peaceful settlement of the current crisis in the country. According to the Liberian Council of Churches, which is serving as mediator, the negotiation will take place in Freetown, Sierra Leone, next week.

15 June 1990, Monrovia Radio ELWA. President Doe has sent two separate messages of congratulation, to Queen Elizabeth II of Britain on the occasion of her birthday, and to the foreign minister of the State of Israel, for his reconfirmation as prime minister, following a vote of confidence passed in the Israeli parliament.

19 June 1990, Agence France-Presse, Freetown. Tom Woewiyu, chairman of the National Patriotic Front rebel delegation which adjourned peace talks with

> Liberian government officials, said there would be no ceasefire 'until Doe is out'. He said, 'There was a cordial environment [at the talks] and we exchanged ideas, but the bottom line is that no decision can be reached until Doe is out of our lives once and for all.'
>
> *22 June 1990, Monrovia Radio ELWA.* President Doe has sent a message of congratulation to the president of Romania on his inauguration.
>
> *2 July 1990, BBC.* Rebels fighting the government in Liberia have advanced closer to the centre of the capital, Monrovia, and are now only about five miles away. For five days, the city has had no water; for four days, it has had no electricity; today, rebels cut the phones off. News is extremely scant. However, our information is that the city is now totally surrounded. The rebels have closed the road to Sierra Leone which, up till now, they had kept open as the last land escape route. The army commander has now gone from Monrovia and only the presidential guard is left to put up any resistance. President Doe, however, shows no sign of quitting. This, in spite of mediation proposal from the Economic Community of West African States that an interim government should be formed immediately until the elections can be held. This proposal has the backing of the US.

Monrovia was cut off from the rest of the world. I now had no way of knowing whether Dennis was alive or dead. Sitting on the sidelines I was becoming increasingly aware that, for civilians such as myself, war is about the loss of control. Speaking with Dennis and knowing he was unharmed had given me the sensation of control; now, unable to sustain the illusion, I felt a terrible foreboding. It was as though the most painful part of my life was about to be played out again.

Dennis wasn't my first husband; I had been married before, to a journalist who worked for the *Los Angeles Times*. We met while reporting on the wars in Central America in the early 1980s, and I fell wildly, madly, cross-eyed in love—as only a twenty-five-year-old can. We were married in the city hall of Tegucigalpa, Honduras, in an impromptu and sentimental ceremony. Ten months later he was dead, blown to bits by an anti-tank mine on the Honduran–Nicaraguan border. It took me a long time to learn to live with the hurt. It took me even longer to decide I could risk that kind of pain again. And now here I was, six months after my wedding, terrified that I was going to become a widow for the second time. I'm not a religious person, but that night as I lay in bed awaiting an elusive sleep, I prayed. As the ocean crashed upon the shore and the short-wave radio whispered its all-night messages from a corner of the room, I prayed to whomever would listen to keep Dennis safe.

> *5 July 1990, BBC.* Last night was a night of terror in Monrovia as soldiers ransacked shops under cover of curfew hours. Rebels have been battling troops in the city's eastern and western suburbs. In the city itself, a serious food shortage is forcing people to beg for life. When this morning broke, frightened Monrovians ventured out into the deserted streets and discovered at least sixteen bodies.

And then I got a letter from Dennis; it was delivered to my beach exile by a foreign journalist who managed to leave Liberia and travel to Sierra Leone.

> 14 July
>
> Dear Lynda:
> This war goes on and on. It's a nightmare that just does not seem like it will end. We, of course, have it easy with generators for light, food to eat and enough water stored for drinking and cooking. I sneak in the occasional brief shower every other day or so. But the people outside of Little America spend their days in search of food and water. Mostly they just stand around, waiting for night to fall so they can lock themselves in their homes and hope the soldiers don't come.
>
> The area of conflict is now so large and the brutality

such that it can't be avoided. Omega [the US-built navigational tower] is in rebel hands, the overpass on the road to Hotel Africa was for a while, but then the rebels faded away. There are displaced people anywhere they feel safe: 500 came over the wall of the American Community School; 6,000 at Voice of America; 20,000 at Omega.

The American flag we hung at home doesn't seem to have much effect outside the gates. Yesterday afternoon, in full view of the international press, three soldiers executed a man on the beach in front of the house. They knew he was a rebel because he said he was going to buy rice and only had $1.25 on him; rice is now two dollars a cup. They dumped his body in our parking-lot across the street. it stayed there most of the afternoon, until we asked for it to be collected.

This morning, three soldiers took a fifteen-year-old boy from one of the embassy's residential compounds, brought him to the Peaceland Car Wash next door to our house and bayonetted him to death. This afternoon, I decided to come home for lunch early when I heard that soldiers were beating up someone else. When I got here, they had pinned this emaciated man—stripped to his underwear—on his back and were holding his feet and arms outstretched. I stood in the driveway watching the two soldiers do this while three other soldiers washed their car. When they finished, the five soldiers threw the man in the car and drove off. I don't know whether being observed by a foreigner made them act differently. If so, it probably only bought the guy a few more minutes of life.

I can't tell you how sick I am of being a spectator to this whole tragedy. Going through it without being able to talk to you is really not fun. The uncertainty is as bad as the separation. If you can get into Freetown to the embassy, we can talk on their radio. They have a ham-type radio that has pretty good quality. We could use Hebranol [Hebrew/Español—our private language] if you want to talk dirty. I want to do a crossword puzzle with you. How's that for romantic? Just know that I love and miss you greatly. This can't go on much longer. Then we can drink a bottle of white wine, I'll let you beat me at Scrabble, and we can forget it ever happened.

Much love,
Dennis

It was during one of these radio exchanges that Dennis mentioned that he'd recently seen what would appear to have been a different group of rebel troops: they wore neat uniforms and advanced in a trained and disciplined fashion—rebels, certainly, but not in the manner of Charles Taylor's rag-tag army. There had been rumours of a rival, splinter force, led by someone called Prince Johnson. These must have been his troops.

6

These soldiers were indeed those of Prince Johnson, an erratic swaggerer given to heavy drinking and deadly rages. He broke away from Taylor not long after their insurrection began; the rumour was that Taylor, sensing a rival in the charismatic Johnson, had tried to ambush him. Prince Johnson then took about 300 of his followers and moved off to the west, as Taylor marched south to Buchanan and then turned west towards Monrovia. Among the three forces now battling one another, Johnson's was thought to be the best; unlike Taylor, the thirty-year-old Johnson had been a military man, a soldier in Doe's army for many years until leaving the country to link up with Taylor. Johnson instilled in his men a great sense of discipline mainly by killing anyone who didn't obey orders. Brigadier General Johnson (the title he had bestowed upon himself, along with Field Marshal) drove around in a commandeered car, shooting on the spot any rebels he found looting or away from their assigned posts. He could keep track of his troops in this manner because his was a much smaller force than Taylor's, which had grown from a band of a hundred or so insurgents to a militia of thousands of untrained, plunderous Gios and Manos.

Johnson set up his headquarters just outside Monrovia, in the former compound of a corporation. A sign outside the main building read: EXECUTIVE MANSION OF FIELD MARSHAL PRINCE JOHNSON. HOURS: 10-1, 3-5. From there he intended to launch his final assault on the port and continue to Monrovia itself.

> *20 July 1990, Agence France-Presse.* Heavy fighting between government troops and rebels seeking to unseat President Samuel Doe is being reported from the Liberian capital, Monrovia, and thousands of people are fleeing, diplomatic sources said here. They said the new fighting, after an apparent lull, was being seen as an indication that the rebels had begun their final assault on the capital.
>
> *25 July 1990, BBC.* Diplomats today reported heavy fighting in the eastern part of Monrovia, where they say rebels loyal to Charles Taylor have resumed their offensive against government troops. The rebels were reported to have waded across a swamp to launch an attack on Spriggs Payne airfield. Rebels commanded by another rebel leader, Prince Johnson, have taken all of the city's northern Bushrod Island, where they control the ports and oil depots. With Taylor's troops attacking from the east and Johnson's from the north, the city appears to be caught in a vice. The acting minister for information, Paul Allen Weah, held an impromptu press conference with gunfire echoing all round, at which he said President Doe remains defiant and has no intention of resigning. Meanwhile, the people of Monrovia are continuing with their desperate search for food and water in a city where all shops are shut and basic utilities have been closed up for more than a month.
>
> *1 August 1990, BBC.* An American official confirmed stories of battles going on around Radio ELWA, a missionary radio station in the eastern suburbs. ELWA fell into rebel hands last week, and the rebel leader, Charles Taylor, used it to make a series of broadcasts. At the other end of the city, where the rebels are part of a different faction led by a commander called Prince

Photo: AP

Above: Prince Johnson.

Johnson, the front line now lies across the middle of the commercial district. The British Foreign Office confirmed that Mamba Point, which houses the American and British embassies, had been overrun and was now in rebel hands. President Doe himself is still in his fortified headquarters, the Executive Mansion, and he contacted the BBC by radio telephone to say he had no intention of leaving. He said that he and his men would continue to fight until the last soldier of the Liberian army was dead. Just because the rebels were now in the centre of Monrovia, he said, did not mean they had won the war.

> *2 August 1990, BBC.* Rebels loyal to Prince Johnson have withdrawn from key positions in Monrovia. A long-time resident of Monrovia, who claims to be close to Johnson, said that the rebel leader was turning his troops around to fight his rival, Charles Taylor. Diplomats said that the Johnson–Taylor rivalry could prolong the conflict for weeks.

On this same night, the night of 2 August, in a part of town that Charles Taylor's rebels had yet to occupy, the government soldiers came for Dr James Mason, a close friend, a pastor, a gentle, bookish man. The government soldiers knew they didn't have long, and were striking out violently and at random. Dr Mason and his wife, Evelyn, were sitting in their living-room at the back of the church they had built, holding hands in the dark—there had been no electricity for weeks—when they heard cars pull up to the house. Someone rapped on the back door, which was locked, and yelled, 'Open up! Open up! There are rebels in there!' Frustrated, the intruders went around to the church door. 'Open this door,' they shouted. 'We know you're in there.' They began shooting and showered the door with bullets until it gave way. Terrified, Mrs Mason dived under a table and pressed her back against the wall; in the gloom, her black clothes made her almost invisible. Dr Mason calmly remained in his chair.

'Where is your wife?' a soldier demanded, as he and his companions set about pulling things off the walls and dumping the contents of drawers on the ground.

'I sent her away.'

'All you Congo [Americo-Liberians] people send your wives to America. OK, let's go. If you're not guilty, you'll come back.'

'Guilty of what?' Dr Mason asked.

'Don't ask questions,' the solder snapped. 'Just come with us.' Before they left, though, the army men stripped the house of its contents. They piled furniture, the television, video recorder, dishes, glasses, cutlery into their vehicles, sprayed the church with bullets and drove off with Dr Mason.

Mrs Mason cowered under the table, paralysed by the sound of shooting. 'Lord,' she prayed, 'direct me what to do.' An hour must have passed, then she heard the soldiers again; having emptied their trucks of her possessions, they had apparently come back to take whatever was left. As one soldier was ripping down the curtains in the pitch-black room, he knocked into her under the table. 'There's someone here,' the soldier said, pulling Evelyn to her feet. She pleaded with him not to kill her; another soldier, on his way to the bedroom to check for booty, looked Mrs Mason up and down and said, 'Oh, leave the old mom alone.' She was lucky: they demanded her wedding ring but spared her life. Then they left with their plunder. Wondering what had happened to her husband, Mrs Mason climbed up to a small balcony in the church, lay down on the floor and covered herself with an old tarpaulin in case the soldiers returned.

The next morning, Mrs Mason went to hide at the house of some friends who lived nearby. But the soldiers who had abducted her husband came back for her after all. They drove her to the swamp near the end of the runway at Spriggs Payne airfield, the killing field where hundreds of corpses lay scattered in the muck. One soldier drew out a large butcher's knife and held it to her throat. 'You're guilty,' he proclaimed and made as though to slash her. In yet another instance of incredible luck, an army man, who passed by at that moment and took in the grisly tableau, said, 'Oh, don't kill that woman, she didn't do nothing.' Inexplicably mollified, the soldier instead demanded money. He and five companions drove Mrs Mason to the house of her sister-in-law, who managed to find forty dollars to give to the soldiers. That wasn't enough, so Mrs Mason went to several other friends in town until she had collected 140 dollars, which satisfied the army men and won her release.

Mrs Mason returned to her neighbour's house. Fearful for her husband and for herself, she didn't know what to do; she waited for a sign. Later that night, a young female soldier came to fetch her. The girl was working as a cook for the government troops camped around Spriggs Payne and had seen Mrs Mason there earlier in the day. She recognized her (having stayed with the Masons when she first moved to Monrovia) and wanted to help. She said she would hide Mrs Mason from the soldiers. She made her dress, then led her about a mile away, to a tent that was concealed under a pile of leaves in a marsh. The bog was infested with rats, which terrified Mrs Mason, and the girl could only provide black, unsweetened tea for her sustenance. After several days, the girl smuggled Mrs Mason past rebel lines to Mamba Point and the US embassy, where her nephew worked as a maintenance man.

Eventually, a friend of Mrs Mason's who had glimpsed Dr Mason in the swamp near Spriggs Payne managed to communicate what she had seen. From then on, the picture of her dead husband—the severed head, the body swollen to a grotesque form, the swarms of flies—allowed Mrs Mason no rest.

> *4 August 1990, BBC.* The Liberian rebels, now divided in their loyalties between Charles Taylor and Prince Johnson, have seemed unable to make their final advance on President Doe's Executive Mansion. But against this background of continuing loss of life, there have been renewed diplomatic moves to try to end the conflict, which could possibly come to fruition at a summit of the Economic Community of West African States on 6 August. Both the United States and the United Nations are showing greater support for the regional solution, while Nigeria said yesterday it was now prepared to intervene in Liberia if it got the backing of other West African states.

> *4 August 1990, BBC.* One of the rebel leaders fighting to overthrow the government of Liberia said he has ordered the arrest tomorrow of all foreigners in the areas he controls. The rebel leader, Mr Prince Johnson, said he was hoping to provoke foreign intervention in the conflict. Nigeria and other West African countries are already planning to send some kind of force to Liberia. But Mr Johnson said they would only be welcomed as part of a wider international effort.

Later I would meet James Samuels, who told me this story after he had walked across Liberia and escaped to Sierra Leone.

James Samuels was sixteen. As the rebels closed in on Monrovia, he had moved to be near one of American compounds where his uncle worked. He thought he might be safer there.

James was given his own room and had food and the freedom to do as he pleased. He made friends with another teenager, Steven Butty, and the two became inseparable. They regularly shared their food with the refugees who encamped around the perimeter fence. There were thousands. After the Americans were evacuated, James felt suddenly like an abandoned child. It seemed very lonely without the Americans. He, Steven and another friend, Sunny Williams, watched as the thousands of refugees around them started to pack their belongings following the Americans' departure. 'Maybe were ought to leave too,' Sunny said. 'Maybe we should go to Kakata.'

'We can't go there, we could get killed at the checkpoints,' scoffed Steven. 'Let's go to Cape Mount, I have a friend there.' After a short discussion, the three agreed they would travel together to the Grand Cape Mount, as it was officially known, the county that bordered Sierra Leone. Grand Cape Mount was about a hundred miles away: the journey would take the three boys away from the war's centre to an area they assumed was unaffected by the conflict because of its remoteness.

The three young men set out the next morning along the highway that led northwest towards Cape Mount, taking only the provisions they could carry—two bags of rice, tins of meat, chicken soup, matches, bedding. There were hundreds of people on the road, civilians like himself trying to get away from the fighting. The presence of all these trekkers was reassuring and after the first day or so of the journey James began to relax. He and his companions settled into a routine of waking at dawn and walking until the first signs of dusk, then stopping at one of the roadside villages to solicit the use of a kitchen to prepare their dinner. They always offered to share their meal and never, therefore, wanted for facilities; close to starvation, the villagers were grateful and treated the youths with kindness. Only once in the early stages of their journey did the three experience any unpleasantness. Having crossed into territory controlled by Charles Taylor's forces, they suddenly found themselves at a checkpoint manned by two, oddly garbed rebels: one adorned in a diaphanous négligée, the other shod in a bedroom slipper and a sneaker. James, who had never encountered the rebels and their inclination towards bizarre dress, stifled a desire to laugh. The rebel with the mismatched footwear slapped Sunny on the shoulder. 'You've got a good build,' he said. 'You're going to be a recruit.'

Sunny looked stunned. 'No, no, I don't want to join,' he protested. The négligée-clad rebel scrutinized Sunny for a tense moment, plucked the sun-glasses from the lad's face, stuck them in his own pocket and, satisfied with the compromise, allowed the boys to pass.

Then they reached Gbai, a village that was of no great significance before the war but now teemed with people, most of whom stood in a line outside a small house. Steven asked a man why everyone had stopped there; this is a G-2 [Intelligence] headquarters, the man explained; you must get a pass from the rebels before continuing along the road. James, Steven and Sunny joined the queue, but after several hours it had barely moved, and they were forced to spend the night in Gbai. They found spaces for their bedrolls in a nearby building and lay down to sleep amid the scores of other refugees. During the night, James was awakened by someone who had crept into the room while everyone was asleep. 'Any ex-army, ex-policemen, government official,' the rebel whispered, 'if you have an identification document on you, throw it away. Throw it away!' The rebel disappeared into the darkness.

The next morning the boys resumed their place in the queue, which now moved at a livelier pace. James watched as a man a few spaces in front of him got to the window of the house; behind the window sat a rebel, who took down everyone's particulars. 'What are you doing here?' the rebel asked the man.

'We're travelling to Freetown.'

'Who are you travelling with?'

'My wife.'

'No children with you.'

'No, just my wife and myself.'

The interrogator told the man to go inside the house to be

Opposite: a masked rebel loyal to Charles Taylor in Monrovia, August 1990.

Photo: Pascal Guyot (AFP)

searched. James could see, through another window, the refugee disrobe to his shorts, and another rebel rummage through his clothing. Suddenly, the rebel began waving a piece of paper about, shouting that he had found a police identification. The rebel tied the man's elbows together behind his back and dragged him outside, where he was made to kneel in the mud. The rebel, who was known as Red because of his bright skin colour (but referred to himself as Young Killer), ordered the man to call his wife from the building where they had slept; seeing her husband half-naked and trussed up, she began to weep. 'Don't cry,' Red barked. 'Your face must remain still or you'll follow him.' Red made the wife kneel in the slime, and told the man to recite to her his last will and testament.

The man faced his wife. 'The boy will get the money I leave,' he said, tears streaming down his cheeks. 'You must use it to educate him.'

Red commanded the wife to say goodbye to her husband, which she did, contorting her face so as not to cry; then Red told her to get up. 'You see how your husband talks?' the rebel said. 'We're going to bring him back, but in a different form.' With those words, Red thrust the knife deep into the man's back. The man gasped and whispered: 'Wait, wait, I want to tell you something . . . ' But Red didn't give him a chance; he fired two shots, point-blank, into his chest. Another rebel sliced off the man's head with a machete and handed it to Red. Holding the head by the hair, Red dangled it in front of the wife's face. 'Clap for your husband's head,' he said, then turned to the horrified people waiting in line. 'You must also applaud this head,' he shouted at them, and they managed to clap their hands. 'Now laugh at this head,' he cried, and the refugees tittered. 'Now sing: up, up, Major Taylor; down, down, fucking Doe.' The people sang. Satisfied, Red asked the wife where she wanted to go; back to Monrovia, she replied timidly, to tell my husband's parents. This clearly wasn't the response he wanted. 'I'll give you a pass to go forward into our territory,' Red said, 'or you can follow your husband.' The woman agreed to the pass.

Watching this scene, James felt himself sicken and grow weak; and when Red went inside the building to arrange for the wife's pass, he began to sob. Steven was furious. 'If you don't stop crying, I'm going to leave you,' he whispered fiercely, trying not to draw attention to himself. 'Just shut up and get your pass.' James knew he had no choice but to stand quietly in the queue. Trembling, barely able to restrain his fear, he approached the rebel behind the window when his turn came. The man stared intently at James. Are you a Krahn? he asked. Mandingo? Have you ever worked for the government? Have you ever lived in the army barracks in Monrovia? James answered no to all the questions and apparently convinced the rebel that he wasn't one of Doe's men; he was told to wait nearby; his pass would be ready in a day or two. Steven and Sunny were also lucky, and the three youths tried to make themselves invisible while awaiting the passes.

To James, Charles Taylor's men seemed diabolical. He watched one rebel—dressed in a reddish wig, cream-coloured skirt, black jacket and stockings—prowl the line of cowering refugees, leering in their faces and cooing, 'Please let me kill you, it's been minutes since I killed anyone, please . . . ' until he lighted upon a victim and dragged him off to the bush. At another moment, the same rebel suddenly announced to the people waiting in the queue, 'I want the number twenty. I like the number twenty.' Counting off the refugees from the back of the line, he promptly shot the twentieth one.

James and his companions finally received their passes and continued their journey. Things were less fantastic at the 'single-barrel' checkpoints, the barriers protected by recently recruited villagers with single-barrel shotguns: the people at these checkpoints were starving along with the rest of the populace and could usually be bribed with a bit of salt or rice. But at the barricades manned by Charles Taylor's Freedom Fighters, James came to expect just about anything. Not long after leaving Gbai, James and the others were waiting at a checkpoint when a Jeep came roaring up and stopped abruptly. A highly agitated rebel emerged from the vehicle, demanding to see the checkpoint's commander. 'Here I am,' said one of the Freedom Fighters, stepping forward.

'I have something to show you,' the rebel said, bringing forth a plastic bag and emptying its contents—a large pile of human penises—on the ground.

'But what did you do with the men?'

'Oh, nothing,' the rebel laughed. 'I just cut off their penises and told them to get going.'

The commander looked pleased. 'Well done,' he said. The two men counted the severed members; there were fifty-two in total, which prompted the commander to decree that the rebel henceforth would be known as the 'Fifty-two Reporter'.

> *20 August 1990, BBC.* There is a lot of speculation about what has been happening in the Liberian capital, Monrovia, following reports that the rebel faction leader Prince Johnson and President Samuel Doe have signed some kind of truce. The suggestion is that the agreement is in part a preparation for the arrival of the Economic Community of West African States peacekeeping force.

> *27 August 1990, BBC.* After initial heavy fighting between the Economic Community of West African States peacekeeping force and Charles Taylor's rebels, there has been relative calm. Today, thousands of hungry civilians milled around outside the port, hoping the peacekeeping force would distribute food. The troops donated some rations, but they could not cope with the overwhelming demand.

> *5 September 1990, BBC.* In Liberia, President Samuel Doe and the smaller of the two rebel factions, led by Prince Johnson, have formalized a two-week old cease-fire arrangement. A spokesman for President Doe said an accord has been signed under which the two sides have agreed not to attack each other and to work together in cooperation with the West African peacekeeping force.

7

A few days after the accord was signed, Doe took a drive to visit the head of the peacekeeping troops. The drive was a dangerous thing for Doe to undertake. Monrovia was still besieged. Doe, however, remained president and expected to be treated as one, even if there wasn't much presidential business to conduct nowadays. Doe had abandoned his double-breasted jackets and his silk handkerchiefs in favour of track suits or camouflage fatigues, the five stars of a general emblazoned on each shoulder. And he had stopped wearing the outsized designer spectacles he thought made him look like a serious head-of-state, but didn't actually need. In effect Doe—with what must have been tremendous relief—had stripped himself to his essence. He had stopped playing the polished and statesmanlike politician; now he was a soldier.

For the last few months, he had lived barricaded inside the Executive Mansion. Every day he met with generals who brought fabricated tales of battlefield victories. Every day, he played checkers with the few cabinet ministers who hadn't already fled to the country; there were outbursts sent by short-wave radio to the BBC; there were the videos. Every day he walked around the terrace of his sixth-floor residence, stopped and stared out to sea where four US ships still floated, their helicopters continuing to evacuate foreign citizens from the country. Then, by early afternoon, the headaches would start: painful, pulsating, migraine-like headaches that drove Doe to bed. He had painkillers, but they didn't help. Sometimes, the headaches disappeared magically at dusk; and if the rains had stopped, Doe would go down to the Mansion's yard. There the families of his 500 Israeli-trained guards were living—along with the policemen, tax collectors, interpreters, mail clerks, secretaries and any number of government workers frightened of rebel retribution. They crowded into the yard with their stew pots, goats, chickens, water jugs, rice bags, sleeping mats, lines of drying laundry. And in the half-light, hazy with smoke from the small cooking fires, Doe would stroll, stopping to talk to some soldiers, pat a child's head, pass around a bit of rice.

The impromptu visit to the headquarters of the West African troops was unusual. Doe had to drive through districts now controlled by Prince Johnson. Although the two men had just concluded the terms of a truce—Johnson had embraced Doe, insisted that he had no quarrel with him and given him a hundred bags of rice—there was still some risk. But Doe genuinely believed he was bullet-proof. He had imported specialists, juju-men from

Mali and Togo, and one from his hometown in the country's interior. Their powers were first proved in a coup attempt against him, one of dozens, five years earlier, when Doe was pulling into the Mansion gates after a night on the town. A sniper hiding behind a broken-down truck across the street opened up with a fifty-calibre machine gun, and two security guards were wounded: Doe escaped unscathed. Later, he said that bullets had passed through his seat and cap and proudly displayed the exit holes to his ministers. Convinced of his invincibility, Doe used to invite the public to the Mansion on Saturday afternoon to witness an eight-man firing squad shoot at him—in vain.

The President's confidence was such that he ventured forth without sending an advance party to scout out the area. For months the streets had been devoid of traffic: suddenly the President's motorcade appeared: a headlight-flashing, horn-honking, siren-blaring parade of police cars and motorcycles and a black Mercedes stretch-limousine. The procession wound its way through town towards the port, the familiar figure at its centre, waving serenely from the Mercedes' sunroof, past the corpses rotting on the roadside, the looted shops with doors smashed open, the broken glass, the refugees jammed into makeshift shelters, listless and weak from hunger.

Doe arrived at the West Africans' headquarters and had gone upstairs to chat with the commander when Prince Johnson and a group of his men appeared. Johnson then set up an M-60 machine-gun aimed at Doe's limousine. The President's guards protested; many had been disarmed in accordance with the rules for visiting the peacekeepers' headquarters. A fight broke out, but before the West African soldiers could intervene, Johnson and his men opened fire. The rebels then entered the Coast Guard building, a small, two-storey structure, running from room to room, hunting down government people. Most of Doe's entourage—more than sixty men—were shot dead; a few survived by rolling under the bodies of those already slain. Cornering Doe, the rebels fired several bullets into his legs, carried him down the staircase and bundled him off to their base at Caldwell.

Photo: Popperfoto/Reuter

Above: Samuel Doe under interrogation, before he was tortured to death.

There is no doubt about what happened next because Johnson, perhaps moved by a sense of history, filmed the events. This weird and grotesque home-movie opens with a tinny-sounding horn playing martial music. White letters then scroll up against a blue sky: THE CAPTURE OF SAMUEL K. DOE BY FIELD MARSHAL PRINCE YEDUO JOHNSON AND HIS GALLANT MEN AND WOMEN OF THE INDEPENDENT PATROITIC [sic] FRONT OF LIBERIA ON SUNDAY, 9 SEPTEMBER 1990. A fluffy white cloud floats across the sky. The camera cuts to the inside of Prince Johnson's headquarters. The rebel leader is seated behind a massive desk. A garland of grenades hangs around his neck; in his hand is a can of Budweiser (several months previously he had looted a container load of the beer from the port). A young woman in a blue shirt fans him with a cloth, occasionally dabbing his temples.

Doe sits on the floor opposite the desk, hands manacled

behind him, legs outstretched and tied primly at the ankles. He is naked except for his underpants and the remains of a camouflage shirt, which two rebels use as a kind of hoist to hold him upright. Doe's head keeps rolling forward. Shreds of flesh hang from his face. He is bleeding from the legs. There are rebels everywhere; screaming at Doe, yelling at one another, crowding around in a circle, resting on sofas, waving to the camera, drinking beer, slapping one another on the back. A desultory sort of interrogation is going on amid the cacophony. 'I want information, I want information,' Johnson shouts from behind the desk, hitting it with his fist. One rebel, sporting a close-fitting cap with flaps, triumphantly plucks a strand of amulets, juju fetishes, from around the President's waist; a small horn had earlier been found in his anus. Everyone claps and cheers.

Doe, meanwhile, is trying to make eye-contact—through the sweat pouring down his face—with another rebel, a tall, massively built man. 'I am your brother,' Doe mutters to him, 'I am your brother.' The rebel beams benevolently at Doe and pats him on the head. At that, Johnson explodes. 'I will kill you!' he roars. 'I don't want to shoot you, I'm a humanitarian. But don't fuck with me!' Johnson stops to take a mouthful of beer. The woman in blue wipes his face and hands him another can. 'So,' he continues, 'what do you want to tell me, Doe?'

'Prince, Prince, listen to me.' Doe slumps forward. 'If you loosen me, I'll tell you. Just loosen my arms.'

But Johnson is distracted by an argument with another rebel. Now everyone joins in and Johnson becomes highly agitated. His shouting is unintelligible, and he gesticulates wildly. All the while Doe is pleading: 'Gentlemen, gentlemen, we are all one.'

Suddenly, Johnson pounds his fist on the desk.

'That man won't talk, bring me his ear!' The camera jerks around to Doe, now held down by several rebels. The one with the close-fitting cap has started carving away at Doe's left ear, amid the President's high-pitched screams.

'Now the other ear, the right ear,' Johnson orders, hitting his desk twice. The woman in blue has stopped fanning Johnson; mouth agape, she moves closer to get a better look. Doe fights back, twisting his body to keep his captors from getting at the remaining ear. A couple of rebels have to step in front and dig their boots into his chest, pinning him down. 'I've got too much blood, too much blood,' Doe gasps, thrashing his head from side to side. The soldier in the cap continues carving. The deed done, Johnson's men push Doe back into a sitting position. One of them mugs for the camera, his boot in the President's back, arms outstretched in a victory pose, pistol dangling from his hand. Doe is covered in blood. The woman in blue is grinning. Johnson is leaning back in his swivel chair. 'Get him out of my sight,' he snaps.

The camera cuts to the outside, where Doe now sits on a concrete patio. Half-unconscious from the loss of blood, he is surrounded by rebels still exhorting him to talk. 'Please be a man,' says one, 'and tell me. What has happened to the Liberian economy?'

'If you loosen me, I will talk,' Doe mumbles, pitching forward.

Another rebel, dressed in a flak jacket, leans over the President. 'Samuel Doe, if you are not willing to confess, just say it. But we are asking you in a polite manner right now. What did you do with all the money?' Turning to a fellow guerrilla, he adds, 'He's a stubborn man.'

'I'm not stubborn,' Doe protests.

'Will you talk?'

'I'll talk, I'll talk.'

'But when? It's getting dark.'

The rebel in the flak jacket squats on the ground, putting his face next to the President's. 'Confess to the Liberian people. That's all we expect of you. Where did you keep the Liberian people's money?'

'You know, gentlemen, if I tell you, you will not believe it.'

'We'll believe it,' the rebels chorus.

'I was always in the interest of the people. I have only one account.'

The flak-jacketed rebel: 'What is the number?'

'I dunno the number.'

'You gotta know your own number.'

'I dunno the number.'

This obviously throws their line of questioning, because the rebels begin to argue among themselves. Doe's eyes are rolling back into his head. 'I'm in a lot of pains,' he moans. 'Let me rest. Please, I'm in pains. My ears are cut. Please, I'll talk later.' Someone empties a can of water over the President's head. Blood and water and sweat drip down from his hair. He whimpers, 'Please wipe my face.'

'Don't wipe his face,' commands one rebel, which causes another argument to erupt about whether to wipe his face. Doe, meantime, is trying to talk to a rebel kneeling beside him. 'I can't hardly lift my head,' he says.

'You don't have to look or see,' the rebel retorts. 'You just have to speak.' He thrusts a microphone into Doe's face. 'Now say: I, Samuel Kanyon Doe.'

'I, Samuel Kanyon Doe.'

'Say: The government of Liberia has been overthrown by Prince Johnson's forces.'

Doe slumps forward again, then throws his head back with effort. 'I order the members of the armed forces to surrender so that we can build our country.'

'Surrender to who?'

'To Prince Johnson.' Doe turns imploringly to the rebel. 'If you save my life, I can learn a lot. I can do things to avoid trouble.'

'Where did you put the Liberian people's money?'

'I want to talk, I want to talk plenty, but please. I'm in pains. Please loosen my handcuffs.'

The video ends abruptly; Doe bled to death sometime during the night. Prince Johnson's rebels took his body to Island Clinic, near the port, where it was placed on a metal operating trolley for public display. Doe lay stretched out on his back, legs and arms extended, so that people cold see where the two fingers on his right hand had been hacked off. Flies danced in and out of the holes where his ears had been, settling on the deep red slashes that scored his limbs and chest. He hardly resembled the ruthless dictator in whose name the orgy of blood-letting and ethnic atrocities had been committed; in the end, chopped up like that, the man who had inspired so much violence resembled little more than a medical school cadaver.

8

I never went back to Liberia. Dennis and I were reunited in Sierra Leone; I then settled in Washington DC and Dennis returned to Monrovia to serve the last year of his posting. I saw him only twice during that year, when he came to Washington on leave. Most of the time, we had no means of communicating except by letters that were delivered by the occasional traveller to and from Monrovia. It was not easy for us, and not at all what I had imagined as the beginnings of our marriage.

Four years after Doe's death, Liberia is still in chaos. Despite several skirmishes with the West African peacekeeping forces that pushed them out of Monrovia, Charles Taylor and his soldiers continue to control about eighty per cent of the country. Several new guerrilla groups—all of them ethnically based—have emerged and now hold chunks of territory in the north-west and south-east. Prince Johnson was forced to flee the country and his army disbanded. A virtually impotent government of national unity, propped up by the West African troops, rules Monrovia.

All the warring parties agreed to a United Nations-sponsored plan to demobilize and disarm their soldiers and to hold democratic elections, but little has been done to implement it. Meanwhile, approximately one million of Liberia's two and a half million people are living as refugees within the country or in neighbouring states; two-thirds of the total population are dependent on food aid.

RWANDA

PAROISSE
IZIHIRWE
YUBILE NZIZA

The Rwandan town of Nyamata is thirty kilometres south of Kigali, the capital. When I went there, the church was still filled with hundreds of bodies. Dogs had torn apart some of the remains, and I had to tread carefully for fear of stepping on a skull or a femur. Journalists had written of vomiting when they came across these scenes. But the smell in Nyamata was not too bad—the massacre had been committed almost three months earlier, and the bodies were dry. I didn't vomit. I wrote my despatch for BBC radio sitting in my borrowed car twenty yards from the church. I began, 'The phenomenon of reporters being shown massacre sites by the rebels cannot be dismissed as mere rebel propaganda. Genocide has been committed and some of the evidence is in Nyamata.' The BBC is very careful about using words like 'genocide', but my report was broadcast exactly as I wrote it.

The killings began with the death of President Juvenal Habyarimana in a mysterious plane crash on 6 April. Within minutes, Hutu death squads began murdering all the late President's political opponents and potential opponents. These categories included moderate Hutus and any Tutsis, the tribe from which the Rwandan Patriotic Front draws most support. No one knows how many died. The Red Cross stopped counting at an estimated half a million.

One of the friends I had made in Kigali was Captain Mbaye Diagne, a Senegalese UN military observer who had come to Rwanda in 1992 as part of an Organization of African Unity observer team. The team expanded into a UN mission in late 1993. The mainly African UN observers were supposed to monitor a ceasefire in the war and the installation of a coalition government.

Mbaye had joined the Senegalese army straight after graduating from the University of Dakar. When I first met him, he appeared to be deeply suspicious of journalists. He was particularly incensed on one occasion when a French reporter stated, correctly, that the militias were fleeing from the rebels in Kigali. 'You are making my job very difficult,' he told the journalist. 'If you say that the militias are fleeing, it will hurt their pride and they might kill more people.' As was usual with Mbaye, the argument ended with a

Photo: Gilles Peress/Magnum

handshake, and his stained teeth were revealed in a smile. 'Do your job. But please be careful.'

Mbaye was a tall man, slim like most Senegalese, and always impeccable in his green combat fatigues. It was a mystery to me how he emerged looking so smart from a tiny room with no running water. Perhaps it was a legacy from his childhood in Pikine, a sprawling suburb of Dakar, Senegal's capital. I have seen the small wooden houses there, also without running water, from which mothers and children emerge into the sandy alleys dressed in magnificent gleaming white *boubous*, the traditional dress of the northern Senegalese.

It was maybe because of the time I had spent in Dakar and the fact that I knew a few words of Wollof, Mbaye's mother tongue, that the Captain and I made friends. We usually spoke French, although he, like most Africans, spoke several languages, including English. One of our favourite subjects was food, especially Senegalese cooking. African soldiers were particularly disgusted by their NATO rations; they were not used to tinned and processed food and dreamt of fish and rice.

Mbaye's job was military liaison between the UN and the Rwandan government troops. He seemed never to stop working. With a cigarette between his teeth and a pile of maps under his arm he was constantly on the move. Fighters on all sides knew Mbaye well because he took the time to stop at the roadblocks and talk to them.

Mbaye knew that the policy of the United Nations was to evacuate expatriate UN staff, not Rwandans working for the various UN agencies. When it was announced that most of the foreigners had been evacuated from Kigali, it meant that most of the *white* people had gone. On the day the announcement was broadcast in Europe, I came across about 5,000 Zairean nationals at their embassy, desperate to leave. They had no food or water, were surrounded by militia and no one except the Red Cross was trying to help them. 'If the UN can't evacuate us,' said a spokesman for the people living in mud on the ruined former lawns of the abandoned diplomatic mission, 'we will walk through the war to Zaire.' A few days later, they had gone. I have no idea how many made it.

While working hard to fulfil his official UN function, Mbaye also set about saving as many members of the Senegalese community and Rwandans as he could. Among the first lives he saved were those of the children of the Hutu Prime Minister, Agathe Uwilingiyimana, who had been murdered early on by the government forces because she was in favour of a negotiated solution with the rebels. Captain Mbaye Diagne knew the government forces and he knew that after the Prime Minister had been killed, her five children would be next. He found them and hid them in his own room before organizing their evacuation.

Thousands of Tutsis and Hutu government opponents had taken refuge in a hotel in the government-held area of Kigali, the once plush Hotel Mille Collines. The swimming-pool was emptied early on by the refugees, who needed drinking and washing water. There was no electricity after a few weeks. The militia hung around menacingly at the gates. A few unarmed UN soldiers provided a thin blue line of symbolic protection. Mbaye Diagne was one of those soldiers. It was his negotiating skill which helped keep the killers from entering the lobby and pursuing their deadly work.

After lengthy negotiations the UN managed to set up some exchanges of civilians trapped behind hostile lines in the city. Tutsis and Hutu government opponents would be removed to safety from the Mille Collines and other places in the government held sector, while Hutus caught behind rebel lines would be transferred from a football stadium to the government side.

The first attempt at a transfer was almost a disaster. The government militia decided that the swap of people was unfair to them and attacked the UN convoy as it pulled out of the Mille Collines. Machete-wielding men and boys in makeshift uniforms hacked at the passengers and blocked the road. One of the people on that first convoy wrote later in a letter, 'Captain Mbaye Diagne saved our lives. He stood unarmed on the lorry and struck out at the militia with his feet, his kitbag, anything. We shall always remember him.'

That particular convoy was turned back to the hotel after several people were badly injured by the militia machetes. But later exchanges did work. Two simultaneous convoys of white UN trucks carrying terrified people crossed at a roundabout on the front line. The trucks, driven by Ghanaian UN soldiers, passed through shaky, UN-brokered truces which were often violated and lasted just a few hours.

There were many other times when Mbaye saved lives. A UN aid worker had a list of Rwandan staff working for UN agencies before the war. Some of the names had a line through them. They were dead. Others had figures next to them—$35, $30. Their lives had been purchased at militia roadblocks; the negotiator had been Mbaye.

Twenty yards in front of a major government army base, Mbaye rescued an entire family that had been hiding in an apparently abandoned house. These people were Tutsis, but the Captain saved many Hutus as well.

And I wonder whether Mbaye saved my own life. I was in his car, travelling through Kigali. We were stopped at one of the city's many roadblocks, and a young militiaman with a Chinese stick grenade came up to my side of the car. 'Are you Belgian?' he asked. The government radio station had said the Belgians were responsible for killing the President. I didn't answer. Mbaye was firm: '*Adressez-vous à moi! Je suis le patron ici!*' The militiaman almost stood to attention despite the fact that Mbaye was unarmed. He went round to Mbaye's side of the car. 'Is that white man Belgian?' he asked. 'Don't be stupid,' the Captain replied firmly—almost too firmly, I thought. Then he smiled and said through his gappy teeth, 'I'm the only Belgian here. See'—he jokingly pointed to his Senegalese skin—'black Belgian.' The militiaman laughed. 'Now,' said Mbaye, firm again, 'Get out of my way. I am a UN military observer and I'm going through this roadblock.' We proceeded as planned.

I often censored my BBC reports regarding Mbaye's work. If it had been revealed that a Senegalese officer was rescuing people, both he and the government opponents still in the area would have been in grave danger. But now, it is relatively safe to write about Mbaye's activities.

I was standing in the car park of the UN headquarters when we heard of what a military spokesman later called 'the accident'. The UN aid worker who had worked with Mbaye to rescue

Rwandans was depressed. 'A military observer has just been hit by a mortar.'

'Who is it?' I asked.

'I don't know yet,' said the aid worker. He was lying. He had heard which officer had been struck but was still hoping his information was wrong. Then he looked out across the barbed-wire fence of the compound: 'I hope to God it's not Mbaye.'

A two-way radio crackled: 'Captain Mbaye Diagne is missing. An ambulance is on its way to his last known location.'

I arrived at the scene five minutes after the body had been removed. The front seat of Mbaye's Landcruiser was covered with blood. He had been killed instantly by a rebel mortar round that landed three metres from the driver's door. He had been chatting to government soldiers at a checkpoint that he himself had named 'Kigali Nightclub Bridge'.

A Hutu civilian who also used to work for the UN tried to take over some of Mbaye's rescue missions. Now it is his identity that must be protected. 'Mbaye is dead,' the man said. 'I must try to carry on his work. There is no one else who knows the town well enough.'

On my last day in Kigali, reporters were offered a trip by the UN from their headquarters in rebel-held territory to the Red Cross hospital on the government side of the city. We would be travelling across Kigali Nightclub Bridge. I had made this trip several times before, usually in a UN vehicle. But as I was gathering my flak jacket and tape recorder, I thought about my friend. I didn't want to die on the final day of my assignment. It struck me, absurdly, that this would be silly. I decided not to make the trip after all.

The photographs on the following pages were taken in Rwanda by Gilles Peress [Magnum].

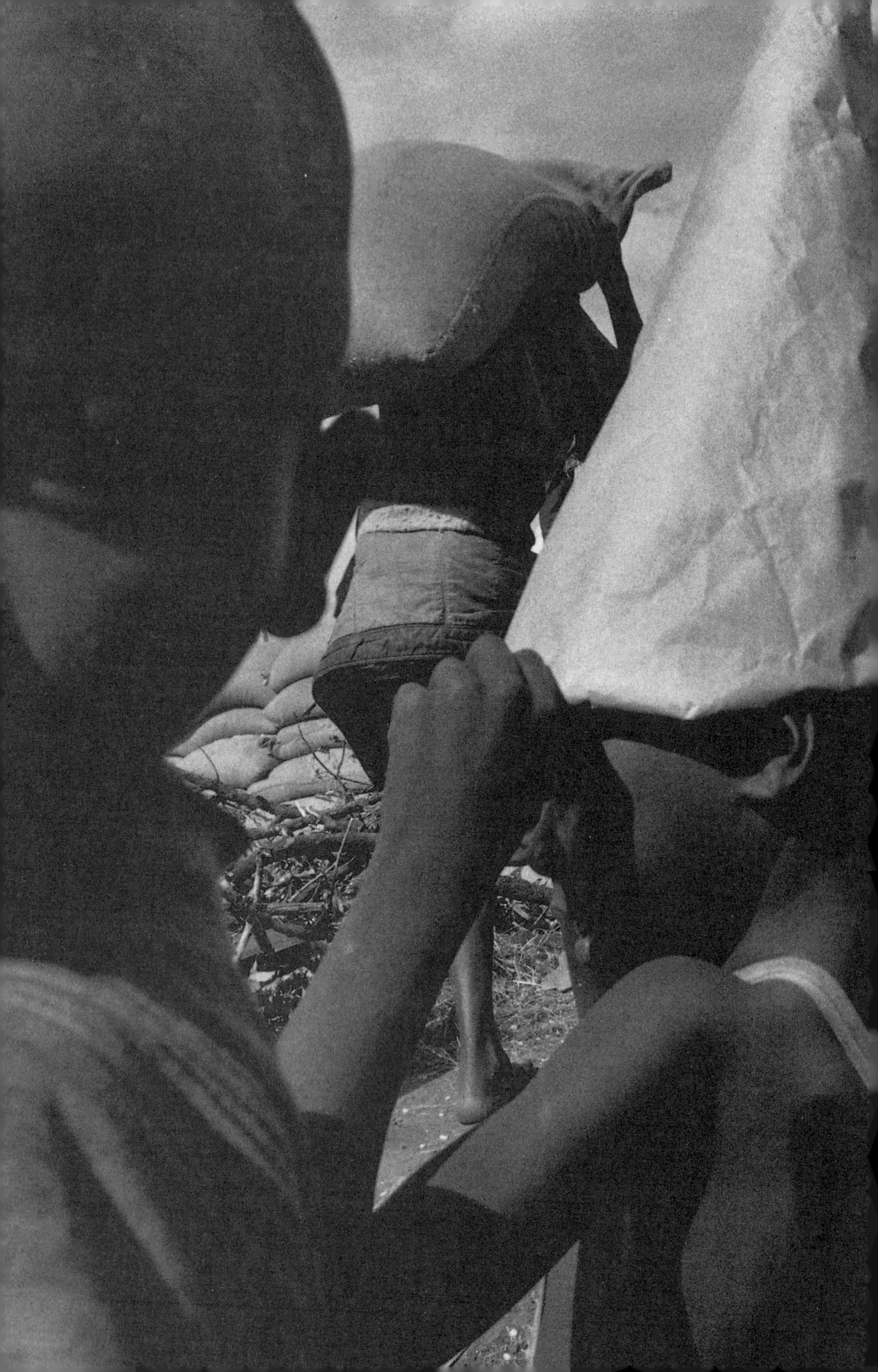

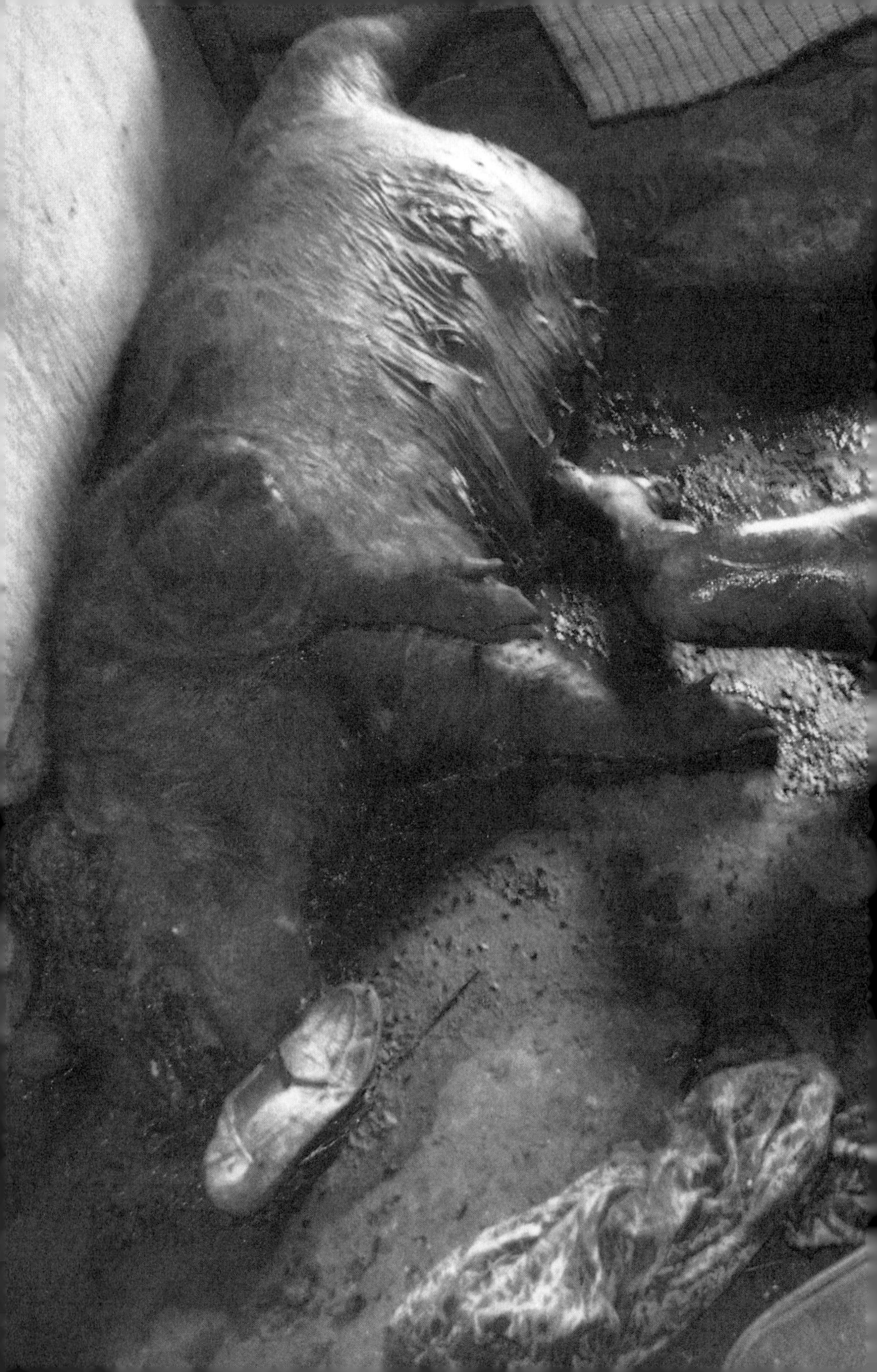

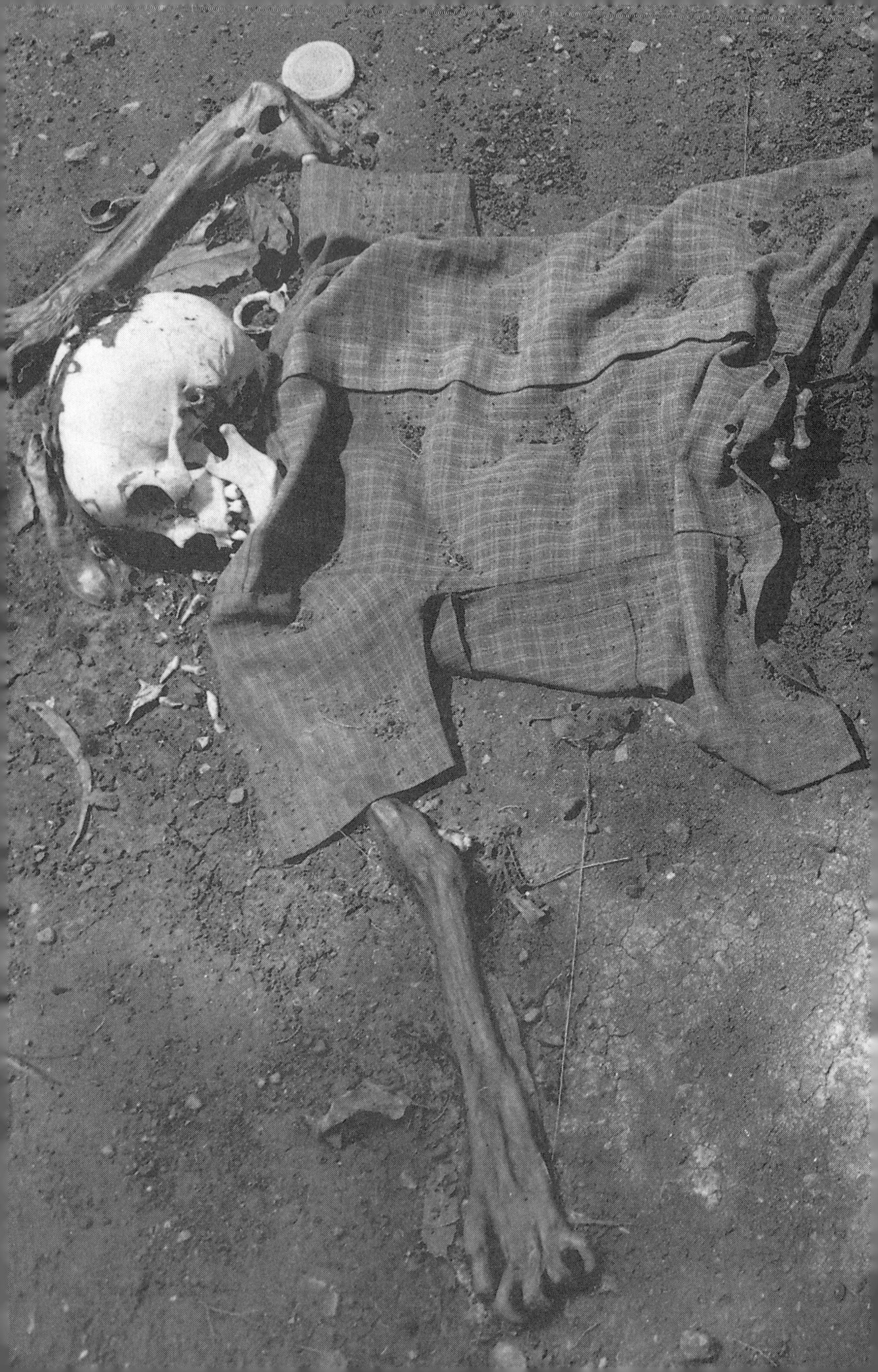

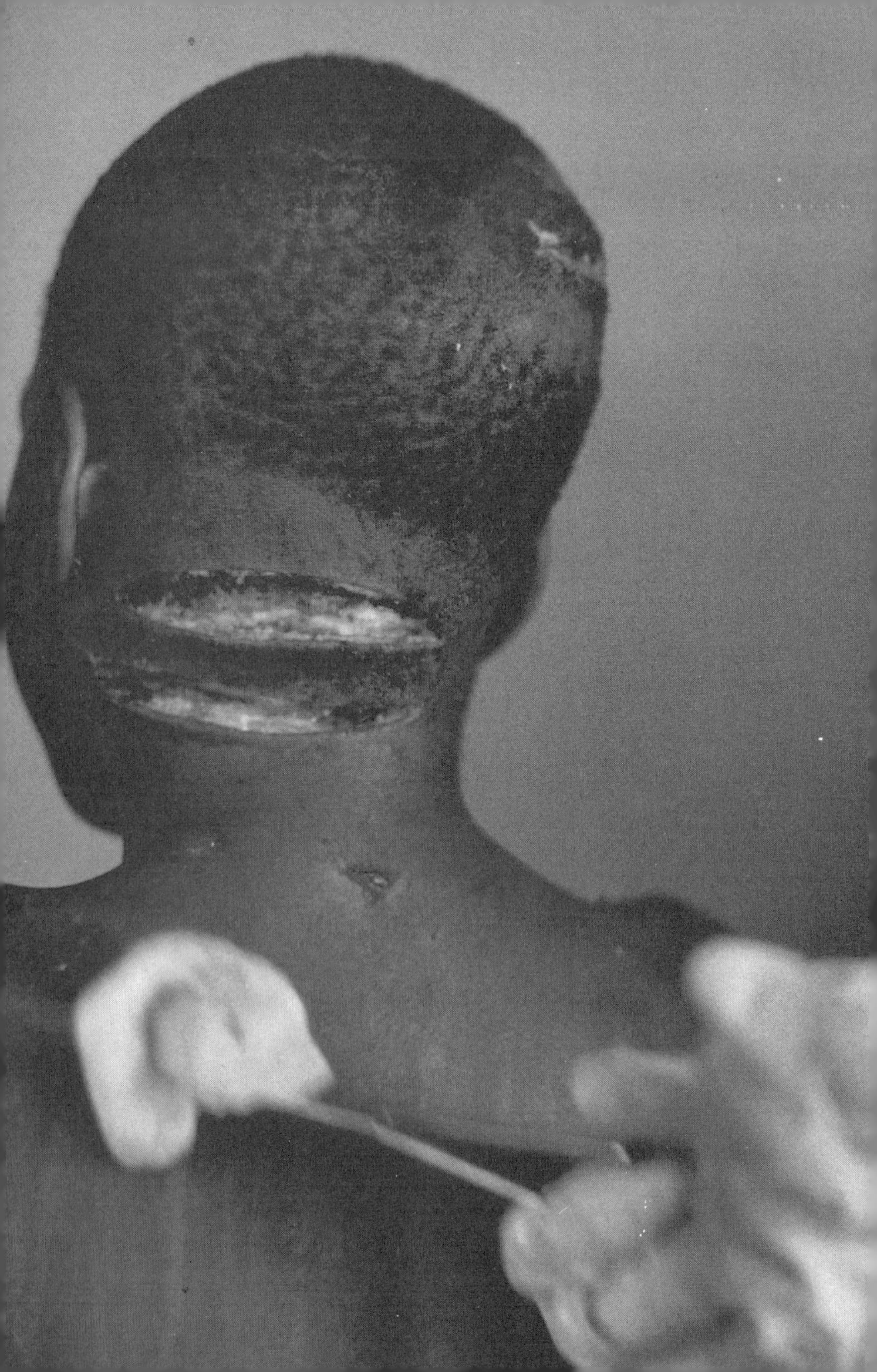

Paul Theroux
The Lepers of Moyo

Boarding the train in the African darkness just before dawn was like climbing into the body of a huge, dusty monster. I rejoiced in the strangeness of entering it, and I felt safe and happy inside, half-asleep on a wooden bench. But after sun-up the train did not seem so huge. And in harsh daylight, the dirty walls confined me, the bars on the windows became black and apparent, and my coach began to stink in the heat. I had a book on my lap, a new translation of *The Diaries of Franz Kafka.* I read only a few pages, in the way you nibble a sandwich, knowing it will have to last, and then I glanced around. The unpainted seats had been brought to a rich, mellow shine, the wood buffed by years of ragged bottoms. The whistle blew; we started to move; and on the first bend I saw the gasping boiler of the old steam engine, the locomotive drooling oil and water—looking wounded. It was just another old colonial train.

Once we were out of town, the huts beside the tracks were poorer—thatched roofs instead of tin, and clusters of them, their skeletal framework of sticks showing through the mud and daub like the bones of their occupants, who squatted nearby, watching us pass. When I caught their eye, they looked fearful and apologetic.

The trees along the tracks were thin, the soil was poor, and this stony land became flatter and drier as the train laboured north, snorting. When the sun was above the spindly branches, slanting into the gaping windows of the train, it heated the rusty bars and the battered interior, and the coach became very hot. I could see the peanut shells, the orange peels, the spat-out mass of bitten and chewed sugar-cane stalks on the floor. A woman in the next seat was nursing a child, but the child was seven or older, and because the woman was young and small and the child was large and greedy, this act of suckling seemed like incest, awkwardly sexual instead of maternal.

Dust stirred by the locomotive and the front coaches floated through the windows with sticky smoke-clouds, reeking of burnt coal. The locomotive dated from the British period, the war

---

Opposite: Paul Theroux in June 1968, when he was director of the Makerere University Centre for Adult Studies in Kampala, with members of his English class, officers in the Ugandan army.

perhaps. The thick engine-smoke left a layer of soot and greasy smuts everywhere, and soon blackened my bare arms. I sweated and smeared it. I had not thought to bring food. I had nothing to drink. And I was alone on this first day of October, known in Malawi as 'the suicide month' because of the intense heat.

This trip should have been miserable. It was magic.

It was my first taste of freedom in Africa. It was drama; it was romance, too. Although I had not published any of the poems I had written, this trip made me feel like a writer. The train was taking me away from the only Africa I knew, a demoralized place of bungalows and shanty settlements, the white club, the black slums, the Indian shops, a town that was no more than one wide street.

For almost a year I had been teaching at a small school just outside Blantyre and the more time I spent there, the more tame it seemed. I had grown used to it. I hated its muddy main street. These towns in central Africa had been laid out by the British and had the look of garrisons. There were bars and a movie theatre and a fish-and-chip shop. I had not come to Africa to drink beer and go to the movies. I needed something darker, stranger; I needed risk—danger, even.

'Going up-country?' my friend Mark had asked the day before I left. He was English, from southern Rhodesia.

'Up-country' said it all.

This was my vacation work. During the African school holidays, we Peace Corps teachers were told to get jobs or do something useful. I could have stayed at my school and catalogued books, or led a team of brush-cutters for the new sports field. Then one of my students mentioned that he was from the Central Province, near the lake. He told me the name of his village and said it was on the way to the mission hospital Moyo.

'The leprosarium,' he said.

I had never heard this English word before and I was bewitched by it. Leprosy was a primitive and dark disease, like an ancient curse. It suggested the unclean and the forbidden. It called to mind outcasts. It was an aspect of old, unsubtle Africa. Leper, leper, leper. I was sick of metaphors. I wanted words to have unambiguous meanings: leper, wilderness, poverty, heat.

I wrote to the father superior and said that I wanted to visit during the long school holiday. I could teach English, I said. Father DeVoss replied saying that I would be welcome. For the next few weeks I thought of nothing else.

I would be travelling by steam train to a remote part of the country; I would be in the bush—alone, in a leper colony. I would be leaving behind politics and order and dullness. It was what I craved: a place in Africa that was wild.

I was twenty-three years old. I wanted to make my living as a writer. I yearned to know the inside of the continent—its secrets.

I looked up from my book and out the window and saw that we were penetrating the bush. I was happy.

I had never been in a train that moved so slowly. It stopped often and everywhere, not always at a station but sometimes in the middle of nowhere, in the yellowy bush, the spindly tree limbs stuck against the window and the wall of foliage so close that the locomotive's racket echoed against it. There seemed no point in these stops, fifteen or twenty of them before noon, and several times the train hesitated, rolled backwards for half a minute, lurched, and then started up again. The sudden stops and reverses made the whole business odd and agreeable.

This African train, burning wood and coal in its firebox, clattered deep into Africa. I dozed and was wakened at one of the stops by the anvil-clang of the coupling—and I smiled when I looked at my arms, black from the soot and smuts settling on my skin.

I compared arms with the small boy next to me.

'Mine is blacker than yours.'

'My arm is not black,' he said.

At one that afternoon we came to the town of Balaka, where dogs slept in the middle of the street. Balaka, a railway junction (another line went to Fort Johnstone and Monkey Bay), was hotter and flatter than any place I had seen. Walking along the platform to ask the conductor what time we were leaving ('Not before tree,' he said), I saw that one of the forward coaches had a good paint job and shuttered windows. A shutter rose, and a small, blue-eyed child looked out—it could only have been a missionary's child—and I realized that I had come upon a first-class passenger. I had not known about this one good coach on the train, shutters down, doors locked.

I had no desire to hide in there and travel with my fellow *mzungus*, first class on soft seats. I did not want to listen to them complain. Shocking train, they would say. Filthy weather. Bloody Africans—

I heard that talk all the time in Blantyre. I imagined the *mzungus* behind the locked doors of their first-class coach, grumbling, killing time by reading the yellow, bound copies of the *Daily Mirror*, months old, that were sent sea mail to Malawi from London.

I found an African restaurant behind the goods shed at Balaka station, and for four shillings and a tickey—threepence—was given a chipped, enamel bowl of chicken and rice. Afterwards I sat in the shade of the veranda, watching the hot street and the white sky, the earth like pale powder, and everything still except the insects. I walked into the sun and immediately felt the weight of it on the top of my head. I stood alone in the middle of the street on the small black island of my shadow, and I thought: *I am where I want to be.*

The whistle blew at about two-thirty, and after some hesitation—shunting in the Balaka tracks—the train set off again, north, through the dusty landscape of yellow bush and low, skinny trees and elephant grass that was taller than the Africans. On this blazing October afternoon, nothing stirred—no birds, no people, no animals. The bush looked stifled. The train was the only moving thing in that whole hot world.

Here and there a station or a siding appeared. Most were wooden sheds with tin roofs and no signs. On their dirt platforms, packed hard by all the tramping feet, women and small girls sold greasy dough cakes and bananas and peanuts, carrying them in tin basins on their heads. They were skinny, ragged, barefoot, and the further north we went the more naked the women were. Most on this hot lakeshore plain were bare-breasted. It was the Africa of my imagination, at last.

I sat at the window, squinting through the coal-smoke as we went deeper. Through the late afternoon I saw shadows rippling in the trees like phantoms, Africans watching the train, and I knew they had seen my white face. On one embankment I saw a funeral, a mass of chanting people marching behind a wooden coffin. I saw naked children. I saw two people, a man and a woman, rolling on the ground in panic, startled by the train in the act of love.

The sun was now below the tattered trees, and dusk was gathering in shadows under a briefly bluer sky.

'Ntakataka,' an African said to me.

That was the station for Moyo.

It was almost six. I had been travelling in a state of great happiness for more than twelve hours.

Father DeVoss met me. He was tall and gaunt, and although he was not old he was grey. He wore a dusty, white cassock and looked at me—fondly I thought—with a sad smile.

'Good to see you,' he said. 'You play cards?'

2

The priests' house was on the only high ground and looked haunted, one of its windows lit by an over-bright pressure lamp, the rest shuttered or in darkness. Its shadows and its size and its crumbling stucco gave it a ghostly, wolfish look.

We passed through the village below it, a place of fires and woodsmoke and voices and yapping dogs. Because of the crude lamps flaring inside the huts, all the shadows were active and black. There was a smell, too, human, sweetish, like decay—the smell of illness and death.

An old priest came fussing down the stone stairs. He managed to snatch my bag over my protests, and passed it to an African in khaki shorts and a white shirt, an African servant's basic uniform. The priest was speaking in Chinyanja and was, I now realized, talking to me, not to the African, slapping at my bag.

'*Moni, bambo, muli bwanji?—eh, nyerere! Eh, Mpemvu! Pepani, palibe mphepo—*'

Hello, how are you? What's that—an ant! A roach! Sorry, there's no breeze here—

The old priest went on jabbering while sweeping away the

insects. It was clear that he did not speak English, and as I did not speak Dutch, this would be our way of communicating.

'*Dzina lanu ndani*?' I said, asking him his name.

His reply sounded like *Fonderpilt*, but when he added in English, 'The poor ones, not the rich American ones,' I understood that his name was van der Bilt. To everyone he was Brother Piet.

He was accompanied by a younger priest, Father Touchette, newly arrived from Canada, still sallow from the trip and rather confused by this torrent of Chinyanja. The African, Simon, put my bag in the corner and then returned and dished up some food. Father DeVoss was already seated and he simply watched me and listened. He was tall and had an air of gentle authority.

I was thinking how white their cassocks had seemed when I arrived, and how dusty and stained and torn they were up close.

Washing my hands at the sink in the kitchen, I glanced at my face in the mirror and hardly recognized myself—my sooty hair and skin, my sunburnt nose, my exhausted, bloodshot eyes. Brother Piet sat me down and gave me the food that Simon had prepared—beans and boiled greens and boiled peanuts and roasted corn and a lump of steamed dough they called *nsima*: African food.

Brother Piet asked me about the train. He travelled on it now and then, he said, to get to the market in Balaka.

'I always go second class,' he said. 'Then I have someone to talk to.'

'When did you come to Africa?' I asked in Chinyanja.

'So long ago'—and the phrase he used, *za kale*, meant in ancient times—'that I travelled down the Nile River. Yes! And I drank the water of the Nile!' He was seventy-four and had not been in Holland for sixteen years.

I went on eating, scooping the food with my hands using a ball of *nsima*, in the African way.

'When I die, maybe,' he said, and laughed, 'they send me back to Amsterdam. I am dead, eh?'

I liked his humour and oddity, speaking Chinyanja in his boisterous way, and occasionally throwing in an English word.

Father Touchette did not have much conversation. He was

new, fearful, with the tense demeanour of a strict believer; no jokes—pious, perhaps because he was afraid. He clutched his breviary as though it were a brick he wanted to throw at a sinner. He seemed to be listening at the window, one ear cocked in the direction of the African shouts and laughter and the random dribbling sound of the drums.

'And how did you happen to come here to Moyo?' I asked him.

'I was sent here,' Father Touchette said sternly, as though it had been a punishment.

'It is his good luck,' Father DeVoss said in a cheery voice, and it seemed to me that he had detected a grievance in what Father Touchette had said and was trying to make light of it.

'I am happy to be here,' I said, truthfully. My smile revealed my weariness. I was exhausted from the trip and from the hot meal in this humid room, all the dark heat of the night hanging like black curtains at the windows.

'Does Paul know where his room is?' Father DeVoss said, seeing that I was tired.

I said goodnight, and with a candle in a dish Simon led me down a long hallway.

'This is a good place,' I said.

'Yes,' he said.

'But some people are sick.'

'This is where they are cured,' Simon said. 'That is why it is a good place.'

He had put the candle down and was throwing open the shutters of my room.

'In the villages'—he meant everywhere else—'people are sick, but they stay that way.'

After he slipped back into the darkness, I lay on the hard bed of this cool room, the candle flame making twitchy shadows on the plaster wall. It was like being in the antechamber of a castle—strange and spooky. I had been reading Kafka. But it was more than Kafka's imagery that inspired this feeling. It was the experience of the train trip and the heat and the dry yellow landscape and the black night and the smell of poverty and illness.

The next morning everything was different. In darkness Africa seems enchanted. In daylight it is hot and pitiless. Most of the trees are so wraithlike, their leaves so slender; there is no shade under them.

The light at Moyo was more intense than where I lived in the south of the country. Was it some effect of the lake near here, its surface flashing back the sun? Perhaps it was the flatness of the land, the high clouds, the thin bush, or simply the time of year. Something made for the glaring leaves and the shine on some rocks and the pale soil and white skies. It made for nakedness.

It was not sunshine, not warm and bright, but a fiery African light that swelled in the sky. It came straight through the threadbare curtains into my room, waking me like a blade piercing my eyes. I saw that the walls were cracked plaster and dusty whitewash, with a wooden crucifix of a skinny, suffering Jesus over my bed. The floor was dusty, and the wood door jamb was pitted with termite holes and the place smelt of ants. Last night, this building on its hill had seemed so substantial, but in this harsh, truthful light the structure was frail and elderly.

In the kitchen, Simon poured me a cup of milky tea. The large screened-in box that looked like an animal cage was, I knew, a meat safe, and its contents—plates of chicken—were going rancid. The smell of dead meat hung in the room. On the table, the bread, the papaya, the margarine and the jam all smelt of the meat safe.

'Where is Father DeVoss?'

'He is saying mass.'

I sat down at the worn table in the blinding light, with my bottle of Koo Ketchup and a dish of Springbok margarine.

'Are there nuns here, too?'

'Yes, there are three,' Simon said.

'What do they do?'

'The nuns take care of our bodies. The priests take care of our souls,' he said, with the sententiousness of a convert. 'And one American *mzungu*.'

'What is the American's name?'

'I don't know. But they call her Birdie.' He pronounced it in the African way, 'Buddy.'

'Like "bird"? *Mbalame*?'

'Yes. She is a sister.'

It was the British usage: a sister also meant nursing sister, a nurse.

'Is the convent nearby?'

'It is near to the hospital.'

'How long has the woman Birdie been here?'

'She was coming this side in July.'

Three months ago.

'What about Father Touchette?'

'He was coming this side in April.'

Simon had been here most of his life. He had been a small child, he told me, when Father DeVoss first came to Moyo. Simon's father had pointed the priest out and told him not to be afraid.

'We thought that white people were ghosts who would eat us. But my father said, 'No, he is a good man.'

'What was your father doing here?'

'He was sick with *mkhate*.'

A leper.

Father DeVoss appeared soon after that. His look of distraction, a dreamy vagueness and inattention, made him seem kind and gentle and a little sad.

'Did you have a full house?'

'Attendance at mass is not so good.'

'Maybe I should go.'

'If you wish,' he said, as though he hardly cared.

'I was about to prepare some lessons. I thought I might start my English classes soon.'

'That is a good idea,' Father DeVoss said. 'But there is no hurry.' He was smiling sadly out of the window. 'Would you like to see the church?'

I said yes, because I suspected that he wanted to show me. It was a short walk from the priests' house. The church was large and dusty, smelling of lighted candles—the tallow, the flames, the burnt wicks. Some of the windows were stained glass, and the Stations of the Cross were African carvings.

'Some of the lepers made them. They are not bad, eh? They are crude, but they have emotion.'

He looked around the church with a crooked smile that seemed to express scepticism, as though he only half-believed what all this represented. He pointed to a plaster statue.

'Saint Roche. You know about him?'

'No,' I said.

Father DeVoss smiled and said nothing. There were other plaster statues and plastic flowers and small gilt ornaments, but even so, from the light alone, streaming through the cracked windows, the church had an odour of sanctity.

'What about the hospital?'

'If you want to see it,' Father DeVoss said, as though surprised.

Since I had arrived, the leper village had been audible. It smouldered and crackled beneath the trees at the foot of the priests' hill. There were always voices and shouts and laughter, the continual cock crows the Africans called *tambala*, and the pounding of the pestles in the mortars as the women made *ufa*, the cornflour that was one of their staple foods. The village was also the smell of woodsmoke and that other more obscure odour, of human bodies, of disease and frailty and death, which was also the smell of dirt.

Father DeVoss was offhand introducing me to the nuns, like a man bringing a stranger to meet a wife or close relation. He hardly looked at them and did not tell me their names, only told them who I was.

'Paul insisted on seeing the hospital,' he said. 'As you know, this is all strange to me.'

He laughed softly and then left to return to the priests' house.

In his self-conscious way, he made me understand that the hospital was not his operation, but theirs, a clumsier, cruder business than saying mass perhaps, the inexact science of doctoring in the bush—knives and sutures and purple disinfectant and lepers always in line, waiting for bandages or pills.

This central building with the tin roof and the veranda was the dispensary, the older nun said. There were several other buildings, lined with cots, for seriously ill people, or disabled ones who had no families. But most of the lepers lived at home, in their huts, and were looked after by their relatives. Their bandages were changed in the afternoon; they picked up their medicine in the morning; and, except for the severe cases who were bedridden, most lepers lived in their village nearby.

As the nun spoke, leading me around, I was thinking of the strangeness of the place, and the word, leper. Leper, leper, leper.

At the next building I saw the woman Simon had told me about, the *mzungu* nursing sister he had called Birdie. She was bandaging a leper's foot, wrapping it like a package. A cheap clock with a stained face of tin ticked on the wall.

The woman was older than me, perhaps thirty, thin, with a sallow complexion, a yellowish pallor that serious *mzungus* acquire in the African bush. Only the fools sat in the sun; the rest stayed indoors or under cover, like this woman, and worked at their jobs.

I smiled while she wrapped the rag-like bandage. She said nothing and did not smile back, as though she resented the nun showing me around the hospital and interrupting the routine. A kind of pointless strictness was another characteristic of people in bush posts, as though such punctuality gave the day a shape and a meaning.

It was unusual in the Africa I knew for strangers not to introduce themselves so I said, 'Hello, I'm Paul.'

'Linda,' she said. 'They call me Birdie.'

'That's pretty.'

'It's short for Birdsall. Everyone in my family gets it,' she said. 'Have you just arrived?'

'I came on the train yesterday.'

'That train is scary.'

'I liked it. I guess I don't scare easily.'

'Then you came to the right place,' she said. 'Wouldn't you say so, sister?'

The nun smiled, but grimly. She had parchment-like skin, very white and wrinkled, as insubstantial as tissue, and a bristly moustache. She wore rubber gloves.

I hated myself for being a spectator here among these women who did this every day.

Birdie was still holding the leper's foot, snipping and

trimming the twisted ends of the knot she had fastened. A man in the next cot groaned. His hands and feet had been bandaged with strips of cloth. But his bandages were dirty and stained, and some foul-coloured liquid had leaked through and darkened his instep.

'What will you be doing here?' Birdie asked.

'Teaching English to anyone who wants to learn.'

Without replying, Birdie went to the next cot, where the leper was softly complaining. She took up one of his legs and began scissoring away his dirty bandages. Her silence made me think I had said something silly.

The nun went to work on another man's bandages and said, 'I'm sure your class will be very popular.'

The mention of an English class among this bandaging made it seem utterly frivolous. Birdie was cutting efficiently through the soiled bandages, using her sharp knife like a letter-opener.

'It seems such a busy place,' I said.

The nun said, 'We have about four hundred lepers and with their families there are about two thousand people altogether. Quite a number, and from all over the country. We have Tumbuka people from the north, Angonis from nearby, Sena people from the Lower River. Even some Yao Muslims from Fort Johnstone.'

'You look after all of them?'

'Oh, yes,' she said, flinging the cut and stained bandages into a bucket. 'Their villages turned them out. There is so much superstition and prejudice connected with this disease. Because for so many years there was no cure. People simply suffered and were treated horribly.'

'But it's not contagious and it's very easy to cure,' Birdie said. She too was discarding bandages and revealing a man's foot pitted with sores. 'There's no chance of any of us catching it. Yet very few of these people will ever go back to their own villages, because they're scarred. A person with toes missing looks like he still has the disease.'

She held the evidence in her hand, as she swabbed it with a damp piece of cotton. I wanted to ask her what had impelled her to do this.

'This is the last illness in Africa,' she said, as though reading my thoughts. 'It's all curable, and when it's gone the curse will be lifted, and there will be no other disease as bad.'

'I like Birdie's spirit,' the nun said.

'But you have them for life,' I said.

'More or less. Some are useful,' the nun said. 'The ones who are cured help us give out medicine and do the bandaging.'

'That guy looks really sick,' I said.

Birdie had moved to a different patient, whose leg was swollen like a club and was greyish and as rough as the bark of a tree.

'This is snakebite.'

'*Mamba akudya?*' I asked him, mentioning the snake whose bite was so venomous, the black mamba.

'*Kasongo*,' he said softly, correcting me, with a strange pedantry for a man in his condition. He had not been bitten by a mamba but by another black snake, as deadly as the cobra, one with a red crest. The hot regions of Malawi were full of huge poisonous snakes, which were so feared that it was a bad omen if one crossed your path, and if you did not manage to kill it you were to return home at once and stay there until the following day.

'His leg looks horrible.'

'Snake venom has an enzyme in it that helps the snake digest its food. That's what meat looks like when it's swallowed. Glad you came?'

'What about that guy?'

It was another man, with bandaged arms and head.

'He was hacked by his neighbour. An argument over a woman.'

Men and women were staring at us through the window.

'They are lepers. They're supposed to be working. They don't care.'

Another nun came into the ward, carrying scissors and a knife, looking businesslike.

'This is the new English teacher,' Birdie said, and it sounded like sarcasm.

After I left the hospital I cut through the village, aware that I was being stared at by everyone, and went back to the priests' house and prepared my English lessons.

The evening meal was the same, *nsima* and beans and boiled spinachy leaves. I asked Brother Piet more questions about Amsterdam, but his answers were the same as last night's. Father Touchette glowered by the window, listening to the racket from the village.

'Deal the cards,' Father DeVoss said at last, and Brother Piet obeyed, chattering in Chinyanja.

Father DeVoss was my partner, Simon was Brother Piet's; Father Touchette clutched his breviary and suffered, looking vindictive. We played six hands of whist and then went to our separate rooms. I read Kafka's *Diaries* by candlelight, no longer rationing them, for now they seemed self-pitying and faintly ridiculous, like the whining of a highly-strung child. It was another language, another world, remote from this one at Moyo.

3

'You can use the old bandaging room in the leprosarium for your English class,' Father DeVoss said, and I thought how striking the remark would have been as the first line of a poem. 'It's just a banda, but it's got tables,' he added.

Where the lepers used to lie, I thought, my students would now sit.

But there were no hidden meanings for these priests and nuns. This leper colony was not a metaphor to them. It was reality, a community of Africans, some sick, some well. It was not subtle. It was their life—the lepers and their families, the priests, the nuns. They would all die here.

The leper colony did not lead anywhere. No one, not even the priests, expected more. Most of the buildings were bare: no books on the shelves, no pictures on the walls, nothing except the simplest chairs and tables. Apart from the hymns in the church, and the drumming in the leper village, which began after dark and continued until eleven or so, there was no music. In this atmosphere, Father DeVoss's deck of playing cards, especially the picture cards, seemed highly coloured and evocative, and I found myself lingering over them, discerning expressions on the faces of the Jack, Queen and King.

The games of whist were to pass the time. At Moyo, there were no other games. There was what you saw and nothing more. No wanting, no desire. The melancholy of it, I thought; but that was my feeling, not theirs. It was not heaven, not hell, but earth as limbo for those who believed in limbo.

There was no talk of the past. The other world was so remote that it had no features. The leper colony had replaced all other realities, and so no one reminisced. The talk among the priests was of practical matters in the present. Except for Father Touchette, everyone spoke Chinyanja. And when they were not being silly—in front of me they always talked in a joky way—they were solemn. They did not talk about the future, though they occasionally mentioned death or eternity.

Their clothes were dusty and dirty, but they did not seem poor. On the contrary, their appearance made them seem indifferent and unworldly and spiritual.

One night while I was making notes for my class, sitting at the dining-table, where the only Tilly lamp stood, its brightness making me see double, Father DeVoss walked behind me, hesitated, picked up the English textbook *Foundation Secondary English*, then examined it—looked it over rather than read it—and set it down. He did the same with Kafka's *Diaries* which was also in the stack. He might have been picking up a pair of shoes, to look at the soles and the stitches. There was nothing inside these books for him. He was utterly uninterested, as though the books were mute objects without any function, like worn-out shoes, and this was, I was beginning to think, precisely what they were: dead weight.

I felt the priests were humouring me about the English class. They were going along with it. I was not dismayed by their low expectations. That they helped me in spite of their lack of faith meant they liked me, and that pleased me. I found them congenial, even nervous Father Touchette, who always winced when the drumming started in the leper village.

I was glad that I had come and for the first time since arriving in Africa I did not want to be anywhere else.

I had put up a sign on the dispensary wall, where bandaging times were announced. My note, in Chinyanja, said there would be an English class on Wednesday afternoon at five. It seemed to me an appropriate time. The lepers spent the morning lining up for medicine and bandages. It was too hot after lunch. Life in the leprosarium resumed when the sun dipped below the treetops, and the shadows lengthened. In the hottest, brightest part of the day, when the sun was overhead, life came to a stop, and there was no one to be seen. People withdrew into their huts, where the dirt was damp and cool.

Wednesday came. At breakfast, Father DeVoss said, 'You don't have to hold your class today. If it doesn't work out, there's always Friday—or next week.'

Time has little meaning here, he meant. But it was for my sake that I needed to make my English class seem urgent; otherwise, I would lose interest in it. I had been in Africa long enough to understand that to survive I had to impose a shape on the long day—break it into three parts—even if it was all a pretence. So I needed the class.

The bandaging room was a large, open-sided shed with a sloping tin roof and a large water-butt under a rusty downspout. At one time, this water-butt must have been important, perhaps a source of water; but as there were now standpipes in the leper village, this big barrel—murky and haunted by breeding mosquitoes—was unused.

At five there were men waiting for me. I knew they were lepers from their walking sticks and bandages. Seeing me approach, some other men got up from under a tree and came over. That made eight. Then an old woman shuffled in, guided by a young girl. It was clear that the old woman was blind: one eye looked as though it were badly sewn shut—an illusion of the lashes—and the other was distorted and as glazed and marbled as an agate. This old blind woman and the young girl were the only females in the class. The girl was in her teens, barefoot, wearing a wrap-around and a purple scarf on her head, a turban, that made her seem exotic. She led the blind woman to a bench, then sat beside her and whispered, while the blind woman made passes in the air with her damaged hand like a clumsy blessing.

'Please write your names on this piece of paper,' I said.

This caused a commotion. Some understood, others didn't. Only three could not write, not counting the blind woman, whose presence baffled me.

One man with a full set of teeth and scars on his forehead that seemed more an accident than a design rattled the paper and began to laugh.

'Do you want to learn English?'

He paid no attention.

'That man is sick in his head,' a man in the back said.

The other men laughed at this. They had big misshapen feet and bruised legs and had brought into the room that earthen odour of sickness and dead flesh.

I ignored them and said to the man, 'My name is Paul. What is your name?'

'Name,' he said. There was a dribble of spittle in the corner of his mouth. He seemed very innocent and helpless, almost childlike in the way his face was about to crumple, either into laughter or tears.

Some of the others laughed, and the man in the back laughed the hardest, commanding attention.

'Why are you laughing?'

'Because he is foolish,' the loud man said.

'Please stand up.'

He did so.

'What is your name?'

'You can read it for yourself on the paper, Father.'

'But I want you to tell me,' I said.

'My name is Johnson Magondwe, and I am very well, thank you.'

'You may sit down.'

'What is your name, Father?' he said, folding his arms and still standing.

'I've already told you that.'

'No. You were telling that foolish man your name, but you were not telling us.'

He grunted *eh*, *eh*, and looked around at the others in the room in triumph.

'My name is Paul. Please sit down.'

'I am having one more question, Father.'

'You can ask it later.'

But he kept his arms folded and set his jaw at me, and I saw that the other men around him were giggling with a sort of submissive fear.

I turned my back on them and spoke to another silent man in the first row, hoping that he was not the simpleton he seemed.

'Hello. How are you?'

He looked terrified. He sucked on his tongue and said nothing.

'He is not understanding, Father.'

'*Moni, bambo*,' I said.

'He is deaf in his ears, Father.'

'*Muli bwanji*?' I said.

'And foolish, Father.'

That was Johnson Magondwe, calling out from the back of the room. I ignored him, but I felt weary in anticipation. So far, one woman was blind, one man was crazy, and another deaf. Several others obviously spoke no English at all. And Johnson was a bore and a bully.

The young girl in the colourful scarf was twisting her fingers, looking anxious.

'Do you speak English?'

'Yes, I do speak,' she said almost in a whisper, lowering her eyes.

'Who is this old woman?'

'She is my granny.'

'What is your name?'

'My name is Amina.'

Then she bowed her head, but even so I could see her long lashes and clear skin, and her shoulders shining. She was thin, but sturdy. Her neck was long, her fingers slender. She had full lips and large eyes. I loved her for my being able to see the suggestions of her bones beneath her flesh, in her face and her hands, her shoulders. She was young, though not so young in African terms. Many girls her age—sixteen or seventeen—already had several children.

The men were surprised that she spoke English. I wrote some lines of dialogue in chalk, on a smooth plank that was painted black. Johnson, and the man next to him, Phiri, could read it easily, and so could Amina. With my coaching, two others learned it. While this went on, the blind woman grunted; the simpleton drooled; the deaf man rocked back and forth.

I was tired, yet they seemed oddly rested and calm. They were not eager but curious, watching me, waiting for me to teach them in the same way they stood at the dispensary with their hands out, empty palms upward, expecting their medicine.

'Repeat after me,' I said. 'It's a dog.'

I chose them at random.

'Is a dock.'

'It's a dog,' I said. 'You.'

'Is a dock.'

'But this is a duck.'

'Thees a dock.'

'A duck,' I said. 'You.'

'A dock.'

While they repeated these words, saying them with little comprehension, I could hear the clank of pots, the murmur of voices, the whack of wood being chopped, the timid complaining of chickens and dogs.

The cooking fires were all alight. The heavy woodsmoke rose so slowly that it became tangled in the jutting bunches of thatch, and hung there, disentangling itself, before seeping upward into the somnolent air in blue rags of smoke. This atmosphere, and the changelessness that it suggested—such villages have always sounded and smelt this way—had a fatiguing effect on me. Its simplicity made me tired.

'That's all for today,' I said.

'It is not yet six o'clock,' Johnson said, in a challenging tone, rising to his feet at the back of the room.

I smiled defiantly at him.

'A class last for one hour. I am knowing that from English lessons. I have been schooling in my district.'

The way he stood, in a domineering posture, his hands on his hips, taking up more space than he needed, seemed to indicate that he was speaking on behalf of the others, or at least trying to. I was already sick of him. I would have preferred a room full of Africans who spoke no English at all.

'This is American English,' I said. 'The class lasts forty-five minutes. We will meet again on Friday.'

The class was silent, attentive in the failing light. But they were not looking at me. At the side of the shed one of the nuns stood, her white robes luminous in the dusk.

'This man is in the wrong place.'

It was Birdie, in a nun's habit, wearing a starched bonnet that doubled as a sun-hat.

'His family is looking all over for him.'

She extended her hand to the silent man in the front row. He allowed himself to be tugged along, and went with her, with a stiffness that looked like resistance. He was obedient, but his eyes were filled with terror.

I dismissed the class and joined Birdie and the man and said, 'I hadn't realized you were a nun.'

'I'm not,' she said. 'It's just that I get more respect dressed this way.' She smiled, she was friendlier than before. 'And this stuff's cooler.'

Just her face was visible, framed by the bonnet that looked as though it was made out of brilliant white cardboard, a prettier face than the one from the other day.

'I mean, I'm naked underneath,' she said.

Without knowing why—perhaps it was my confusion—I looked at the African, his glassy eyes, his fists at his sides, his rigid way of walking.

Birdie laughed at me and steered the clumsy African towards his hut.

For a long time afterwards I could not think of anything else. I was dizzy with the words *I'm naked underneath*. Her saying that had a physical effect on me and made me slightly deaf and near-sighted and stupid. She must have known that, from the way she laughed. Over cards that night, and in the darkness of my room, and the dusty heat the next day and especially during meals, while I was swallowing something, I thought of what she had said, and went stupid again.

On Friday I held another class: again a dozen Africans, big and small, sick and well. The simpleton was not there, and some of the others had not returned. But Johnson was in his same seat, and Amina and her blind granny had come. Two other young women were also there, and from the whispers and the gestures between them and two of the men, I could see they were being courted as the class progressed. At the end, they paired up and sneaked into the bush.

I was almost fearful that Birdie might show up as she had on Wednesday, but she was nowhere to be seen. It was one of the characteristics of the leprosarium that people kept to themselves, each person to his portion of the place, the priests in their house, the nuns in their convent, the lepers in their village. I missed mass on Sunday and I realized it was because I thought I might run into Birdie. Her laughter had excited and disturbed me.

The Monday class was smaller than Friday's. Amina and her granny were missing, and of the others, the same two young women, fewer men. They giggled among themselves. They were inattentive. I was sure the class was now simply a pretext for a liaison in the bush later on. Aware that no one was listening to me, I became tired and hoarse.

I wondered why Amina had dropped out. When she did not show up at the next class, I took it as a rejection, taught for half an hour and then disgustedly sent them all home.

4

The leper village had an air of being industrious and yet nothing seemed to change. Was there something African in the way that all this energy and motion left no trace? Women carried firewood; big girls carried small children or else buckets of water; boys played or hoed the rows of corn; men squatted in groups, muttering and smoking pipes. Food was grown and cooked and eaten. Firewood was burnt. The buckets of water were emptied. The people were sustained, and the achievement of the work was that life continued. All this effort was to hang on to life and remain the same.

It was only at midday that it became apparent that something had been happening—the sudden stillness was proof that there had been work going on, but it was only noticeable when it stopped, like a hum that goes dead or a clock that stops ticking. On Saturdays the silence was more obvious because nothing followed it. The shop closed; the dispensary was locked; gardening ceased; the market emptied; and the women who sold bananas and peanuts and boiled potatoes and the black, bony smoked fish stacked up like shingles all drifted away. Then the leprosarium, this village of pale mud huts, lay silently baking in the sun. The only sounds were barks or cock crows or the howl of locusts like vibrant wires: no voices. Saturday was like a day of mourning.

I sat on the veranda of the priests' house. Father Touchette read his breviary, turning the pages with clean, white fingers. Brother Piet dozed, his hands clasped over his stomach. His snoring was like an obvious form of boasting. Father DeVoss had gone to the lakeshore on his motor cycle to say a Saturday mass at a village church.

I unbuckled the belts on my leather satchel and slipped out a cheap Chinese-made notebook, its spine covered in red cloth. I wrote *11 Oct 1964, Moyo Leprosarium, Ntakataka, Central Province*, and then I looked up, beyond the tin roofs to the thatched roofs, to the treetops, to the smoke mingling with dusty sunlight and to the Africans looking as upright as exclamation marks. I thought that, but I did not write it into my notebook. Writing seemed irrelevant.

My poems, about a dozen of them, I had copied carefully into the back of the notebook. I turned to them and read some lines, and then I began to skip. They were lifeless and trivial; I hated and was bored by the repetition of the word 'black'. My eye fell on the words 'pulpous' and 'gorgeous' and 'taut'. I disliked them, too, and shut the notebook.

There was no point in a letter home. I seldom wrote anyway, and I wouldn't know how to write about this place without embellishing it, and I knew that it would be a mistake. Leprosy was accepted; snake-bite was normal; work changed nothing. Except for the foreigners, everyone was a leper or a relative of a leper.

The reality was that no one was sentimental. They came here

ill; they declined; they died. No one advanced or prospered. It was a small world in which there were no illusions about making choices. And no one minded. I did not know why this was so, although I suspected that it was because everyone was always in the presence of death.

My poems were pointless. The very word '*poems*' irritated me. *Look at me*, all poems said. They called attention to themselves rather than their subject. I wanted to throw them away, but paper was such a luxury that someone was bound to retrieve them and I would be ashamed. So I hid them and vowed to destroy them in my own secret way.

I turned to the Kafka *Diaries*, and found them gloomy and tormented with morbid self-pity. The worst was Kafka's hypochondria and his repeated expressions of anxiety and the minutiae of his exaggerated ill health. *Sleeping badly*, he wrote. *Shortness of breath and a tightness in my chest*, he wrote. And then my eye fell on the word *leper*. *Sometimes I feel like a leper*. He had no idea how a leper felt. I could not read any more.

I thought: You could stay here and learn to hate all written words and despise literature most of all. I decided to find a shovel and dig a hole and bury my notebook of poems and my Kafka book.

I got up and walked along the path to the edge of the village where I had seen a stack of smoking bricks. They made bricks the old way here, digging a hole in clayey earth and pouring in water and straw and then tramping on the mix which they then crammed into a mould and baked.

I wanted to dig a hole here. Anything buried here would (to use a word from one of my poems) become friable—it would crumble to dust and one day, wetted and moulded and baked, would be turned into bricks for a latrine, a fitting end for these paltry poems.

The earth was dry. It seemed hard at first, but it cracked and gave and came apart, and soon, digging with a rusty shovel, I had a deep enough hole to bury the Kafka and my notebooks and my typescript of poems. I flung them in casually, liking the way they plopped into their pauper's grave, and then I covered them with dirt.

'Great,' I said loudly.

In that same moment I heard a startled yelp and looked up. A little distance off, beyond the stack of bricks, I saw a woman running away and a man hitching his shorts up and dusting off his knees, slapping at them. He coughed loudly, glanced in the direction the woman had gone and then hunkered down, elbows on his knees, and stared at me.

He was as black as the shadow of the mango tree where he crouched.

'These bricks'—I was mounding the dirt over the corpses of my papers—'are they yours?'

Now I saw his sweating face and bandaged feet, smeared with dust.

'They belong to the hospital,' he said, using the word *chipatala*. The sick ones called it a hospital; the healthy ones referred to it as a village or a mission.

I walked nearer to him. Like many other Africans, he looked as though he had been worn down by the weather, skin roughened by wind and sun like a tree stump or a fence post.

'They are for the kitchen,' he said.

I looked round and saw then a partly-made wall, the mortar hardened as it had oozed out from between the bricks. This was perhaps the foundation, the outline of fireplaces that were like a row of barbecue pits. It was to be a communal kitchen.

'Is it your kitchen?'

'It is anyone's kitchen.'

He seemed bored, but it was the way most of the lepers talked to *mzungus*—offhand, faintly jeering.

'Are you working on it?'

In the same bored tone, he said, 'No, I am sick.'

He held up his bandaged hands.

'I thought maybe your woman was helping you.'

'Not to work, but to play.' He laughed in a rumbling way, and coughed and then spat, and all of that too was like a pronouncement.

'I just buried some rubbish,' I said, realizing that he might have seen me. In Chinyanja the word rubbish suggested something that was contaminated and unclean. I did not want him to become curious and dig it up, as a scavenging African might.

'If I complete the work on the kitchen, will you help me?'

'How much will you pay me?'

'Nothing.'

'Then I will not work.'

It was a leper's response and verged on insolence. He was blunt; he was not afraid. In Blantyre, an African would have humoured me and still not done any work.

'Why should I?' the man said, because I had not replied to him.

I thought of Franz Kafka in Prague confiding to his diary, *I feel like a leper*. The book belonged in the ground with my bad poems. Kafka was not a leper. He was a middle-class insurance clerk with a bat-like face, pathologically timid and paranoid and guilt-ridden, developing various personal myths as he wrote long, fussy letters to lonely women desperate for the chance to love him.

This was a leper: guiltless, maimed, seeping into his bandages. He had just copulated under a tree with a leper woman and was now staring me down. In many ways he was healthy—certainly healthier than Franz Kafka. Reading meant nothing to him; a book was a mute object. He was patient and contemptuous because he was powerless and knew it. Nothing would change for him, nor would he change anything. He had no illusions, and so he was fully alive every moment, looking for food or water or shade or a woman.

'What is your name?'

'Wilson. And yours?'

'Paul.'

'From England?'

'America.'

'Americans have so much money.'

'I don't have any.'

He laughed at me and hobbled away. One foot was bandaged; the other was big and yellow and cracked, with twisted toes. He wore a ragged shirt and tattered shorts. His hands were wrapped like mittens.

That evening I recalled his confident mocking laugh and was ashamed of what I had told him. Did the disease make them frank because it made them clearsighted? Of all the people I had met in my life they had the least to lose.

That night, during a lull in the game of whist, I said to Father DeVoss, 'I'm giving up the English class.'

'That's a good idea.'

They had been his exact words when I told him I was planning to start the English class.

'I think I'll work on building the outdoor kitchen instead.'

'If you like, yes,' he said. He smiled—but he might have been smiling at his hand of cards. 'That's a good idea.'

'Maybe Father Touchette will help me.'

Father Touchette looked startled.

'I am busy with baptisms,' he said. 'So many these days.'

'I suppose the lepers might help me.'

'*Pepani, bambo!*' Brother Piet exclaimed—Sorry, dad!

'You really can't do anything,' Father DeVoss said. But he was speaking of the game. He collected the last trick and then began counting the cards stacked in front of him. His satisfaction and his remoteness touched me. Nothing of what I had said really mattered to him. He was very happy.

'The kitchen and the bricks were Father LeGrande's idea,' he said, smiling again. 'He is now in Basutoland.'

The next morning, in the mottled shade of the scrawny trees, the half-built kitchen looked like an old ruin, one of those useless walls or battlements the British had left behind. I carried and piled bricks for an hour or so, and then, as I was mixing some mortar in a pit, I looked up and saw some Africans staring at me. I had not seen their approach; they simply materialized, squatting, three ragged men.

They muttered among themselves but none spoke to me as I continued the wall, scraping mortar and setting the bricks in place.

'Do you want to help?'

I used the plural, but there was no reply. I said it again in a matey way, using the word *iwe*—eeway—the bluntest *you* in the language.

They laughed and grunted as though I had nudged them

with my elbow.

'Pay us some money,' one said in English.

'*Ndalama*,' another said. Cash.

I ignored them and went on laying bricks. They were still talking softly among themselves, and I had the impression that they were debating the issue of whether to help me.

'It is your kitchen—not mine,' I said.

'Then why are you working on it?'

'To help you.'

'It is your choice,' the English-speaking one said.

'*Mzungus* like to help,' the third one said, an old man.

They left soon after, crept silently away, leaving patches of shadow, deep black in the white dust, where they had been.

I stayed there, laying bricks, feeling stubborn. I worked through the lunch bell and was pleased when Birdie came over with a plate of *nsima* and beans and a cup of tea.

'Father LeGrande would be happy to see you working here,' she said. She was wearing a long, blue skirt and a floppy hat.

'I wish I had some help.'

She was smiling. 'They're lazy,' she said. 'They just don't want to work. They don't care whether it's done or not. We do everything for them.'

I was shocked by the casual brutality in her tone—and by her healthy, confident face.

'They pretend to be sick,' she said. 'They laugh at us behind our backs. And they're bloody rude. If we went away, they'd die or kill each other. They can't go home—they don't fit in.'

She was still smiling. She wanted to shock me.

'I'll send someone for the bowl and the cup,' she said, and gathered her skirt so it wouldn't drag in the dust and headed for the dispensary, leaving me flustered.

What she had said made her repulsive to me. I repeated it in a whisper to myself, and, watching her making her way down the path, I found fault with the way she walked, her ridiculous hat, her raised elbows, the jumping of her skirt.

The Africans did not come back that day. I worked until dusk, when the mosquitoes came out, and then I headed for the priests' house for dinner. I was too tired to play cards, or read, and the priests were still awake when I went to my room.

I did the same the next day. Birdie brought me food, and she said, 'So where are they? Sleeping in their huts while you work.'

'This is my idea, not theirs,' I said.

I ate the food while she watched, standing over me.

'Why don't you sit down?'

'Dust,' she said, and smiled.

'Have you stopped wearing your nun's outfit?'

'I'll start wearing it again if you want.'

She went away laughing, and I thought: Do I dislike her because she says what I secretly think? I had begun to resent the Africans at Moyo for the very reasons she said.

But I kept at it the following days, always starting just after breakfast and working through lunch until Birdie showed up with a plate of *nsima* and beans, heading home at dusk, guiding myself by the pressure lamps blazing at the windows.

I like this place because no one knows me, I thought.

As I was walking through the leper village, I heard a shriek and a gasp and a groan—the sounds of suffering coming out of the open window of a mud hut. I suspected that it was a woman being beaten by her husband. That kind of random, domestic violence was fairly routine. The sudden brutality seemed like another aspect of the sexuality of the leper village.

I went to the door of the hut, but seeing two women, one a nun, kneeling beside a mat on the floor, and a woman lying between them, gasping, I hesitated. A kerosene lamp lit the room and the women; it distorted everything else.

The woman on the mat called out again, and I could tell from the way she gasped, and the naked heap of her belly, that she was in the throes of childbirth.

The white nun and the African woman spoke to her gently, and the nun held the woman's legs, bracing her. The African chafed the woman's hand to comfort her, and I could see that the woman who was about to give birth had a hollow between her thumb and forefinger—the tiger's mouth—and that the fingers themselves were mangled: a leper.

There were no screams or hysteria, only a muttering now, and a laboured breathing, a kind of sighing, as the midwives encouraged her. After another grunt the child was lifted into the yellow lamplight.

'*Mwana*,' the nun said. It's a boy.

It was a perfect child, pinky grey with a full head of hair, all his fingers and toes intact. He dripped for a moment and then pissed—a narrow stream in the air—while he howled, growing pinker, as the women laughed in relief.

When I got up to go, I staggered and almost fell, and wondered why. My eyes hardly focused. I seemed to see a small group of people, gathered in the shadow just beyond the reach of the lamplight. Was one of them Amina? I saw the smooth face and bright eyes and blue turban. I had the sense that she was looking at me and not at the hut, where the women were rejoicing. Then I was groping on the path in the darkness, and I thought of the man beneath the tree telling me, *I'm sick*.

5

'I think I'll lie down,' I said as I entered the priests' house. My voice was quacky and echoey in my ears, and I felt terrible, though I pretended to be well—just tired, as I had been each evening on returning from the kitchen outside the leper village. Tonight I tottered like a drunk trying to pass for someone sober.

As I reached my room, I collapsed, my head aching, all my bone joints cracking. In seconds my skin was on fire and every sound was a howl in my head. It was as though my skin had been peeled from my flesh to expose the naked white threads of my nerves.

I lay in the hot darkness, dust in my nose. A fever had taken hold. I felt I was in the grip of a fatal illness, and was suddenly so sick that I couldn't even raise myself to tell anyone. I heard the clatter of plates; they had finished dinner. Simon was gathering the dishes; Father DeVoss was snapping the playing cards. Brother Piet was humming as he sewed; Father Touchette was clutching his breviary. I groaned but could not get up from my bed. I had shut and bolted the door.

The voices in the next room sounded in my dream. They

were rough, indifferent men in stained robes, laughing as they played cards, gambling while I lay dying. I was greasy with my sweat; I felt frailer and more fearful.

Help me.

But the moan stayed in my mouth because I was too weak to cry out.

I thought: They could come in here, any of them, and they could help me.

I shivered, I sweated. My heart drummed. The laughter—was it Brother Piet?—was sudden and explosive, and the racket of it tore into my head.

A shadow rattled against my eyes. It was a bat, flying back and forth in the room, the way I had once seen one flap in a barn. This fever bat was cut by the stripes of light from the cracks in the doorframe. I watched the creature seeming to crackle in the broken light. I was not afraid, but I was helpless. The pain in my head and my bones paralysed me, and my sense of my powerlessness frightened me. I sensed the thing swoop near my face, beating its skinny wings, and got a whiff of its stink. The bat seemed part of the paraphernalia of my death, like a funeral prop, a candle or an owl.

I implored the darkness for one of the priests to look up from his hand of cards and think of me and show concern and break the door down. But I was alone and I was trapped in this room. I was lost. They would not miss me until tomorrow, noon at the earliest, and by then I would be dead.

This terrified me and made me so sad I began to cry again, like a child, not sobbing but whimpering and squeaking as I cowered.

Then I was dreaming of enormous women, Birdie and others, with green skin and stupendous breasts and scorching mouths, laughing at me and biting me, wrestling joyously with each other and casting me aside. Quite near me a leper woman with stumps where her limbs should have been turned away, and I realized that I was even uglier than she. Laughing at me, she twisted her nose off—it was like the damp prune of a dog's nose—and reached for me.

That woke me, but moments later I was in another dream.

By dawn, I was reassured by the cock crows, and when I

woke at last to knocking on the door, I struggled out of bed and slid the bolt and collapsed. And then Brother Piet was kneeling near my bed and murmuring, *Pepani, pepani*—sorry, sorry—and fumbling with a thermometer.

My temperature was 103. I thought: I know something I did not know before, but I could not remember what it was.

I lay there too weak to raise my head, yet I was glad that I had been found. It had been a long, painful night, at the edge of death. I had sensed myself slipping away, unable to call out.

Father DeVoss visited me, his hands behind his back. He said, 'It's lucky you decided to spend your holiday at a hospital.'

I had not thought of Moyo as only a hospital. It was everything—a mission, a church, a village, a leper colony. It was for castaways—lepers and syphilitics and snake-bite victims, mostly men, with extravagantly ugly afflictions; and they lay disfigured and hopeless, because they had been cast out of their own villages. Not a hospital, but a refuge for desperate people. They were not sick; they were cursed.

'It could be malaria,' Father DeVoss said, lightly speculating. He did not seem concerned, and he stood to one side as Brother Piet set down a tray.

'You drink this while it is hot and then I give you *mankhwala*,' Brother Piet said. The seriousness of the occasion inspired more English words than I had so far heard him use. He offered me a cup of sweet, steaming tea. He dosed me with chloroquine, six tablets now, six more at noon, and paracetemol, to bring my temperature down.

'Or blackwater fever. Even cholera. Or one of the fevers that doesn't have a name,' Father DeVoss said. 'But we'll treat you for malaria first, because we have the *mankhwala* for that.'

I nodded and tried to smile and thanked them both in a croaky voice, glad that I had survived the night and that I had witness now to my fever.

'I think Paul is feeling better already,' Father DeVoss said.

It had been an awful night. But now the attention of these kind men had raised my hopes and dulled my pain. I felt looked-after and I was reassured by Brother Piet's fussing. He carefully changed my sheets, and once in dry sheets I felt calmer.

Father DeVoss still smiled at me but in such a melancholy and benign way I felt he were blessing me. His forgiving eyes seemed to bestow grace. He was looking beyond my fever and my frailty to my soul, while Brother Piet was tending to my body.

All that day Brother Piet served me tea and made me gulp chloroquine tablets. When I grew feverish again in the early evening, he folded wet towels on my head to cool me and bring my temperature down. In the darkness of the night I still burnt with fever, but I was less afraid. I prayed that I was on the mend, and when morning came—with the first light—I was more hopeful. I had made it through another night. Then it was hot tea and sour quinine and watery chicken soup. As each day waned my temperature went up, my skin burnt, my nerves ached, my eyes began to boil in their sockets. And I was afraid again, that I might falter in the darkness and die.

And then I began to think that it was my lesson. I had to be sick and feverish and lying on my back, unable to form a word with my scummy tongue, to realize that any effort here was pointless.

Brother Piet went through the motions of bringing me wet towels and tea and soup and medicine. But neither he nor any of the other priests seemed unduly alarmed. They did their duty and they were watchful. But their attitude was as fatalistic as the lepers'. How in this world of lepers could I expect sympathy for my fever? In spite of what they said, they looked upon me as someone who might die.

Eating did not make me well or even strong. It simply gave me diarrhoea. But instead of using the chamber pot, I hobbled to the latrine. I had always used the one outside the kitchen. But there was one in an overgrown part of the garden, all mossy bricks and weeds, just outside my room. It was as old as the house itself.

This shed—mud walls, thatched roof, sagging door, spider's webs—was built near my part of the corridor. Now and then I heard it being used because its door hinges squeaked, sometimes at the oddest hours of the day. This squeaking in the dark hours of the morning had been part of my feverish hallucination.

I was surprised to find that there were no door hinges. I stood dizzy from being upright and saw that the door was fixed with loops of knotted rope. But I had not imagined the rusty scrape of metal—I heard it again as I stood in the sun, just outside this old latrine. The squeaking was louder inside. When my eyes grew accustomed to the dark I saw that bats—three or four rat-sized ones—had attached themselves with dirty claws to the rough edge of the wooden seat hole. I banged the seat with my fist, and they took off, dropped into the pit, where they flew in fluttering batty circles. Still they flapped and squeaked under me while I sat wincing, trying to hurry the business.

A week of this: sleep, fever, dysentery; and Brother Piet. *Pepani*—sorry. Most nights, the drumming. My fever subsided, and one day I woke without a headache. My eyes did not hurt. The day was fresh, and the film of moisture on the leaves and the darkening of the dust under the trees with dew gave the illusion that it had rained during the night. I marvelled at the sky, which was an ocean of light, and for the first time I felt hungry and wanted to eat, and I thought: I'm alive.

'What was wrong with me?'

'A fever,' Father DeVoss said.

'What kind?'

'In Africa most fevers have no names,' he said. 'But what does it matter? You've pulled through.'

6

I had survived the fever but I had not recovered. Light-headed and weak and trembly, I was hungry but could eat little. My heart was fluttering, my hands unsteady; a walk with Brother Piet's carved walking-stick to the bat-haunted latrine left me breathless, and a trip to the dispensary took all morning.

In this watchful, passive state of convalescence, I understood the leprosarium's indifference to the world. Before, no one could explain exactly what it was. On my arrival I had accepted what they had said about the disease, but you had to be ill in this place to know it. My nameless fever had done it. They were naked, and now I was naked too.

Naked meant no clothes; it was not a figure of speech. That

kind of talk was unknown. Words here had definite meanings. There were no metaphors, no symbols, nothing poetic or literary. Sick meant leprosy; fever meant a week of suffering; hot meant this pitiless sun; dust, this sour powder that covered the ground and was the grit in every mouthful of food. And desire—I had seen it enough times—was a man kneeling against a woman in the dust, behind a blind of crackling cornshucks at the edge of the village, pumping while she thrashed, and it was brief and brutal.

This was the bush, and had its own bush rules. It was foolish of me to think that I could teach English here. And it was ludicrous to think of the outdoor kitchen as something that had to be completed. No one cared. Anyway, the leper village of the day was just subsistence and struggle: staying alive. The leper village of the night was pleasure. And both were outside time. Today was like yesterday or like tomorrow or like forty years ago; and forty years from now, there would be the same dust and drums and hunger. There were no expectations. Used to their illness and grateful for their blessings, they embraced life, they were roused by sex, they shrugged at sickness, they accepted death.

I understood words I had not known. And still feeling brainsick and lame I saw people clearly. They took me more seriously too—the lepers, their families, the nuns, Birdie. Amina now said hello—slyly murmuring and waving while her granny, hearing her, demanded, 'Who is that?'

The priests had sympathized with me in my fever but were calm in the presence of illness. I knew that from the way they spoke of a young man, Malinki, who lay without moving in a corner of the men's ward, wasted like a castaway—yellow eyes, his tongue swollen, struggling to breathe. Never mind his collapsing body, and everything that leaked from it. His soul was their mission. It was almost as though, trapped by his unknown illness, unable to move, he could be claimed: they'd snatch his soul while he was flat on his back.

We had resumed our after-dinner card game. One night, after losing a trick, I asked how Malinki was. I wanted to hear stories of recovery.

'He's very ill,' Father DeVoss said, picking up his hand, concentrating on each card as he arranged them in a fan.

The next night, during the whist game—as though a lost trick were the reminder—Father DeVoss turned to me and said, 'That young fellow didn't make it.'

'*Pepani!*' Brother Piet said.

'We have the funeral tomorrow,' Father Touchette said from across the room. He was not playing whist tonight. Simon had taken his place. Simon played without speaking, with a kind of anxious caution that made him lose.

'What would you have done if I had been as sick as that African?'

'We would have taken care of you,' Father DeVoss said, surprising me with his vagueness.

'I'm talking about an emergency,' I said. 'Who would you have called?'

'We have no telephone.'

'And there is no one to listen!' Brother Piet said bluntly in Chinyanja: *Palibe anthu senga!* And the card game resumed.

When the lepers died, they had a funeral, with a mass, and were buried in the cemetery surrounded by the stone wall, in the shade of the mango tree, where I sometimes saw a man and woman coupling.

'Maybe Paul will be our altar boy.'

'All right,' I said.

The Africans at Malinki's funeral sang in a moaning harmony. The men groaned, the women shrieked, they all wept. And they carried Malinki's corpse in a battered coffin that would be re-used after he was dumped out and buried in a burlap sack.

Later, in the sacristy, Father DeVoss said, 'That soutane looks good on you.'

He stood and admired the white cassock that I had started to unbutton.

'You don't have to take it off. You'll find it very cool to wear, because it's loose. Better than your heavy trousers. Go on, try it.'

I wondered whether I ought to. I was too weak to work. I had abandoned my English class and laying bricks for the outdoor kitchen. So I kept the cassock on and I walked down to the dispensary. I needed more aspirin, but I also wanted to walk among the Africans while dressed as a priest.

'Hello, Father,' Africans said as I passed by. That was a usual greeting: *Moni, Bambo. Bwana*, master, was more respectful; *achimwene*, brother, was more intimate. I thought 'Father' was about right, even though I had just turned twenty-three. Yet when they said it they hung back, bowed and clapped their hands, and some women and most children dropped to their knees.

Seeing me approach the dispensary, the nuns smiled, knowing that I was an imposter; nevertheless, they regarded me as an ally. And Birdie, who was doling out white tablets in paper cups to a long line of lepers, laughed out loud, as though seeing an old friend.

'Yes!' she called out.

She let her African assistant take over and hurried towards me, smiling.

'It gives you a feeling of power, right?' she asked, and touched my sleeve.

'It's just cooler, wearing it.'

'Oh, sure,'

And I remembered how I had seen her in her nun's outfit and her saying *I'm naked underneath*, and her watching my reaction.

Now there was a different look on her face—more sympathetic and animated, quicker to respond, brighter and kinder. Even the way she touched my sleeve seemed like a gesture of affection.

She said, 'I'm glad you're feeling better.'

'So am I.'

'I was starting to miss you,' she said. And, perhaps detecting a look of scepticism on my face, she added, 'There are so few people here.'

'Two thousand is a lot.'

'I mean *mzungus*.'

All this time she was glancing at my cassock. Her scrutiny had started to make me feel uncomfortable, because she was looking at my clothes and not at me. I wanted to change the subject.

'Are these people getting their medicine?'

'The second batch,' she said. 'We give them a hundred milligrams a day, half in the morning, half in the afternoon.'

'What is it?'

'Dapsone. It's a sulpha drug. We're getting low—not that the lepers care,' she said. 'We do their worrying for them.'

'You don't look very worried.'

'Does it matter?' She gestured to the line of men and women who were waiting to receive their Dapsone tablets. There were some children too. All this patience and submission. Towards the end of the line I saw Amina and her granny.

'Some of these people don't look like lepers.'

'Looks are deceiving. A child may have leprosy but won't know it until he or she is an adult.'

Seeing her stare at them, some youngsters in the line lowered their eyes.

'A bunch of these older people are almost cured,' Birdie said. 'But they have to go on taking medicine for ten years to be completely clear.'

As she spoke, she glanced at me and saw that I was smiling at Amina. Birdie turned towards Amina and gave her a swift, pitiless look, as though sizing up a rival, then walked over, pulled her out of the line, lifted up Amina's slender arm and pinched her skin, holding it between her fingers.

'You see this hard, dry spot? It is dead. That's the body's reaction to the bacillus. It's like a wall, sealing off the germs. That helps, but it also makes parts of the body die.'

Yet Amina was lovely. She was murmuring to her old blind granny, who had asked, '*Ciani?*'—what is it? I had not known that Amina was a leper. I had thought she was there only to help the old woman.

'Arms and legs can become useless,' Birdie said, still watching Amina closely. Was I imagining that she sounded triumphant? 'It can turn the hand into a claw.'

Amina touched the spot on her arm and shrank back into the line of lepers waiting for medicine, her granny groping for her shoulder.

'It cuts off the nerves.' She indicated a man whose hand had become cup-shaped as it had withered. 'He feels no pain.'

But I was looking back at Amina. 'I don't get it. I thought leprosy disfigured people.'

Amina was standing shyly among the lepers, her scarf wound around her head like a turban, her hands clasped, a cloth wrapped around her, so that she seemed like an upright bundle, very slender and straight. And just behind her was the old blind woman, gripping Amina's shoulder with a diseased hand.

'On some people it doesn't show for years. And it's not the leprosy that disfigures, but the body's reaction to it. By fighting the bacillus the body destroys its own tissues. It starves and hardens them.'

'Is that how their fingers and toes fall off?'

'That's a myth. We amputate them when they harden and become useless.'

I saw Wilson, the African man who had refused to help me with the kitchen. I saw Simon the cook, and Johnson Magondwe and the rest of the people from my English class, including the deaf man and the feeble-minded man, some of them twisted and limping on bandaged feet, others looking perfectly all right. A few seemed much healthier than me.

'That disfigurement is its success. It stops the bacilli.' Birdie turned away from the line of people. 'It stops the body too.'

The lepers were moving past a barred window which was like a ticket window, and each took a paper cup of tablets from Birdie's assistant. They swallowed the tablets or held them in their mouth while a nun filled the paper cup with water. Then they went outside.

'That girl you were staring at. She has a nodule on her arm. A lot of these people have nodules. That's why it's called tuberculoid leprosy.'

The nun with the pitcher said, 'But it's not all like that.' And pouring water into a man's paper cup, she went on, 'This man Yatuta is lepromatous.'

He had a heavy face and a shrivelled nose and thick, coarse, bunched up skin. The nun explained that the cells in this type of leprosy were unable to fight the disease, which slowly destroyed the body, as the extremities—nose, fingers, toes—collapsed.

'It's terrible,' I whispered, as the man gulped the pills with the water and moved slowly outside, stabbing his walking-stick into the dirt floor.

Birdie was smiling at me, as though to ridicule my sympathy.

'These people aren't dying,' she said.

I turned sharply at her, disliking the expression on her face and hating her dismissive tone. But what did I know?

'You don't die of leprosy,' she said. 'You shrink and become crippled. You live out your life. But you're disfigured and covered with scars.'

I felt self-conscious talking about the lepers in their presence, as they moved in the long line and took their medicine. They were glancing up at us and looking helpless, as though they knew they were being discussed.

But Birdie went on chattering. In a hospital everyone was naked, and this leper colony was an extreme example of nakedness.

'That fever you had was much more dangerous,' Birdie said.

I had wondered whether she knew how sick I had been.

'This disease will be completely cured,' she said, belittling leprosy the way she always seemed to belittle me. 'But there are other diseases. Some aren't in the medical books. People are brought in ill. We think they have TB—they have all the symptoms. But they don't respond to treatment. They waste away, becoming thinner and thinner until they die. We stand and watch and then we bury them, like that young guy Malinki. We never found out what was wrong with him.'

The nun with the water pitcher said, 'But we have a good idea of how leprosy is spread. Probably from mucous, probably from running sores.' She shrugged and filled another paper cup.

'That's why we keep the wounds clean,' Birdie said. She was standing very close to me and still smiling, and her smile seemed to have nothing to do with what she was saying. 'All this bandaging.'

'If you have friends in America who can send us bandages or old bed sheets,' the nun said, 'we'd be happy to receive them.'

'What about these children?' I asked, seeing some small boys and girls in the medicine line clinging to their mothers. 'Do they have it?'

'We don't know. But if a child is born to a leper woman it's almost certain the kid will get leprosy.'

I recalled the birth I had witnessed just before I fell ill. It had appeared in my feverish dreams: the leper woman, the perfect child; it had seemed miraculous.

'Do you separate them?'

'No. The mothers won't let us. We give them *mankhwala*.'

The nun said, 'We had leprosy in Holland once, long ago. Europe was full of lepers. That was when Europe was poor and people lived in dirty conditions. Now the dirty conditions are in the tropics—Africa especially. That is why leprosy is here. It is a disease of dirt—of people living and breathing in one hut.'

Another nun folding bandages said, 'When I came here in 1946 we treated people with oil. That was the old remedy for leprosy.'

'Did you say oil?'

'Chaulmoogra oil. It worked!' she said. 'But now we use the sulpha drugs. They are better and stronger. This disease will be gone some day.'

The other nun frowned. 'Europe was full of huts once,' she said. 'Little dirty huts.'

I was on the path walking back to the priests' house, thinking that Birdie and these nuns were admirable, when I heard footsteps behind me. I turned to see Birdie hurrying. Such a rare sight, someone running in the heat of this slow-motion world.

'Almost forgot,' she said. 'Here's your aspirin, Father.'

'That's not funny.'

'I meant it, Father.'

She glanced around. She seemed hesitant and self-conscious. In such a frank and wide-open place, any hesitation seemed obvious, even furtive.

'Have you been to the lake, Father?'

'Stop saying that.'

'You're wearing a cassock. I can't help it,' she said. 'What about a picnic at the lake?'

I had nothing—no work, no reading, no writing. I had time to fill.

'How would we get there?'

'Father DeVoss will let you use his motor cycle.'

I had started again to walk along the path, thinking that she would accompany me. But she did not move.

'Aren't you coming this way?'

'Yes, but—' She smiled instead of finishing the sentence.

'What's wrong?'

'It's not a good idea for us to be seen alone together here,' she said. 'That's another reason to head for the lake.'

Only when she said that did I realize that the whole time we had been discussing leprosy she had been flirting with me.

Father DeVoss's motor cycle was a black, older model Norton, with fluted plates on its twin-cylinder heads and two wide, dish-like seats. Its fenders curled front and rear like the visors of Roman helmets, and it had roomy leather saddlebags. Like every other material thing in the priests' lives, it was simple and practical and well-cared for.

'I love it,' Birdie said.

'So do I'—and I gunned the engine.

'Not the bike,' Birdie said. 'The outfit.'

My white cassock, she meant. But wearing it I felt more like a choirboy than a priest.

'It was Father DeVoss's idea. He said that I would be safer dressed as a priest because of the road blocks.'

Smirking, as though she did not believe me, Birdie got on to the rear seat. She was wearing Bermuda shorts and a loose blouse and knee-socks. She clung to me instead of to the leather loops, and I could sense a nervous impatience in the way she held me.

It was two in the afternoon—a late start because of extra bandaging. At this dizzying time of day, the sun at its hottest, the village was empty and not even the small boys were outside.

We passed the dispensary, the hospital, the village, and then we were out of the leprosarium, jouncing on the rutted road through the stands of thin yellow trees. I slowed down for the railway tracks. Beyond them, there were no huts, no people, no dogs, no gardens, only baked earth and dusty sunlight and the narrow road. I settled the bike into a wheel rut and took off.

I had done this before in the south of the country, travelling fast on a motor cycle in the groove at the side of the road, but after so many weeks of following the routine of the leprosarium there was something unreal about this. It was not just the speed; it was that I was hurrying away from an existence I had begun to understand.

I felt uneasy and somewhat unsafe—insecure, anyway. I had, I realized, no desire to see the lake nor the roadblocks Father DeVoss had warned me about. There was also something less definite in my anxiety. Outside the leprosarium I was in the big, unstable world. It was a mid-afternoon of hot stillness and slanting shadows. Here and there were baobab trees, looking like a child's monstrous version of elephants, distorted and fat and grey. I was already anticipating being late on the return trip. No one travelled in the dark on a bush road in this part of Africa.

Behind me, Birdie was talking excitedly. I could hear the sound of her voice, but the slipstream of rushing wind muffled her words.

I had been put off by Birdie's first reaction to my wearing a cassock. 'I love it.' Farther along, an African woman on the road dropped to her knees when she saw me and made the sign of the cross, almost spilling the load of wood on her head. Birdie clutched me tightly and called out in triumph. That repelled me too.

Soon after, we passed a cluster of mud huts, and there was a horizontal bar across the road, an iron pipe resting on two oil-drums: a bush road-block. At either side of the road were about eight men and boys, looking hot and bad-tempered, wearing the faded red shirts and smocks of the Malawi Youth League. They held wicked-looking sticks and vicious slashers and crude, lumpy truncheons. Yet seeing how I was dressed, they backed off, seeming sheepish and awkwardly respectful, handling their weapons with obvious embarrassment.

'Good day, Fadda-sah,' one said.

'You can pass this side,' another said, raising the iron pipe.

It was all just as Father DeVoss had said.

They were staring at Birdie now, their mouths slack and hungry.

'What's the problem?' I asked.

'We are assisting wid da security situation, Fadda-sah.'

The man who said this was dressed like the others—faded

red shirt, khaki shorts, barefoot—but he was grizzled, with a nasty face: a little old man in a boy's clothes.

Assisting with the security situation was the opposite of what they were doing. They were the paid thugs of the government, obstructing the road in order to intimidate anyone on it into buying (for five shillings) a membership in the Malawi Congress Party. Like other hacks in this one-party state, they were making trouble while pretending to keep the peace. At Moyo I had forgotten the political nuisance in the country.

There were two more road-blocks (grubby men, a dusty iron pipe, 'You can pass, Fadda') before we got to the lake. Then Birdie was shouting into my neck. I saw the lake shining through the trees, not cool or blue, but a hard, metallic glitter, like tin foil, a great wrinkled expanse of it, and I felt helpless. There was too much of this emptiness, and this was not where I wanted to be. I wanted to ride straight back to Moyo. I said so to Birdie.

'But I brought food,' she said.

Because she had food was I obliged to eat it? I parked the motor cycle but I did not walk far from it.

'I'm not hungry.'

'I am,' she said. 'Very hungry.'

She said this in a good-humoured way, paying no attention to my ill-temper.

'I hate those road-blocks. I hate those horrible guys and their dirty faces.'

'They respect your cassock, Father. Doesn't that give you a sense of power?'

'No. It's like scaring someone by wearing a mask,' I said.

'They do it all the time.'

'It's cruel.'

'They're cruel.' She said this with a shrug while poking in the saddlebags for food.

'I'm thinking about the trip back.'

'I know, Father.' She unwrapped a sandwich and took a bite.

'Stop calling me Father.'

She ignored me and said, 'I sometimes think I don't belong anywhere else.'

The way she chewed the bread made her seem innocent and defenceless, and I thought how a person's character was never more apparent than when eating. There seemed to be a brainlessness about eating, too: poor, dumb, hungry animal.

Perhaps sensing my pity and mistaking it for compassion, she swallowed and looked grateful. Then she touched my hand and, in the kindest way, said, 'What would make you happy?'

I was glad that she had put it that way. It gave me the confidence to say plainly that I was uneasy here on this great sloping shore, among the boulders and the stones and the blowing trees and the splash of the lake. It was almost four-thirty. It would be dark at six or so. Couldn't we just leave?

Birdie said, 'I was imagining a picnic by the lake. But we could have it somewhere else.'

'What about back at Moyo?'

'I have a bottle of cream sherry in my room back at the convent.'

'Let's go home.'

7

This abrupt change of plans was like a reprieve and put me in a good mood. Everything seemed simple now. Instead of killing time at the lake, we would forget the picnic and go back. I had not had an alcoholic drink in over a month, and the prospect of it, the novelty, and the way Birdie had tried to please me, made me willing. She said, 'OK, let's go,' and without realizing it I was following her directions for a short-cut back to the mission. I was glad we were together and liked her high spirits and this haphazard outing that had just proved to me that I too felt at home among the lepers of Moyo.

It was growing dark when we got back—dark enough for me to need my headlight. The road and the paths were empty, the whole mission occupied with eating their early supper. I drove slowly behind the dispensary and up the hill to the motor cycle shed, which was near the church, and between the priests' house and the convent.

As I propped the bike, Birdie said, 'Let me go first, to see if the coast is clear.'

I did not wonder what she meant by that. It seemed just another expression of her unpredictable high spirits.

At this time of day the fading light gave everyone a ghostly appearance, the threadbare look of an apparition that might quicken or fade. Birdie turned and glowed for a few moments and then was gone.

I waited—longer than I expected—wondering what to do. Then I saw a light go on in an upper room of the convent. Birdie came to the window, said nothing, but raised her head, beckoning me.

And I obeyed. I did not question all the randomness that had led me this evening to climb the back stairs of the convent to Birdie's room. I did not take Birdie seriously because I knew that if I did I would have to conclude that I did not like her very much.

She opened and shut the door so quickly that I was inside before I realized that she was dressed as a nun, in the white robe and bonnet of this severe order of the Sisters of the Sacred Heart. Birdie had switched her lamp off. Two candles burned on her dresser, giving it the look of an altar and the room the feel of a dim chapel.

'Just a joke,' she said.

People said that self-consciously of their most passionate acts. I did not know what to reply.

'Did anyone see you?'

I shrugged—what did it matter whether anyone saw me?

'Because you're not supposed to be here, Father.'

She was whispering, she was barefoot, she had a crazed nun look of sacrilege. She must have put her nun's habit on hurriedly because a lock of her hair was loose at the side of her face, and the gown itself—the robes, the sleeves—was dishevelled. I could see her naked breasts through the wide, hitched-up sleeve.

When I turned to push the door open, to leave, she stepped quickly over and held it shut. This was a nimble move, swift and serious, and when she put her finger to her lips to shush me, I heard other voices.

'This box of bandages has to be sorted for size.'

'Did you see this other stack?'

They were nuns outside in the hall, speaking through an open door.

'We can start now and go on with it after dinner.'

Go, I urged with my whole mind.

'I will do some. Sister Rose can wash the vegetables and then you both can come to help.'

Sorting bandages, washing spinach—good plain chores. It was what I wanted, what I valued most in the place, simplicity and completeness. For this I had gladly rejected my writing and buried my books. And this was why I was so uncomfortable in Birdie's room, with a bottle of South African sherry, by candlelight, dressed as priest and nun.

Her tongue was clamped between her teeth, in a parody of concentration. She slid the heavy dead-bolt in the door, then plucked my sleeve and led me across the room to the only place to sit, the edge of the bed.

The nuns were still fussing, some of them muttering in Dutch.

'I feel sorry for them,' Birdie said. 'But sometimes they're awful.' She thought a moment, biting her lip. 'I'm as bad as they are.'

I did not need to be convinced that it was unwise of me to leave just then, with nuns hurrying back and forth in the hallway. But I realized how great a mistake it was for me to be here. What convinced me of my error of judgement was Birdie's energy: my enthusiasm waned as hers rose. She liked this game of dressing up—she in her habit, me in my cassock, nun and priest clinking glasses of sticky South African sherry, sitting side by side in the narrow convent room, the door locked and bolted.

She seemed very excited, licking wine from her lips and watching me with shining eyes. But each thing that roused her only made me more gloomy.

I said softly, 'This is ridiculous.'

She opened her mouth eagerly, as though shaping the word *yes*. It was the absurdity of it that she seemed to like best. She sipped more wine and kissed me, forcing my lips open with her tongue and spat this sip of wine into my mouth. My surprise as I choked and swallowed only thrilled her more.

'Father,' she said, and kissed me, holding my head, searching my mouth with her tongue again. At first I was so startled I began to pull away, but her boldness challenged me. I was astonished by the strength of her hunger.

Outside the room a nun said, 'Twenty-eight. All folded. The rest are stained. We'll have to bleach them. It's never enough.'

Birdie was probing my ear with her tongue. Her breath was hot and she whispered, 'No, Father. Don't make me. I'm so afraid.'

And still she held me. I was going blind and deaf, fooled with the inklings of desire.

I would have taken my cassock off, but I was stuck in it—it was like a sack around me—and her gown and robe were caught in its folds. So we embraced, pleaded in our different ways, in a great, soft knot of white cotton: her gown, my cassock, the starched wings of her bonnet askew, and all her nakedness shifting beneath this tangle of cloth. My fingers, trapped in the plackets of her robe, touched her warm skin, and breaking free of her kissing I dislodged her bonnet with my chin and her hair tumbled between our faces.

'Don't touch me, Father,' she implored, her breath harsh with heat.

Her irrational sincerity scared me, and then her hands were on me, searching through the unbuttoned flap of my cassock. I was confused. I drew back, saying 'No, wait,' though I could feel her pleading in the pressure of her fingers.

'Not if you don't think they're clean,' a nun said in the hall.

Birdie took hold of the inert slug of my penis and began pumping it, as though trying to start some odd primitive engine with a churning, chafing motion of a little handle.

It hurt. I wriggled free, keeping her away by holding her shoulders.

'Don't rape me, Father,' she said, and now her eyes were unfocused and she lay back as though she were my victim.

There was drumming—was it from the village or from the throbbing of my temples? Whatever, it too made me hesitate.

I was overcome with embarrassment and anxiety. My heart was not in it. I had no interest in her—did not even like her much.

I was too afraid and self-conscious and too remote from her fantasy to be able to perform in this sad comedy of dressing up.

'Then just hold me,' she said. She was trembling.

I could not even do that simple thing. I was preoccupied with the problem of how to escape.

'I have to go,' I whispered, though it probably sounded to her like a wicked hiss.

She said nothing, and then, 'You can go at any time. You don't belong here.'

Her face was in shadow, and she was a rumpled mass of hair and tangled clothes.

I stood up and undid the rest of the buttons on my cassock and took the thing off. I had a T-shirt and bathing suit on underneath. I folded the cassock and sat and put it on my lap. Birdie lay across the bed in a tragic posture, looking grotesque, a mass of shadows, sorrowing.

Nothing, not even laughter, kills sexual desire quicker than tears. The spell was broken. There was no more to be done. I could not determine her mood, whether she was disappointed or embarrassed.

I hugged her, and she went rigid against my arm, pretending to be stubborn and unyielding. I imagined her to be very angry.

'This was a bad idea.'

'I don't think so,' she said. 'But if you do—'

I held my breath, waiting for her to finish the sentence, because she was on the verge of tears.

'—then you're useless.'

She began soundlessly to cry, making a horrible face.

8

It was said at the leprosarium that there were no secrets. No matter what happened in darkness, it was known; no matter how soft your whisper, it was heard. That was another aspect of the reality of the place. Nothing was hidden. A leper was a leper, and everything was easily visible. It was like a doctrine. We were naked.

And yet no one seemed to know what happened between me and Birdie in the convent that night. Perhaps it was too absurd, too outlandish—inconceivable in a place so lacking in fantasy and pretence. Perhaps it was because we really had no secrets: the truth was that nothing had happened.

It was not a scandal that I sneaked out of the convent, wearing my cassock. I took the long way back to the priests' house in order to conceal where I had been. By then the priests were asleep. If anyone else saw me, they did not say anything. I crept into bed, scarcely believing what had happened, and I was so exhausted by the suspense and the fear of being caught that I went straight to sleep and did not wake until the sun was in my face, blazing into my eyes through my eyelids.

Now it will never happen, she had said.

She was probably right. And it cured me of dressing up in a cassock—of dressing up at all.

Now my days were orderly. I woke squinting and blinking like an animal, and then foraged for my breakfast and kept busy until the next mealtime. When I thought of reading or writing, I felt a giddy thrill knowing that I would do neither. I had that same feeling waking from a dream in which something important and difficult was expected of me, one of those dreams in which the last words I heard were from a large, grey figure insisting that I meet his deadline. I felt inexpressible relief when I had woken, and then the whole day stretched ahead, all sunlight. The burden of writing had been lifted from me. Not writing meant not having to remember; I was excused from having to notice details. I lived now in a luxury of forgetfulness.

I had never known such easy days. Birdie and I greeted each other as friends, and I understood her better. I saw her difference, her weakness. She was like a nun, like a leper—she belonged here, more than I had imagined. This interested me, yet I had very little to say to her.

Father DeVoss was the only person who mattered, now, but his mind was on more pressing matters.

It had begun one night when Father Touchette burst into tears during our game of whist. His crying was like an audible form of bleeding. You could not play cards when he was doing it. It was messy and shocking; it upset anyone who witnessed it, and it seemed to weaken him. And then one morning, I heard

Africans grunting and their hard feet scuffing on the cement floor. They were laboriously moving furniture, I thought—no, not furniture. It was a large tin trunk, new enough to be only slightly dented. The three men struggled trying to share the weight.

'*Katundu* of Father Touchette,' Simon said.

I had breakfast alone. I kept out of sight; spent the morning in my new way: cleaned the spark plugs on the Norton, talked to an old man about witches, looked for snakes to kill. On my way back from the withered cornfield I bumped into Father DeVoss.

'Is anything wrong?'

'No,' he said. He glanced aside. The tin trunk rested on the veranda of the dispensary. 'But Father Touchette is leaving us.'

He said it as though it were no great occurrence: it was in the nature of things—not wrong, no one to blame. People came and went. I had asked the wrong question.

'He will be happier somewhere else,' Father DeVoss said.

The old priest did not elaborate, but now I understood Father Touchette's sobs, and the way he had stood trembling at the open windows, glaring at the sound of the drumming at night from the leper village.

A solemn White Father, his bulky body obvious under his creamy robes, arrived at Moyo that evening on the train. He was Father Thomas, come to take Father Touchette away. There was no card game after dinner that night. Instead, Father Thomas conferred with Father DeVoss. The next day a high mass was said in the church—because we had an extra priest, Father DeVoss explained. I suspected that the service was being held to offer prayers for the troubled soul of Father Touchette, who sat with his hands in his lap in the front pew, looking stunned and shamed, like a fallen angel.

There was singing and drumming and solos with Angoni fingerharps; hearing this, more Africans came from the village and crowded into the church. The front pew was all nuns, with Birdie at the end. She did not look at me. I knelt just inside the communion rail while the priests sang the mass, and in between—dressed in black pants and a white shirt—I served as altar boy.

I rang the bell, I genuflected, I uttered the responses. I

brought the tray of cruets at the consecration. I bowed and I gloried in the strangeness of it—the heat, the ceremony, the singing, the drumming that rattled the loose panes in the church windows. No one outside Moyo knew that we existed or that this ritual was taking place. As always there was a dusty sense of remoteness here, but I found an intense pleasure in it, knowing that no one else that knew or cared about us.

The mass was sung in Latin; the hymns in Chinyanja; the drumming, too, was African—filling the gaps of the ritual. The drumming seemed to unnerve Father Touchette again. His mask of sadness grew tighter on his face, as the drumming grew louder, echoing against the walls of whitewashed plaster while incense rose from the thurible drifting past the glitter of the monstrance. Then the smoky incense curled as thick as drug fumes in the shafts of sunlight that pierced it.

Amina sat in one of the rear pews with her blind granny. I watched Amina closely, the way she followed the priests with her eyes, the passing back and forth, the sudden chants and sung prayers, my spoken responses, the jostling at communion.

In her eyes this must have seemed strange, like a ritual of magic, the kind of sorcery that went on in a village to cast a spell, drive out devils, make a person whole again. In a sense, this sort of purification was the aim of the mass—the holy sacrifice of the mass, as I had been taught to call it.

Afterwards I put out the candles and gathered the cruets and tidied the sacristy, while Father DeVoss whispered to Father Thomas. And I knew exactly what he was saying—practical things, like the mood of Father Touchette and the time of the train to Balaka and Blantyre. Lunch was a long silence. We sat, eating *nsima* and chicken in the heat, while Father Touchette paced the veranda. Then Father Thomas led the weakened priest to the Land-Rover and helped him in, taking him by the arm. Father Touchette climbed in slowly, like someone elderly or ill and without a word folded his arms, waiting to go. His eyes were sunken and dark, he looked haunted, his mind was elsewhere. I heard someone in the watching crowd of lepers say the word *mutu*, referring to Father Touchette's head—something wrong with it. Talking louder than the others, Amina's blind granny was asking questions: Who is it? Where is he going? Will someone else come to take his place? Is he sick?

With the old woman monopolizing the attention of the crowd, I sidled over to Amina and was glad when she did not move away.

'I saw you in church, Amina.'

'Yes.'

'But you are a Muslim.'

'I went because of my granny. To help her. She is a Christian.'

'Did you see me watching you?'

'Yes.' She sniffed nervously. 'I did not know why.'

'Because looking at you makes me happy.'

She sniffed again, she blinked. What I had said embarrassed her.

'How did you know I was looking at you?'

'Because I was looking at you,' Amina said.

This touched me, and though she spoke with her eyes averted, she was bolder than I had expected.

There was confusion in the dusty road, as Father Touchette's big trunk was hoisted into the back of the Land-Rover. Already Father DeVoss was gunning the engine, and beside him Father Thomas had the grim resignation and grumpiness of a parent who has been inconvenienced by his son's expulsion from school. Father Touchette was in the rear seat, looking defeated, watched by lepers who seemed stimulated, even thrilled, by the sight of this ruined *mzungu*.

In a place where very little changed from year to year, this departure counted as momentous, an event that would be remembered and distorted in the years to come.

'*Alira*,' someone muttered. He is weeping.

It was odd seeing this grown man sitting in the vehicle with his face in his hands, tears running through his fingers. The crowd of lepers gaped at him—they were skinny, crippled, crooked, barefoot, ragged. So many of them wore large, dirty bandages. They watched impassively, with hardly a murmur. It was the lepers' pitiless curiosity that made Father Touchette especially pathetic.

I had always disliked the way Father Touchette carried his breviary around with him, consulting it and seeming to wrestle with its verses. I resented his saying, 'I have baptisms,' when I needed help carrying bricks. The book seemed like a talisman against his ever having to work. He used it the way the lepers used their mutilation as an excuse. The young priest wore socks with his sandals, which made him look silly. I thought how madness is often a way of dressing.

'He is your friend?' Amina asked.

'No.'

'But he is a *mzungu*.'

'I would rather talk to you.'

I wanted to tell her that I was glad to see him go. He was a worrier, a baptizer, a converter, a scold. *That's savage*, he had said of the drumming almost every night. Perhaps I had alarmed Amina by being forthright, for after the Land-Rover had driven off she disappeared.

The drumming was louder that night; there were shouts and yells, a kind of whooping, like panic. In my fever that same drumming had filled my imagination with vivid images of Amina dancing—her slender body gleaming, her mouth open, her glazed eyes looking drugged.

Desire for me was always the fulfilment of a fantasy—not a surprise or a shock, but something studied in advance, dreamed and premeditated. It was pleasure prepared, the completion of a thought begun in a vision. Desire was familiar and fixed; not something new, but an older deeper wish, with a history, an embrace that had already shadowed forth in my mind. It was something specific, like a gift I yearned for. And later, when it seemed to be granted—flickering into reality and becoming attainable—I seized it.

I had heard that same drumming many nights before, rattling through the heat to reach me in my bedroom where I lay alone on my cot. It was also the sound the village women made when they pounded corn into flour, thumping a heavy pestle into the mortar. When there was more than one woman pounding it set up a syncopation in the trees and a chorus of grunts and thuds.

'No cards tonight,' Father DeVoss said. He did not have to explain that this was out of respect for Father Touchette, who hated our card playing. Among other things, the sight of us flipping cards and collecting tricks had driven him crazy. Never mind, we would play tomorrow.

'No cards,' Brother Piet exclaimed, taking up his sewing. '*Pepani, palibe sewendo*!'—sorry, no games!

It was as though we were respecting the memory of someone who had just died. Perhaps leaving Moyo would be like death, as life outside bore no resemblance to life here.

'I hope he gets better,' I said.

Guessing what was in my mind, Father DeVoss said, 'He won't come back.'

There was a great cry from the village, and a surge of brightness, as though a mass of dry straw or cornshucks had been dumped in the fire and exploded into flames.

'They never come back,' Father DeVoss said.

At just that moment it seemed that the only life in the place was down in the leper village—the drumming like a faulty heart beating; not wood at all, but the racing pulse of the place.

Brother Piet was sewing by the light of the pressure lamp, while Father DeVoss sat near him, with shadows on his face. In any other place they would have been reading, writing a letter, looking at pictures. But this was Moyo, as stark as anything else in the bush. They were like an old married couple.

I said goodnight and went to my room, where I stood by the window. I was restless, impatient, ready to leap into the darkness. The trees beyond that darkness were lighted by the fire in the village. Because of the flames each branch was distinct and black.

Slipping down the back stairs I went outside, avoiding the path but following the firelight and the sounds of the drumming.

Though there was a thin circle of spectators, almost the whole village was dancing in the clearing, women on one side, men on the other, shuffling and stamping their feet, nodding their heads, raising their arms, calling out.

The men clapped their hands, and the women yodelled in a shrill ululation that was both fearful and triumphant—a sort of war whoop. There were no carved masks, but there were painted faces, none more frightening than the man whose face was dusted with white flour. He was a leper, wearing a bedsheet and carrying a crucifix. A woman opposite him was also wrapped in a bedsheet—priest and nun, writhing in a suggestive dance that was a riotous sexual mockery or a ritual, or both.

The lepers danced on dead feet swollen with bandages, making the sound of clubs. Small boys dressed as dogs or monkeys, naked except for the mangy pelts flapping on their backs, moved on all fours through the chanting, stamping crowd.

Another group entering from the shadows of the huts lifted an image on a set of poles. It was a small building like a doll's house, and I guessed from its cupola and crude steeple that it was meant to be a church. It rested on a little platform that had been set on poles that were used like handles, as though they were carrying a stretcher.

I had missed the preliminaries, I knew. The dance had been going on for an hour or more. I had been listening to it throughout dinner and afterwards, while I had sat in silence with the two priests. It had now grown to a pitch of excitement that had bystanders joining in. It was impossible to tell the dancers from the spectators, there was so much movement, the stamping, the drumming, the clapping, the flapping rags.

The man dressed as the priest and the woman as the nun were at the head of a frenzied procession.

I recognized many of the dancers as the people I had come to know since my arrival in Moyo. It was strange to see them so active. The leper dressed as a priest looked like Johnson from my English class. He carried a book—not a Bible nor a breviary, but the message was clear enough. This was Father Touchette, and because he had just left, they were dramatizing what they knew of him. He performed a baptism on one of the dog boys. He read his book with rolling eyes. He pranced, looking haughty. He rebuffed a flirtation from the nun. The drumming was both music and a hoarse, hectic commentary.

Among the moving bodies it was easy for me to pick out Amina. She stood to one side, in the shadow of a hut's eaves, the firelight on her face, watching, nodding at the dancers and clapping to the stamping rhythm.

Had Amina been among the dancers, I would not have been able to get near her. But because she was next to the hut, watching, I could approach her. I touched her arm. All the physicality of the dance seemed to make touching permissible. She did not draw away.

'I want to visit you at your hut.'

'Yes,' she said.

She faced the throng of dancers, the dust, the lighted smoke, the dog children, the dirty feet, the drummers beating on logs and skins, the swaying image of the church.

'But what will your granny say?'

'She will not see you,' Amina said. 'She is blind.'

9

I had been hearing these drums since the night of my arrival. They had been part of my fever, they had been a feature of our card games, always pulsing in the background. I was certain that they had driven Father Touchette out of his mind.

The drums of Moyo had penetrated me too, but they had energized me. It was a physical sensation, like a drug or a drink. It was brainless, making me dumb and incoherent.

I tried to speak to Amina, but there was so much noise that I could not hear what she said. *What next*? I wondered. But I could tell from Amina's expression that it was no use. She could not hear me either. Perhaps that was for the best.

Without a word, Amina led the way, Granny right behind her, her leprous hand gripping Amina's shoulder. I followed and was glad for all these shadows, for the crowd and the confusion and the fire and the drums.

Amina's hut—more likely her granny's—was in the outer circle of older huts, the ones nearest to the bush that surrounded Moyo. It had its own tree—I could just make out its shape in the rising firelight—which was larger than the other stunted trees. The smell of the old, trampled cornshucks in the nearby garden was linked in my mind with the snakes and scorpions and biting spiders that lurked in the warm, broken rubbish of the shucks.

Hunched over, trying not to stumble, I banged my head against a heavy pole that served as a rafter for the thatched roof.

The old woman said something and reached for me.

'*Fisi*,' Amina said. Hyena.

The old woman had muttered in a dialect that was probably Yao. It was a bush language associated with Muslims in Mozambique that I did not understand. But I could translate Amina's replies. She may have been speaking Chinyanja for my benefit—as it was not odd for the Africans at the leprosarium to converse in several languages. The granny was still talking.

'Because I am very tired,' Amina said in Chinyanja.

She lit a candle and placed it in a large tin can which had holes punched in it.

To the old woman's croak, Amina said, 'I want to keep the hyenas away.'

Gabbling again, her granny seemed to be praying. She was at the far end of what was, by Moyo standards, a spacious hut, rectangular, a large single room, with two mats on the floor. She lowered herself to the distant mat and faced in our direction.

Except for the mats, the exposed floor was hard-packed dirt, and the walls were mud, and dust trickled from the straws in the thatch bundles of the roof. The room stank of dirt and termites, and on the looser and untrodden part of the floor there were wormcasts. There were some cardboard cartons and lanterns and a sturdy wooden crate shoved against the wall that had the look of an heirloom.

I held my breath while the old woman gazed with white eyes, and then murmured.

'I am moving my mat,' Amina replied.

She motioned me to her mat, and I sat down next to her, carefully pulling my legs under me.

Amina's face in profile was as smooth and simple as a carving with the candlelight behind it. She had long lashes, and her mouth looked solemn in silhouette. She sat very straight, her neck upright and so fragile-seeming that I reached to touch it. She hardly moved. I passed my fingers across her lips, and she opened her mouth and bit them. She was swift, and I could feel her hunger in the sharpness of her bite.

The old woman grunted several words, her face on us, and I watched her closely as I slipped my hand under Amina's cloth, feeling for her breasts.

Was that what the old woman was saying? Now I could recognize some of the dancers' chanting.

Sursum corda! Habemus ad dominum!

Cupping Amina's breast, I moved nearer, and she sighed and moved towards me to make it easier.

Agnus dei, qui tollis peccata mundi!

I kissed her and although I could smell the dirt floor, the ants, the sweat, the mice, the dust sifting down from the thatch, there was a sweetness on her lips, and her skin had the heavy sensuality of freshly turned earth. She received my kiss and moved nearer still, shifting to face me, the candlelight flickering in her eyes.

Had we made any noise? The old woman uttered another remark.

'It is the *zinyao*,' Amina said.

The old woman grumbled as I leaned over and whispered to Amina, 'Let's go outside.'

She shook her head: no.

I clutched her as though questioning.

'The people will see us,' she whispered, as she stared at the blind old woman.

Then we lay on the mat, side by side, while I went on stroking her breasts and breathing in shallow gasps, afraid that I might be heard. The old woman's face was fixed on us. She was still muttering, but nothing she said was clearly audible. I wanted her to sleep, yet she sat bolt upright, her eyes unblinking.

The drumming was so loud the thatch bundles trembled in the roof. The voices of the dancers cried out, *Christe eleison! Kyrie eleison!* and other snatches of the mass responses, as though they were incantations.

Amina's body was hard and thin. It made me think of the saplings at Moyo, their long narrow branches and small leaves. She was so small I could caress her easily with one hand.

I put my lips against her ear and said, 'When I saw you at

the English class I wanted to touch you.'

My face was so near to hers that I could feel the change in her expression. She was smiling, I knew. But she did not reply.

'So why did you come to the class?'

'To see you,' she said.

'Did you want to touch me?'

She hesitated.

'Tell me.' I moved so that her mouth was at my ear.

'I wanted to play with you,' she said at last. The word for playing was also the word for dancing and foolery.

I stroked her arm, and my fingers touched the leprous patch, the disc of dead skin. I had been here long enough to know there was no danger to me. I slipped my hand into hers and guided it against my body, so that she would touch me. She knew what to do, without my suggestion, and her knowledge excited me; she was a woman not a girl. Leaning towards the little lamp she pursed her lips as though kissing the candle flame.

Just then the old woman grunted again.

'I am putting out the light,' Amina said, and her one sigh against the flame killed it and brought darkness down on us.

Seconds later, when my sight returned, the moonlight made angular shadows in the room. There was also the glow from the *zinyao* dance outside. We embraced and touched and kissed and moved our bodies closer.

The blind woman spoke again, sounding irritable.

Amina, gripping my hand, said, '*Ndiri ndi mphere kwabasi.*'

I have a serious itch. Brother Piet had taught me that word. It was one of the sexiest things I had ever heard, and as she said it she moved my hand between her legs and helped me, working my fingers.

Amina was smiling as I touched her, her face even more beautiful in the moonglow, animated with desire. Her mouth was open as the old woman spoke a whole rattling sentence as though uttering a proverb.

Amina put her mouth against my ear again and spoke breathlessly. 'She says, "then scratch it."'

She slipped her leg over me and clumsily steadied herself. I propped myself up on my elbows. And she opened her cloth as I fumbled with my shorts. Then she was on top, straddling me.

The old woman had started moaning to the drumming and the yelling outside, while Amina shut her eyes and strained not to make a sound, as she rocked back and forth.

Sursum corda!

Deus meus!

Amina hitched herself forward and moved her hands to my face and held me as she drove her body against me, riding me. I could still see the old woman at the far end of the room, the light and shadow broken over her body like patches of liquid. It was like being in the presence of an old African idol, a great impassive lump that might spring to life at any moment and become a demon.

Yet I had no fear. I took Amina by her hips and jammed her against me, and she threw her head back as though convulsed. And when she bowed down and clutched me again I thought I heard her say, 'I am not crying.' I could not hear her cry, yet her tears were running down my face.

It was heat and noise and skin and drums and fire and smoke, and the feeling of silk in every opening of her body. It was also the growl of the crowd, and it was our old blind witness. I struggled with Amina and held her tight feeling like a cannibal gorging on her. Soon my body was sobbing, caught in a desperate panic of possession that made me reckless. And then we too were blind.

After this singular act of love we turned into two people, and I knew I had to get out of her hut. It was not easy to leave, for as soon as I got up, the old woman mumbled, saying to Amina, 'Don't go,' or something like it, because she, too, stood up and began shambling to the door.

I could not go out alone or the old woman would hear. The only way I could avoid detection and not rouse her suspicions was to stay so close to Amina that we would sound like one person.

In all the clatter of the drumming there was another snorting noise.

'*Fisi,*' the old woman said.

I knew that word.

'Yes. A hyena,' Amina said, as a big bristling and humpbacked dog blundered out of the darkness next to the hut.

That was how I left, startling the slavering creature and covered by its noise. We were the noise, the hyena and me. The thing was alert but did not seem afraid. It was mangy and misshapen, and it snarled at me, not angry but annoyed, as though I was the intruder.

10

When that scavenging animal bared its teeth at me I knew it was the end. I would have to leave Moyo and I should pack up and go before I was sent away. Expulsion would have been so hard: facing Father DeVoss's melancholy eyes. I was ashamed on the path back. I skulked like the hyena. I went guiltily to my room, sneaking up the stairs, knowing that anyone could hear my feet.

Even so, when I said the next day, 'I have to be getting back to my school,' Father DeVoss did not protest or make an ironic remark. He nodded as he sometimes did when he was dealt a certain hand of cards.

It was settled, his silence meant that it would be soon. Perhaps he was grateful to me for sparing him the bother of having to banish me from Moyo.

I had lost my right to remain. I had interfered. I had used Amina and that was wrong, because it violated a strict rule. I knew the rule, but I had been curious. I had created an area of disorder. I had to go. It was just as though after being warned of the consequences I had plucked a fruit. There was no way I could deny it or undo it. There were no secrets here, and now Father Voss knew mine.

And what made me ashamed was that I felt strongly that everyone else knew, too. I could not look into their faces, and when I glanced at them they seemed different—not more familiar but a great deal stranger, almost menacing. And if this was so, that everyone knew what I had done, I could never go back to Moyo.

'I am sorry to be leaving,' I said to Father DeVoss.

He did not ask why. That shamed me, too.

'Because this is the real world,' I said.

'Yes,' he said, and smiled. 'It is all here.'

He was not being ironic. It was a complete world, perhaps the only real world, and I was leaving it for the feebler and less secure world of metaphors, where leper did not mean leper.

'Maybe you can write something,' he said.

He had watched me struggling. He had seen me abandon my writing. Moyo was not the place for it. Moyo's reality did not require interpretation, and anything imaginative was an offence to the lepers and their families. And not even the expatriates needed it, for in their way they had become lepers too—so different and adapted to the place that they were not able to leave. Books and pictures were not wanted. It was playing cards and prayers and simple medicine; it was dust and sunlight and drumming. If I stayed I would be handing out Dapsone and tying bandages. I now knew that these simple tasks were the best things to do in Africa, something totally practical; not showing movies or teaching English and making Africans lonelier, but healing their wounds and pulling their sore teeth.

'I don't know about writing,' I said, remembering how I had shovelled my books into the ground in an attempt at a great purifying act of finality. 'It's so hard.'

'*Papier is geduldig.*' Father DeVoss had never spoken Dutch to me before. He smiled, as though he had revealed a secret. 'Paper is patient.'

At the station at seven the next morning, Father DeVoss said, 'Don't forget us.'

It was perhaps just a pleasantry, but I knew I never would. Then he touched my elbow, and I felt the charge of his hand travelling through my arm.

The train drew into Ntakataka, and it was a confusion of shouting and boarding, the women with baskets, the men with chickens. This was near the beginning of its run but after just four stations it was littered with peanut shells and chewed sugar-cane stalks and orange peels. And the carriages seemed much more battered than they were six weeks ago. Decrepit and uncomfortable, they looked a hundred years old.

I sat in second class again and even before we left the station I began to list what I had seen at Moyo. I wanted to write something, but I felt as though I would never write again, about Moyo or anything else.

Was I a writer? A writer had to get used to looking on and not interfering—being a witness. I had been passionate. Should I have kept back and been colder? I did not know whether I had made it hard on myself. I did not know that I would only see this over an enormous distance of time and space. I felt sad because I did not know how to live.

The low woods, the yellow leaves, the elephant grass, the dust, the mud huts, the unvarying bush: every landscape feature seemed to turn its back on me in my departure.

I would miss Moyo, I knew, and what made the loss of it a burden was that no one there knew what missing meant, nor wanted to be anywhere else. In that sense it was paradise.

To console myself, I looked for a young girl who might resemble Amina. I searched inside the train and looked at the people we passed in villages. No one looked like her. That thought uplifted me, but made me sad.

Moyo was unlike any of these mud-hut villages by the tracks. It was static and settled, a place of monumental inertia and no drama. It was not dark, not dangerous. It went against all my notions of Africa. It was snakes and insects and curable diseases. You accepted it and left all other ambition behind.

The lepers and priests and nuns were all happier than anyone I had met. They had found what they were looking for. What luck. It bothered me that I had not been able to fit in; that through my own fault I had been cast out; and that having left I would have to keep going—searching for the rest of my life for a similar place, and my mind always returning to Moyo.

I thought of what the people said at the leprosarium: There would never be a disease like this again, never a plague or scourge, and certainly nothing like it in this part of Africa, which in a clumsy way was being purified. No plague, no scourge, and even words like this would be archaic or quaint when leprosy was gone.

Yet I was uneasy, feeling naked again, certain that I was leaving this for a greater ignorance.

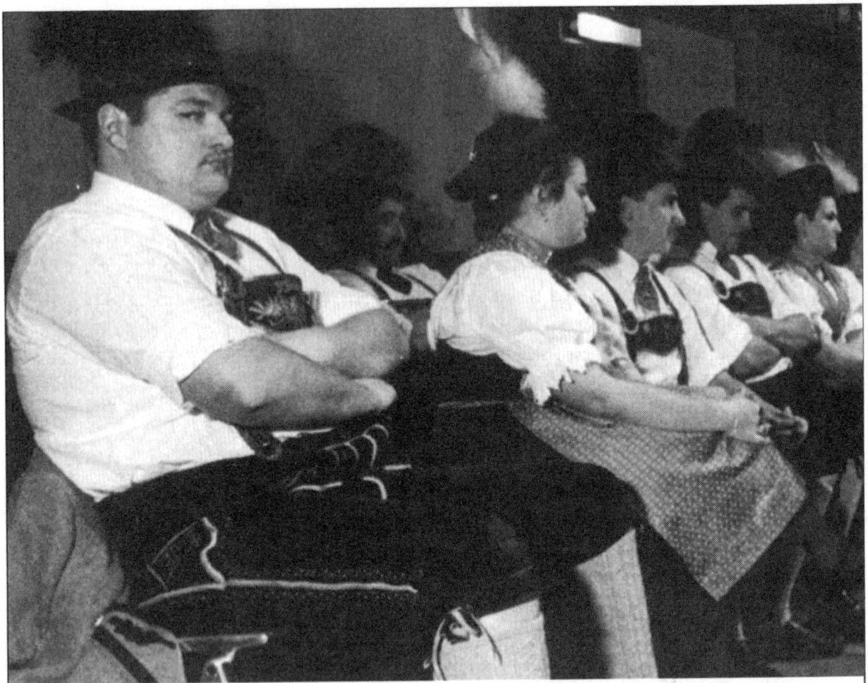

NO
STAMP
REQUIRED

FREEPOST
2-3 Hanover Yard
Noel Road
London
N1 8BR

NO
STAMP
REQUIRED

FREEPOST
2-3 Hanover Yard
Noel Road
London
N1 8BR

GRANTA

Sousa Jamba
Brothers

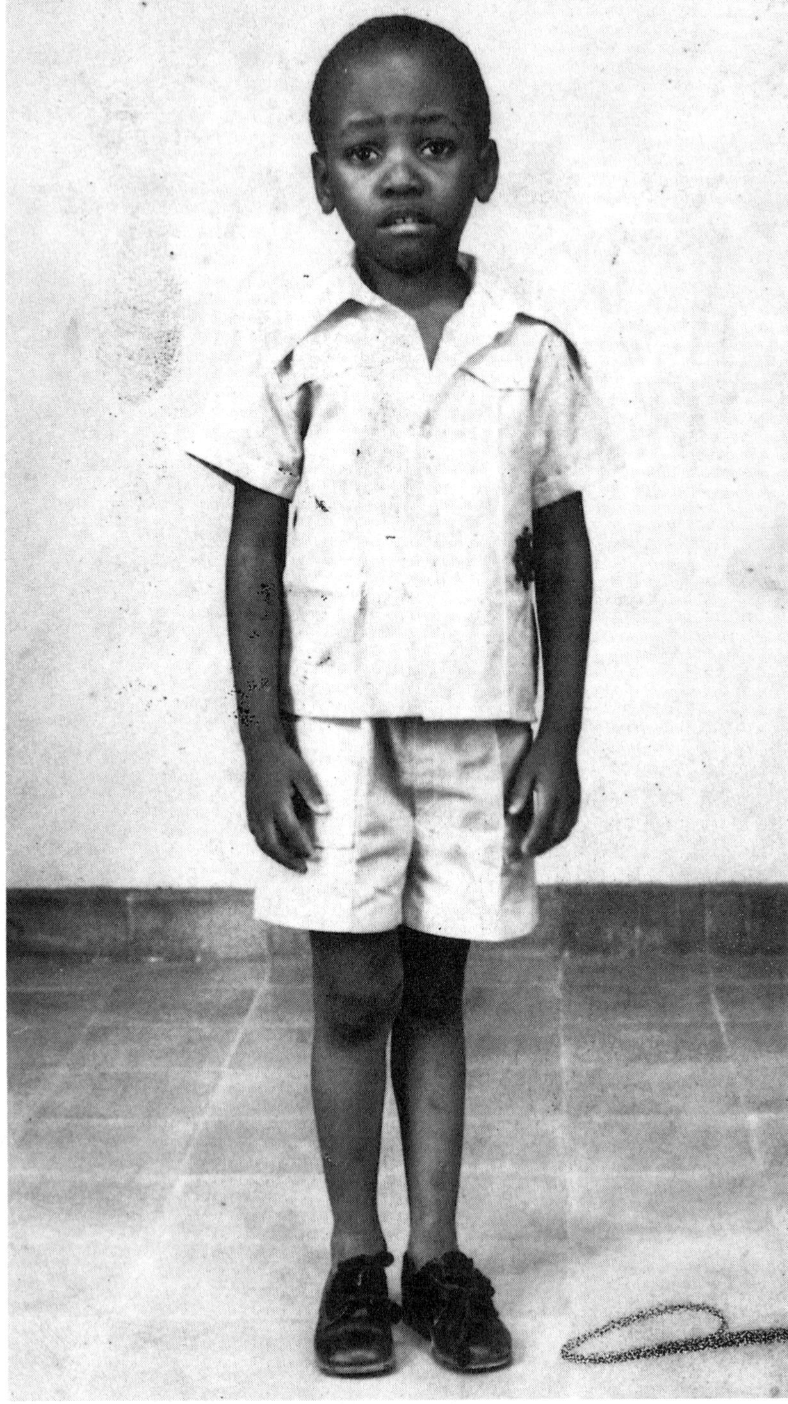

'Please, do whatever you can to help me get out of here.' It was Davide, my younger brother, his voice faint on the telephone from Angola. Then a man who spoke Portuguese with a strong French accent came on the line and said, 'Either you help your brother get out of the country or he will be dead. They are recruiting men his age.' A day later, Davide, whom I had not seen for eight years, managed to call again. This time he told me that he had just spent three months in prison.

I knew that getting Davide out of Luanda was not going to be easy. Angola was now back at war, and the authorities were ensuring that no man eligible for military service slipped through their net.

This was June, last year. Nine months earlier, in September 1992, Angola had been a very different place; a peace accord had been signed and had, despite a few glitches, endured, ending the eighteen-year civil war; Angolans were going to vote for the first time; from London I could phone and speak to my relatives in Luanda without fearing that the Angolan security services were listening in.

The elections themselves were remarkably peaceful, but after the results were announced Unita, the main opposition party, claimed that they had been fraudulent. The MPLA, which had won most of the seats, insisted that they had been free and fair, and the international observers and the UN concurred. A battle ensued between the government and Unita forces, and the vice-president of Unita, Jeremias Chitunda, was killed. He had been part of a Unita delegation in Luanda which, with the help of United Nations mediators, was trying to negotiate a settlement to the post-election crisis. His car was hit by a rocket as he and other high-ranking Unita officials were trying to leave the city.

Unita installations all over the country were destroyed, and hundreds of Unita activists were thrown in jail; many thousands were killed. Davide was working in Namibe, a small town in the southern Angolan desert near the Namibian border, where he had been part of a Unita team monitoring the elections. I had heard reports of fighting in Namibe and was worried about Davide. I also knew that captured Unita soldiers were being imprisoned or forced

Opposite: Davide Jamba aged four.

to fight on the government side. The idea of Davide marching against Unita with a rifle horrified me. Now I had heard from him: at least he was still alive. I had to get him out of Angola.

The civil war had scattered my family. I had last seen Davide for six hours in 1985 when he was thirteen, and I was passing through Zaire on my way to Angola. Before that, I had not seen him for ten years. In my memory, Davide was still a baby.

As I sat in London, trying to work out how to rescue my brother, I kept thinking of my childhood. I come from a family of eleven; I am the tenth, Davide is the eleventh. In our ethnic group, the Ovimbundus, last-borns—*kuasualas*—are fêted like first-borns. When I was a child, the elders gave me presents and held me on their laps, but I was dethroned in 1972, when Davide was born. I was six years old. Davide was a sickly baby who cried a lot and needed my mother's constant attention—I felt that she loved him more than she loved me.

After the Portuguese left Angola in 1975, the three liberation movements—the Popular Movement for the Liberation of Angola (MPLA), the National Union for the Total Independence of Angola (Unita) and the National Front for the Liberation of Angola (FNLA)—came to our home city of Huambo in the central highlands on recruiting drives. Most of my family joined Unita, which was led by Jonas Savimbi who, like us, was not only an Ovimbundu but also a Protestant. Joining Unita was something we did as naturally as attending church.

Political analysts both in and out of Angola have often characterized the civil war in terms of the cold war—as a struggle between competing ideologies in which the ruling MPLA was the defender of communism and Unita its arch-enemy. The truth is far more complex: what was really at stake was which ethnic élite would prevail in Angola. The MPLA drew most of its support from urban Mbundu people from Luanda and people of mixed race. It was backed by the Soviet Union and Cuba. The FNLA was mainly Bakongo and had its roots in a movement founded in the sixties by Angolan exiles in Zaire who hoped to revive the famous Bakongo Kingdom. It was backed by the United States. Unita was an offshoot of the FNLA and drew most of its recruits from the Ovimbundu. At first it received assistance from China, then later from the United States and South Africa.

In 1975 my mother joined the Unita Women's League. Until then she had been a full-time housewife, but now, to the consternation of my father, she started travelling around Angola, dressed in trousers made of Unita flags, attending rallies and addressing meetings through a megaphone. My father believed that a woman should stay in her adobe kitchen. He was further incensed by the news that she had taken to putting her hands in her pockets—grossly unfeminine behaviour.

My mother often took Davide along with her on these trips. I still recall her description of the *welwitschu mirabilis* that she had seen in the Namibe desert, a woody plant with a long taproot which can live up to a hundred years; I had often heard the elders repeat the legend that this plant could eat people, and I was jealous that my mother had taken Davide to see it, not me.

In 1976, as hundreds of Cuban troops approached Huambo with tanks and planes, most of my family fled. I got into a car with my sister Noemia and her husband. Davide and my mother (now separated from my father) went with Jaka, one of my older brothers, and his wife. We thought we would only be away for a couple of days—the Unita activists had told us that the Cubans would soon be forced out; that there was a large shipment of arms coming from China for the Unita soldiers; that the Unita men were invincible. We believed them. But as it turned out, the members of my family were to be separated for more than a decade.

Noemia, her husband and I reached Menongue, a town in Eastern Angola on the banks of the Cubango river. Here we met my mother and Davide, who had also ended up there with Jaka. During Portuguese rule, Menongue was a prosperous resort, but by this time the walls of the plush hotels had been sprayed with bullets, and the rooms were full of refugees. Everyone was panicking. Jaka managed to get my mother on a plane to Zaire. Davide went with her. Jaka then joined the Unita army and went for military training deep in the bush. I stayed with my sister and her husband, and we joined a large group of about a thousand people who were planning to walk through the Angolan jungle to Zambia. Our only guidance was provided by an old map someone had plucked from a classroom wall. The map proved on many occasions to be disastrously inaccurate; what was marked as a river often turned out to be a huge, impassable swamp. We were trying to avoid the main roads because we thought they would be filled with Cubans and MPLA troops. Many people died of starvation and disease; others got lost in the jungle and were attacked by wild animals. Of the original group, only fourteen of us made it to the Zambian border. We survived by eating mushrooms and caterpillars. One rainy night, I remember shivering under my wet, cold blanket, crying, wanting my mother, imagining her and Davide sitting somewhere having hot chocolate with bread and jam.

I spent most of my childhood in Zambia; I couldn't join my mother and Davide in Zaire because no one knew where they were. I went to primary school in Lusaka, the Zambian capital, and then to a secondary school in Mwinilunga in the north. Noemia did everything she could for me, sometimes going without shoes herself to support my studies.

I left school when I was nineteen and returned to the part of Angola under Unita control. I had finally made contact with my mother through a businessman who travelled between Zaire and Zambia, and on my way home I managed to meet up with her and Davide; he was now thirteen, spoke fluent French and Ligala and was obsessed with break dancing. He was fascinated by me and kept asking my mother questions: why I didn't look like him? Why was my hair so long? My mother would not stop apologizing for having left me behind eight years before; she seemed to feel both guilty and nervous. In the short time we spent together, she tried to say a great deal, but I was a very different person from the child she had known. I now spoke Portuguese and Umbundu with a slight Zambian accent, which she found very strange. One thing hadn't changed; I still envied Davide his closeness to her.

I spent a year in the Angolan bush where I worked in the Unita propaganda section, spending most of my time writing pro-Unita articles which were then broadcast on Unita radio, known as the Voice of the Black Cockerel. Then, in 1986, I was sent to Britain on a scholarship.

Two years later, my mother decided to return to Angola with Davide. She had been very homesick in Zaire, and the Unita-controlled area was now very large and very safe. Davide studied at the Unita school in southern Angola and had a job sorting diamonds, one of the major sources of Unita's income.

After the 1991 peace accord, Unita moved into the main cities, and the party leaders sent Davide to Namibe to help campaign for the elections. When war broke out, Davide was trapped.

To get Davide out of Angola, I had first to go to Portugal. Although there were still flights out of Luanda to other parts of Africa, there were so few passengers that it was easy for officials to spot people who were trying to flee the country. Portugal was a much more popular destination, especially for young people, which made it easier for Davide to slip through the Angolan controls. I had several Portuguese friends, including the novelist Pedro Paixao who offered at once to serve as Davide's guardian, and the Angolan emigré community in Portugal had created networks to support new arrivals. The real problem was getting a visa for Davide. Since the peace accord had collapsed, the Portuguese authorities, mindful of the large numbers of young men who would be trying to escape from Angola, had clamped down on immigration.

I called Davide in Luanda: I could tell he was nervous; he was often afraid to go out because the army recruiters were picking up every young male they came across. I tried to keep his spirits up, telling him to be strong. I told him that if he got the chance to get to some other country—Namibia, or Brazil, or South Africa—he should seize it, and not count on making it to Portugal.

For more than two years I had been writing a weekly column in *O Independente*, a large-circulation Portuguese weekly. The paper was also widely read in Angola, which was how my brother made contact with me in the first place—he spotted my byline. I frequently criticized the way in which Unita members were being treated by the government, which I later learned had led to members of my family still in Luanda receiving threats. Davide had managed to keep our relationship secret, but I was very worried that the authorities would work it out. When we spoke on the telephone, we talked in code.

In the early hours of a Thursday morning in September 1993, Pedro Paixao and I were at Lisbon airport awaiting Davide's arrival. I had not slept the previous night. I knew that the immigration officers in Luanda were on full alert; if they found out who Davide was or realized that he was fleeing the country they would send him straight to prison and from there to the army.

After an hour's delay, the plane from Luanda landed, and eventually Davide came through the gate. He was taller than me, but very thin—to me it looked as though he was suffering from malnutrition. His hair was red; his eyes were slightly bulgy. As I hugged him, I tried hard to hold back the tears. My own brother looked almost like the starving Africans I had seen in photographs. He was carrying a small black bag which contained a tattered track suit. He wore a white shirt, jeans and a pair of ill-fitting boots. As we drove to Estoril, where Pedro lived, Davide looked around at the beauty of Lisbon; he could scarcely grasp that he was really here.

When we arrived at Pedro's house, Pedro's first act was to throw open his wardrobe and invite Davide to choose whatever he wanted. Davide could not believe his luck, faced with so many clothes, but I kept telling him to take the oldest things so as not to abuse our host's generosity. This was the beginning of some tension between us; Davide could not see why he should hold back—Pedro had told him to take what he wanted—and thought that I was being difficult.

Later that morning, we went out to buy Davide some shoes. I thought he should buy a sensible pair; he wanted something snazzy and felt that I was imposing my taste on him because I was paying. I insisted that I knew what was best for him. He insisted that I was treating him like a child. I tried to reason with him; he threw a tantrum. We had different ideas about what being brothers meant. He was still the *kuasuala*, the last-born, and he expected me to indulge his every whim; I wanted to help him become as independent as he could.

As time went on, I sometimes did not know exactly how to deal with Davide. I had never had a younger brother. I kept wondering what brothers did with each other. How much, for instance, could I tell him of my private life? Were there special things I had to do to keep his respect? We did agree on one matter—the importance of food. We went to restaurants and ordered huge meals; I wanted Davide to put on weight.

We spent so much time with other people that we scarcely had a chance to talk. I also sensed that Davide did not really want to dwell on what he had been through. He was more interested in how he could get to study business management. But he still bore the marks of someone who had been living in fear: in restaurants he would suddenly begin to whisper to me if there was a black person within earshot. We shared a room, and he talked in his sleep—he just couldn't escape from his past. I tried everything to distract him; I bought him the Portuguese translation of Mario Vargas Llosa's novel *Aunt Julia and the Scriptwriter*, but it became clear that Davide didn't really enjoy fiction—he said that life was too short. He preferred reading Edgar Morin, the French sociologist.

One evening, we were sitting in a seaside restaurant, when suddenly Davide said, 'You know, sometimes I wish I wasn't Angolan.'

'Why?'

'Oh, some of the things we do to each other. I have seen so much in Angola. I was almost killed. I was saved by some women who kept pleading with the policeman who was about to pull the trigger. I am very lucky to be alive. I saw a man being forced by the police to eat a Unita flag. He was vomiting and shitting all over while his children were watching.'

I asked him what prison had been like. Davide shook his head. 'I will tell you all about it some day. All I can say is that I know what hell is like.'

'How did you survive?'

'We got into the wrong lorry. After all the Unita supporters were rounded up, they started sorting out who was Ovimbundu and who was Mucubal. Four of us got into a lorry filled with Mucubal people, and luckily no one denounced us. The Ovimbundus were all taken to Bentiaba and shot.'

Davide was weeping. I said that Unita too had committed human rights abuses, and that no party in Angola was beyond reproach. Davide agreed, looking straight out at the yachts on the sea. The waiter brought us large sirloin steaks with salad, and we dug in.

Davide found a place in college to do a diploma in business studies. I left Lisbon for London feeling relieved.

I returned to Portugal six months later, and Davide met me at the airport, accompanied by his new girlfriend. He had put on so much weight I found it hard to believe that this was the same person I had met off the plane from Luanda. He was bubbling over with excitement, telling me all about a college trip he had taken to Spain.

Davide had made many friends. He took me to his college, where his lecturers told me that he often came top of his class. I noted that he had already adopted some Portuguese traits, including a passion for football. He slept with a small Benfica flag next to his pillow. Flashy shoes and baggy trousers no longer interested him—he now wanted to look as dowdy as any other Portuguese student, dressing in black jeans, canvas boots and T-shirts.

The sight of my own brother transformed from a difficult, emaciated youth to a zestful, curious student brought home to me the depth of Angola's tragedy. There were hundreds of young men who could be busy at school and at college, preparing for the future. Instead, they were in prison or on the front line.

For more than three months now, the Angolan government has been meeting with Unita in the Zambian capital, Lusaka, to try and negotiate a solution to the Angolan imbroglio. Nothing has come of the negotiations so far. There will only be peace if the powerful élites from the many regions of the country are allowed to exist in their own spheres of influence. Angola will only survive as a federal state in which power is not concentrated within an élite from a specific area. For years, each of the two warring sides had convinced itself that it could crush the other. In truth, they will have to learn to co-exist.

GRANTA

Ryszard Kapuściński
Startled in the Dark

Morning and dusk are by far the best times of day in Africa. The sun is scorching, but these times allow you to live.

The gesture of a boy

We are heading in the direction of the Sabeta Waterfalls, twenty-five kilometres from Addis Ababa. Driving in Ethiopia you have to be prepared to make constant compromises. The roads are old and narrow, packed, to the point of overflowing, with vehicles and people, and, one way or another, they all have to be accommodated. Every so often the driver (or herdsman or passer-by) has a problem, an obstacle, a puzzle: how is he to avoid colliding with that oncoming vehicle? What should he do *not* to tread on those children under his feet or the invalids who seem to be crawling everywhere, while driving his cattle (or his sheep or his camels)? How exactly is he meant to cross the road and not get knocked over by a passing lorry? Just when is he meant to step out of the way of that bull? And will he really be able to stop himself from knocking down that woman carrying a twenty-kilo parcel on her head? And yet no one gets angry or abusive. There are no shouts or curses or threats. Silently, patiently, everyone progresses in his or her own manner, manoeuvring, ducking and diving and dodging, pirouetting, twisting this way, then that way, but—above all—somehow moving forward. Hold-ups on the road are normally solved by amicably agreeing to advance—millimetre by millimetre.

The river that flows over the Sabeta Waterfalls first comes down a creviced, stony canyon. The river here is shallow and rocky and full of rapids. Then it drops, falling lower and lower until it reaches the sharp edge of the waterfall's precipice. This is where a small Ethiopian boy, about eight years old, makes his living. He starts up-river. He undresses in front of the tourists who have gathered here, slips into the water and is then immediately carried off by its rapids, sliding down the stony river bed, racing to the very edge of the precipice, where he then comes to a dramatic stop—to screams of terror and relief from all the people assembled to watch. The boy then rises, turns round and climbs back up, his naked behind conspicuously displayed to the members of his audience. A gesture of scorn? An insult? Quite the

Photo: John Vink (Magnum)

opposite; the display is an expression of pride (that also serves to reassure the spectators)—showing off the well-tanned hide of his behind, one so calloused that it allows him to slide down a river-bed bristling with sharp-edged boulders without being harmed. The skin genuinely has the appearance of the soles of a pair of climbing boots.

The annihilation of a great army

The following day we are outside a prison in Addis Ababa. At the gates, there is a queue of people standing under a tin roof, waiting for the prison to open. The barefoot and half-clothed men milling near the gate are the prison guards. The government is too poor to provide them with uniforms. We have to accept that they have the power to allow us inside—or turn us away. We are resigned to recognizing that this is the case and that we must wait for them to stop talking among themselves.

The prison is fairly old. It was built by the Italians and then used by the Moscow-supported regime of Mengistu to detain and torture the opposition. Above the gate is an enormous star and the familiar hammer and sickle. In the courtyard, we discover a bust of Karl Marx. Today, the present government has ordered Mengistu's closest associates to be imprisoned here—former members of the Central Committee, ministers, army generals and policemen.

The summer of 1991—when Mengistu fell, fleeing to Zimbabwe at the last possible minute—marked the seventeenth anniversary of his regime. Until that moment, he had—with the help of his friends in Moscow—built the most powerful army south of the Sahara: 400,000 strong, armed with some of the world's most sophisticated missiles and chemical weapons, dedicated to fighting the guerrillas from the northern mountains (in Eritrea and Tigre) and in the south (in Ogaden). The guerrillas were barefoot peasants; many were children; they were poorly armed, hungry and bedraggled. But in the summer of 1991, they forced this powerful army to retreat to Addis Ababa, as Europeans fled fearing that a terrible slaughter would follow. Nothing of the kind took place. What ensued might have been a scene in a film—with the possible title: *The Annihilation of a*

Great Army. Mengistu's powerful army broke up within hours of his leaving the country. The soldiers—now demoralized and famished—had turned into beggars, pleading for food, still bearing their Kalashnikovs. Their tanks, rocket-launchers, planes, armoured cars and artillery abandoned (a vast heap of the stuff can be found in the suburbs of the city today), the soldiers dispersed in all directions. On foot, by mule or by bus, they made for their villages. In Ethiopia today, you still come across healthy, virile young men sitting idly on doorsteps or on the stools of shabby, dark roadside bars. They are the ex-soldiers of the great army of Mengistu, once poised to conquer Africa, which, during the course of a single day in the summer of 1991, completely disintegrated.

We have come to see Shimelis Mazengia. He was one of the ideologues of the Mengistu regime, a member of the politburo, and the secretary of the Central Committee for matters ideological—an Ethiopian Suslov. Mazengia is forty-five years old. He is intelligent and takes great care in choosing his words. He is wearing a sporty, light-blue outfit. All the prisoners here are indistinguishable from the civilians; the government does not have the money to provide them with prisoners' uniforms. I asked one guard if the prisoners were ever tempted to escape, given that, once they did, they would look like any other man in the street. Escape? He looked at me with genuine incredulity. Here, he said, they get a bowl of soup. Out there they would be dying of hunger like everyone else. The prisoners, he stressed, are our enemies—this is true. But they are not idiots.

Mazengia says that Mengistu's flight caught everyone associated with him by surprise. Mengistu was tireless, working day and night, ostensibly untouched by material possessions. He had a passion for power, absolute power. He was incapable of compromise, of any kind of flexible thinking. He regarded the massacres—the so-called red terror that decimated the population of the country—as a necessary feature of power. (Mengistu, it is claimed, is held responsible for 30,000 deaths; some put the figure as high as 300,000.) I remember the sight of the 'nightly harvest'—the bodies of those killed the previous night—from the late seventies as I drove through the city in the early hours of the morning. I was curious to know how Mazengia now viewed his own role in the highest echelons of a discredited government, the collapse of which led to such widespread misery and death.

Mazengia answers philosophically. History is a complex process, he says. It makes mistakes. It dodges, searches, shifts and sometimes gets stuck in a blind alley. You need the correct means by which to judge the past. Nothing but the future is able to fulfil this requirement.

Along with 406 others, all connected with what is referred to—in Ethiopian nomenclature—as the 'old regime', Mazengia has spent the past three years in prison not knowing what will become of him. Will he be sent to another prison? Be tried? Executed? Released? The government, too, would appear to be pondering the same question: what should be done with the prisoners?

We sit in a small room; it could have been a guard's room. No one eavesdrops on our conversation; no one insists that we stop. People come and go constantly, chaotically; the phone rings on the next table but no one can be bothered to answer it.

Before we part, I ask Mazengia to show me where he is locked up. I am taken into a courtyard flanked by two-storey galleries. The prison cells run along the galleries, their doors opening out on to the courtyard. It is crowded with prisoners. I scrutinize their faces. These are the faces of university professors, their assistants and their students. The Mengistu regime was supported by people who believed fervently and idealistically in the Albanian version of socialism as practised by Enver Hoxha. When Tirana broke with Peking, there were killings on the streets of Addis Ababa: such was the power of their conviction that the Ethiopian pro-Hoxhists took to shooting the Maoists. The blood bath lasted a month. But after Mengistu fled and the army dispersed and the soldiers returned to their homes, the academics remained in the city: they didn't know to leave. They were easy to apprehend and lock up in this crowded, teeming courtyard.

Far from Africa

Perusing a copy of the summer 1993 edition of the Somali quarterly *Hal-Abur (Journal of Somali Literature and Culture)*, I notice that out of the seventeen contributors—leading Somali intellectuals, scientists and writers—fifteen are living abroad. Therein lies the problem. Most African intellectuals do not even live on the continent. If persecuted, African academics will not seek refuge in another African nation. You'll find them in Boston, Geneva, London, Paris or Rome. Those who stay behind are—at the bottom of the social ladder—the ignorant masses of cowed and exploited peasants; and—at the top—they are members of a heavily corrupt bureaucracy or of an arrogant army ('lumpenmilitariat' in the words of the Ugandan historian Ali Mazuri). How can the continent develop without its own middle-class intellectuals?

Maybe then?

I visit the university in Addis Ababa, the only one in the country. I look briefly at its library—the only library in the country. The shelves are empty. No books, no newspapers. It is the same in so many other African countries. There was once a good library in Kampala (in fact, there were three). There was a good library in Dar-es-Salaam. Now there is nothing. The land mass of Ethiopia is as large as France, Germany and Poland put together. At present it has a population of fifty million. In a few years, it is predicted, it will rise to more than sixty million; in a few more years, it will exceed eighty.

Maybe then?

At least one?

The African bible in Addis

When I have the time, I go to Africa Hall, an enormous, decorative building on one of the hills of the city. In May 1963, Africa Hall was the venue for the first African summit. I was here and saw them, the big names of the time: Nasser, Nkrumah, Haile Selassie, Ben Bella, Modibo Keita. They met in this very hall, where today they would find boys playing ping-pong and a woman selling leather jackets.

Each time I visit, a new building is being constructed near Africa Hall, each one more imposing and luxurious than the last. Although African society can be seen to be changing, and, in the process, becoming ever poorer, the business of government seems to grow uncontrollably. There is the example of Africa Hall. It is not subject to any conditions or regulations. Corridors as well as conference rooms and offices are buried under papers stacked as high as the ceiling. There are more papers bulging out of the cupboards and filing cabinets. There are even more spilling out of drawers, tumbling off the shelves. And everywhere, behind every desk, packed as closely together as possible, are beautiful women.

They are the secretaries.

I am interested in a paper entitled *Lagos Plan of Action for the Economic Development of Africa 1980-2000*. It contains the details of a meeting of the heads of all African states that was convened in Lagos in 1980 to address the crises in Africa. The plan devised there was seen as a bible, a panacea, a great strategy for Africa's development.

My enquiries led nowhere. Most people have not heard of the paper. There are some who have heard of it but know none of its details. A few say that they have read it but do not possess a copy. They are, however, able to give me details of one of its resolutions, the one concerning peanut production in Senegal and how to increase it. Or the one pertaining to the tsetse fly in Tanzania and how to exterminate it. Or the one about the drought in Sudan and how to limit it. But the answer to the question of the plan itself—how to save Africa?—no one seems able to remember.

A paradox of our world

In Africa Hall, I speak to the young and energetic Babasahola Chinsman, deputy director of the United Nations development agency. He comes from Sierra Leone and is exceptional in being one of the few Africans represented in the new 'global class'. He has a villa in Addis Ababa (it goes with the job), his own villa in Freetown (which he lets to the German embassy), a private apartment in Manhattan (he dislikes hotels). He has a car with a driver, and servants. Tomorrow he is in Madrid for a conference; in three days' time, he will be in New York; next week, he flies to Sydney. And the question informing every discussion is invariably the same: how to help the starving in Africa?

Our conversation is friendly and interesting.

Chinsman tells me: 'It is not true that Africa stagnates. Africa is developing. It is not solely a continent of hunger; the problem is greater, worldwide; a hundred and fifty underdeveloped countries clamour at the doors of twenty-five developed ones, which are themselves suffering from a recession and whose populations are not expanding . . . And in the meanwhile, Africa cannot get past the obstacle posed by its own hugely underdeveloped infrastructure: the inadequate transport, the bad roads, the insufficient supply of heavy-goods vehicles and coaches and buses, the bad communications system.

'One of the paradoxes of our world is illustrated by the cost of providing one meal—usually a fistful of corn—for one refugee in a camp in, say, Sudan: the expense of transporting this fistful of corn, its storage and the service that gets it to a refugee is higher than the price of dinner at the most expensive restaurant in Paris.

'It has taken us thirty years to understand fully the importance of education. The economies in which the peasants have been educated are ten to fifteen times more productive than those in which the peasants have received no education. Education alone brings material benefits. It is not necessary to have investment.'

I speak to John Menru from Tanzania: 'Africa needs a new generation of politicians who will think in a new way,' he says. 'Today's politicians should resign. They don't think about development; they concentrate on staying in power. We need politicians with a vision.

'What is our great threat? Ethnic fundamentalism. It can develop to the point where the principle of ethnicity assumes a religious dimension, becomes a substitute for religion.'

Sadig Rasheed from Sudan—a director of the Commission for Economic Affairs in Africa—says: 'Africa has to wake up! African societies have to develop a new, self-critical attitude; otherwise Africa will always be marginal.'

The spirit of criticism and the spirit of pride

I speak to an old English settler, who argues that the strength of Europe and European culture lies in its ability to criticize and, most importantly, in its ability to be self-critical. European cultures practise the art of analysis and enquiry. They are restless.

The European mind is willing to acknowledge its limitations, accept its imperfections. It is a sceptical mind. The spirit of criticism does not exist in other cultures. They are proud, believing that what they have is perfect. They see themselves in an uncritical way, tending to blame others (subversive agents, various forms of foreign domination). Criticism is an attack, a manifestation of extreme prejudice. It is interpreted as a personal insult, a deliberate attempt to humiliate or as an expression of persecution. If you say that the city is dirty, it is taken personally. It is as if you were saying that its citizens don't wash behind their ears, that their necks and nails are filthy. They resent your observations; they sulk; they develop grudges. This renders them culturally, structurally, incapable of progress, of creating in themselves the will to grow.

Are African cultures—and there are as many as there are African religions—really beyond criticism and untouchable? Why is Africa perpetually lagging behind in the race of continents? It is the question Sadig Rasheed and Africans like him are trying to answer for themselves.

The revolution of a plastic bucket

We have driven 2,000 kilometres into Ethiopia. The roads are deserted. At this time of year (it is winter in Europe), the mountains—so high that they reach the clouds—are green and magnificent in the sun. The silence is piercing. If you stop and sit on the roadside, you hear high, monotonous voices in the distance. They are from children singing in the hills, the sons and daughters of herdsman, collecting wood, cutting grass for their cattle. You do not hear the voices of their parents. It is as if the world belonged to children.

Half the population of Africa is under fifteen years old. Children are everywhere: in the armies and the refugee camps, working in the fields and trading in the market places. And at home it is the child who performs the most vital function of the family: fetching the water. At dawn, while so many are still asleep, small boys start up in the dark and hurry off to wells, ponds or rivers. The new technology has proved to be their great ally. It has provided them with an essential instrument: a plastic bucket.

The plastic bucket has revolutionized the lives of Africans. You cannot survive in the tropics without water—the shortages are always acute. And so water has to be carried long distances, frequently dozens of kilometres. Before the invention of the plastic bucket, water was carried in heavy vats made of clay or stone. The wheel—and vehicles that use it—was not a familiar aspect of African culture; everything was carried on the head—including the heavy vats of water. In the division of household labour, it was the woman's task to fetch water. A child would have been unable to lift a vat. And the conditions of acute poverty meant that few households could afford more than one vat.

The appearance of the plastic bucket was a miracle. To start with, it is relatively cheap (although in some households it is the only possession of value), costing around two dollars. And it is light. And it comes in different sizes: even a small child can carry a few litres.

And so now it is the child's job to fetch water. The sight of flocks of children playing and bantering on their way to a distant well is common. What a relief for the overworked African woman! What a change in her life! In fact, the positive features of the plastic bucket are endless. Consider the queue. When water was brought in by cisterns, it was often necessary to queue for a whole day. The tropical sun is relentless. You could not risk leaving your vat in your place in the queue and retiring to the shade. It was too expensive. Today it is possible. The bucket has taken the place of the individual in the queue, which, today, frequently consists of a long, colourful line of plastic containers, their owners waiting in the shade, off to the market or visiting friends.

A request for one pen

If you stop in a village or a small town, even at a farm, you find yourself suddenly encircled by a brood of bedraggled children, with tattered shirts and shorts. Their only possession is a gourd with a little water. A banana, or the smallest piece of bread, disappears within seconds. Hunger is a permanent presence. And yet the things they beg for are not bread, fruit or money.

They ask for pens.

A ballpoint pen. Price: ten cents.

But where can they get ten cents?

They want to go to school; everyone wants to learn. But even those lucky enough to have a school to go to (in a village, commonly a place in the shade of a mango tree) cannot learn to write; they have no pens.

Walking from the north to the south

Near Gondar (a town of Ethiopian kings and emperors which you pass as you make your way from the bay of Aden through Djibouti and carry on in the direction of El Obeid, Tersaf, Njamena and Lake Chad), I meet a man who is walking south from the north. That is all I can say about him; that is what distinguishes him. I learn that he is looking for his lost brother.

His feet are bare, and he wears a pair of patched shorts and what once could have been called a shirt. He carries three objects: a walking stick; a piece of cloth that serves as a towel in the morning, a head covering from the sun during the day and a blanket to sleep under at night; and a wooden bowl with a lid that he carries over his shoulder. He has no money. He lives on the kindness of strangers. If he does not get food, he goes hungry. He has always been hungry.

He is walking south because that is the direction in which his brother set out when he left home. When was that? I ask. A long time ago. The whole of this man's past seems to be summarized in that phrase: 'a long time ago'. He set out from the mountains of Eritrea, from Keren. He set out a long time ago.

He knows how to get to the south. In the morning he walks in the direction of the sun. He asks each person he meets if they know Solomon, his brother. Nobody is surprised by such a question. The whole of Africa is on the move. Some are fleeing wars back home, or drought, or hunger. And they often lose their way. The man walking south is merely one of many others.

I ask him why he wants to find his brother. He shrugs his shoulders. To him, the question answers itself. His shrug is one of pity for this man, this stranger, who may be well dressed, but is clearly deprived, in some fundamental way, of something more truly valuable.

I ask him if he realizes that he has crossed from Eritrea into Ethiopia. He answers with the smile of a man who knows. For him, there is one scorched earth, and one brother looking for the other.

Debre Libanos
Along the same road, but down a hill and then deep into a precipitous canyon, stands a monastery—Debre Libanos. Inside, the church is pleasantly cool, and it is as if I have been dropped into total darkness. After a while, my eyes adjust and I see fresco-covered walls and Ethiopian pilgrims, dressed in white, lying face down on a floor covered only with straw matting. In the corner an old monk is singing the psalms in Gyz, now a dead language. His sleepy voice is faint—as if at any moment it might fade away entirely. It is a moment of silence and mysticism, a moment that is more than a moment, beyond measure and weight, beyond existence, beyond time.

How long have the monks been lying there? I do not know. I know only that I leave church and I return. I do this several times over the course of the day. And each time, the monks are lying there, unmoved.

A day? A month? A year? As long as eternity?

Translated from the Polish by Alicja Buford

GRANTA

AHDAF SOUEIF
SANDPIPER

Outside, there is a path. A path of beaten white stone bordered by a white wall—low, but not low enough for me to see over it from here. White sands drift across the path. From my window, I used to see patterns in their drift. On my way to the beach, I would try to place my foot, just the ball of my foot, for there never was much room, on those white spaces that glinted flat and free of sand. I had an idea that the patterns on the stone should be made by nature alone; I did not want one grain of sand, blown by a breeze I could not feel, to change its course because of me.

I used to sit where the water rolled in, its frilled white edge nibbling at the sand, withdrawing to leave great damp half-moons. I would sit inside one of these curves, at the very mid-point, fitting my body to its contour, and wait. Sometimes the wave would touch my feet, sometimes it would swirl around me then pull back, sifting another layer of sand from under me, leaving me wet to the waist. My heels rested in twin hollows that filled, emptied and refilled. And subtle as the shadow of a passing cloud, my half-moon would slip down the bank—only to be overtaken and swamped by the next leap of foaming white.

I lean against the wall of my room and count: twelve years ago, I met him. Eight years ago, I married him. Six years ago, I gave birth to his child.

For eight summers we have been coming here; to the beach-house west of Alexandria. The first summer had not been a time of reflection; my occupation then had been to love my husband in this—to me—new and different place. To love him as he walked towards my parasol, shaking the shower water from his black hair, his feet sinking into the warm, hospitable sand. To love him as he carried his nephew on his shoulders into the sea, threw him in, caught him and hoisted him up again; a colossus bestriding the waves. To love him as he played backgammon with his father in the evening, the slam of counters and clatter of dice resounding on the patio while, at the dining-room table, his sister showed me how to draw their ornate, circular script. To love this new him, who had been hinted at but never revealed when we lived in my northern land, and who, after his long absence, had found his way back into the heart of his country, taking me along with him. We walked in the sunset along the water's edge, kicking at the spray; my sun-hat fallen on my back; my hand, pale bronze in his burnt brown; my face no doubt mirroring his: aglow with health and love; a young couple in a glitzy commercial for life assurance or a two-week break in the sun.

My second summer here was the sixth summer of our love—and the last of our happiness. Carrying my child and loving her father, I sat on the beach and let my thoughts wander. I thought about our life in my country before we were married: four years in a cosy flat built on a roof in a Georgian square, him meeting me at the bus-stop when I came back from work, Sundays when it did not rain and we sat in the park with our newspapers, late nights at the movies. I thought of those things and missed them—but with no great sense of loss. It was as though they were all there, to be called upon, to be lived again whenever we wanted.

I would look out to sea, trying to work out my co-ordinates. I thought a lot about the water and the sand as I sat there, watching them meet and flirt and touch. I tried to understand that I was on the edge, the very edge of Africa; that the vastness ahead was nothing compared with what lay behind me. But—even though I'd been there and seen for myself its never-ending dusty green interior, its mountains, the big sky—my mind could not grasp a world that was not present to my eye. I could see the beach, the waves, the blue beyond and, cradling them all, my baby.

I sat with my hand on my belly and waited for the tiny eruptions, the small flutterings, that told me how she lay and what she was feeling. Gradually, we came to talk to each other. She would curl into a tight ball in one corner of my body until, lop-sided and uncomfortable, I coaxed and prodded her back into a more centred, relaxed position. I slowly rubbed one corner of my belly until *there*, aimed straight at my hand, I felt a gentle punch. I tapped, and she punched again. I was twenty-nine. For seventeen years my body had waited to conceive, and now my heart and mind had caught up with it. Nature had worked admirably; I had wanted the child through my love for her father and how I loved her father that summer. My body could not get enough of him. His baby was snug inside me, and I wanted him there too.

From where I stand now, all I can see is dry, solid white. The white glare, the white wall and the white path, narrowing in the distance.

I should have gone. On that swirl of amazed and wounded anger when I first sensed that he was pulling away from me, I should have gone. I should have turned, picked up my child and gone.

I turn. The slatted blinds are closed against a glaring sun. They call the wooden blinds *sheesh* and tell me it's the Persian word for glass. So that which sits next to a thing is called by its name. I have had this thought many times and feel as though it should lead me somewhere; as though I should draw some conclusion from it, but so far I haven't.

I run my finger along a wooden slat. Um Sabir, my husband's old nanny, does everything around the house, both here and in the city. I tried, at first, at least to help, but she would rush up and ease the duster or the vacuum-cleaner from my hands: 'Shame, shame. What am I here for? Keep your hands nice and soft. Go and rest. Or why don't you go to the club? What have you to do with these things?' My husband translated all this for me and said things to her which I came to understand meant that tomorrow I would get used to their ways. The meals I planned never worked out. Um Sabir cooked what was best in the market on that day. If I tried to do the shopping the prices trebled. I arranged the flowers, smoothed out the pleats in the curtains and presided over our dinner-parties.

My bed is made. My big bed into which a half-asleep Lucy, creeping under the mosquito-net, tumbles in the middle of every night. She fits herself into my body and I put my arm over her until she shakes it off. In her sleep she makes use of me; my breast is sometimes her pillow, my hip her footstool. I lie content, glad to be used. I hold her foot in my hand and dread the time when it will no longer be seemly to kiss the dimpled ankle.

On a black leather sofa in a transit lounge in an airport once, many years ago, I watched a Pakistani woman sleep. Her dress and trousers were a deep, yellow silk, and on her dress bloomed luscious flowers in purple and green. Her arms were covered in gold bangles. She had gold in her ears, her left nostril and around her neck. Against her body her small son lay curled. One of his feet was between her knees, her nose was in his hair. All her worldly treasure was on that sofa with her, and so she slept soundly on. That image, I saved up for him.

I made my bed this morning. I spread my arms out wide and gathered in the soft, billowing mosquito-net. I twisted it round in a thick coil and tied it into a loose loop that dangles gracefully in mid-air.

Nine years ago, sitting under my first mosquito-net, I had written, 'Now I know how it feels to be a Memsahib.' That was in Kano; deep in the heart of the continent I now sit on the edge of. I had been in love with him for three years, and being apart then was a variant, merely, of being together. When we were separated there was for each of us a gnawing lack of the other. We would say that this confirmed our true, essential union. We had parted at Heathrow, and we were to be rejoined in a fortnight, in Cairo, where I would meet his family for the first time.

I had thought to write a story about those two weeks, about my first trip into Africa: about Muhammad al-Senusi explaining courteously to me the inferior status of women, courteously because, being foreign, European, on a business trip, I was an honorary man. A story about travelling the long, straight road to Maiduguri and stopping at roadside shacks to chew on meat that I then swallowed in lumps while Senusi told me how the meat in Europe had no body and melted like rice pudding in his mouth. About the time when I saw the lion in the tall grass. I asked the driver to stop, jumped out of the car, aimed my camera and shot as the lion crouched. Back in the car, unfreezing himself from horror, the driver assured me that the lion had crouched in order to spring at me. I still have the photo: a lion crouching in tall grass—close up. I look at it and cannot make myself believe what could have happened.

I never wrote the story, although I still have the notes. Right here, in this leather portfolio which I take out of a drawer in my cupboard. My Africa story. I told it to him instead—and across the candle-lit table of a Cairo restaurant he kissed my hand and said, 'I'm crazy about you.' Under the high windows the Nile flowed by. Eternity was in our lips, our eyes, our brows—I married him, and I was happy.

I leaf through my notes. Each one carries a comment, a description meant for him. All my thoughts were addressed to him. For his part he wrote that after I left him at the airport he turned around to hold me and tell me how desolate he felt. He could not believe I was not there to comfort him. He wrote about the sound of my voice on the telephone and the crease at the top of my arm that he said he loved to kiss.

What story can I write? I sit with my notes at my writing-table and wait for Lucy. I should have been sleeping. That is what they think I am doing: sleeping away the hottest of the midday hours. Out there on the beach, by the pool, Lucy has no need of me. She has her father, her uncle, her two aunts, her five cousins; a wealth of playmates and protectors. And Um Sabir, sitting patient and watchful in her black *djellaba* and *tarha*, the deck-chairs beside her loaded with towels, sun-cream, sun-hats, sandwiches and iced drinks in Thermos flasks.

I look and watch and wait for Lucy.

In the market in Kaduna the mottled, red carcasses lay on wooden stalls shaded by grey plastic canopies. At first I saw the meat and the flies swarming and settling. Then, on top of the grey, plastic sheets, I saw the vultures. They perched as sparrows would in an English market square, but they were heavy and still and silent. They sat cool and unblinking as the fierce sun beat down on their bald, wrinkled heads. And hand in hand with the fear that swept over me was a realization that fear was misplaced, that everybody else knew they were there and still went about their business; that in the meat-market in Kaduna, vultures were commonplace.

The heat of the sun saturates the house; it seeps out from every pore. I open the door of my room and walk out into the silent hall. In the bathroom I stand in the shower-tray and turn the tap to let the cool water splash over my feet. I tuck my skirt between my thighs and bend to put my hands and wrists under the water. I press wet palms to my face and picture grey slate roofs wet with rain. I picture trees; trees that rustle in the wind and, when the rain has stopped, release fresh showers of droplets from their leaves.

I pad out on wet feet that are dry by the time I arrive at the kitchen at the end of the long corridor. I open the fridge and see the chunks of lamb marinading in a large metal tray for tonight's barbecue. The mountain of yellow grapes draining in a colander. I pick out a cluster and put it on a white saucer. Um Sabir washes all the fruit and vegetables in red permanganate. This is for my benefit since Lucy crunches cucumbers and carrots straight out of the greengrocer's baskets. But then she was born here. And now she belongs. If I had taken her away then, when she was eight months old, she would have belonged with me. I pour out a tall glass of cold, bottled water and close the fridge.

I walk back through the corridor. Past Um Sabir's room, his room, Lucy's room. Back in my room I stand again at the window, looking out through the chink in the shutters at the white that seems now to be losing the intensity of its glare. If I were to move to the window in the opposite wall, I would see the green lawn encircled by the three wings of the house, the sprinkler at its centre ceaselessly twisting, twisting.

I turn on the fan. It blows my hair across my face and my notes across the bed. I kneel on the bed and gather them. The top one says, 'Ningi, his big teeth stained with Kola, sits grandly at his desk. By his right hand there is a bicycle bell which he rings to summon a gofer—' and then again: 'The three things we stop for on the road should be my title: "Peeing, Praying and Petrol".' Those were light-hearted times, when the jokes I made were not bitter.

I lie down on the bed. These four pillows are my innovation. Here they use one long pillow with two smaller ones on top of it. The bed-linen comes in sets. Consequently my bed always has two pillows in plain cases and two with embroidery to match the sheets. Also, I have one side of a chiffonier which is full of long, embroidered pillow-cases. When I take them out, I find their flowers, sheltered for so long in the dark, are unfaded.

Lying on the bed, I hold the cluster of grapes above my face and bite one off as Romans do in films. Oh to play, but my only playmate now is Lucy, and she is out by the pool with her cousins.

A few weeks ago, back in Cairo, Lucy looked up at the sky and said, 'I can see the place where we're going to be.'

'Where?' I asked, as we drove through Gabalaya Street.

'In heaven.'

'Oh!' I said. 'And what's it like?'

'It's a circle, Mama, and it has a chimney, and it will always be winter there.'

I reached over and patted her knee. 'Thank you, darling,' I said.

Yes, I am sick—but not just for home. I am sick for a time, a time that was and that I can never have again. A lover I had and can never have again.

I watched him vanish—well, not vanish, slip away, recede. He did not want to go. He did not go quietly. He asked me to hold him, but he couldn't tell me how. A fairy godmother, robbed for an instant of our belief in her magic, turns into a sad old woman, her wand into a useless stick. I suppose I should have seen it coming. My foreignness, which had been so charming, began to irritate him. My inability to remember names, to follow the minutiae of politics, my struggles with his language, my need to be protected from the sun, the mosquitoes, the salads, the drinking water. He was back home, and he needed someone he could be at home with, at home. It took perhaps a year. His heart was broken in two; mine was simply broken.

I never see my lover now. Sometimes, as he romps with Lucy on the beach, or bends over her grazed elbow, or sits across our long table from me at a dinner-party, I see a man I could yet fall in love with, and I turn away.

I told him, too, about my first mirage, the one I saw on that long road to Maiduguri. And on the desert road to Alexandria the first summer, I saw it again. 'It's hard to believe it isn't there when I can see it so clearly,' I complained.

'You only think you see it,' he said.

'Isn't that the same thing?' I asked. 'My brain tells me there's water there. Isn't that enough?'

'Yes,' he said, and shrugged, 'If all you want to do is sit in the car and see it. But if you want to go and put your hands in it and drink, then it isn't enough, surely?' He gave me a sidelong glance and smiled.

Soon, I should hear Lucy's high, clear voice, chattering to her father as they walk hand-in-hand up the gravel drive to the back door. Behind them will come the heavy tread of Um Sabir. I will go out smiling to meet them, and he will deliver a wet, sandy Lucy into my care, ask if I'm OK with a slightly anxious look and maybe pat my shoulder. I will take Lucy into my bathroom while he goes into his. Later, when the rest of the family have all drifted back and showered and changed, everyone will sit around the barbecue and eat and drink and talk politics and crack jokes of hopeless irony and laugh. I should take up embroidery and start on those Aubusson tapestries we all, at the moment, imagine will be necessary for Lucy's trousseau.

Yesterday when I had dressed her after the shower she examined herself intently in my mirror and asked for a French plait. I sat behind her at the dressing-table, blow-drying her black hair, brushing it and plaiting it. When Lucy was born, Um Sabir covered all the mirrors. His sister said, 'They say if a baby looks in the mirror she will see her own grave.' We laughed but we did not remove the covers; they stayed in place till she was one.

I looked at Lucy's serious face in the mirror. I had seen my grave once, or thought I had. That was part of my Africa story. The plane out of Nigeria circled Cairo airport. Three times I heard the landing-gear come down, and three times it was raised again. Sitting next to me were two Finnish businessmen. When the announcement came that we were re-routing to Luxor, they shook their heads and ordered another drink. At dawn, above Luxor airport, we were told that there was trouble with the undercarriage and that the pilot was going to attempt a crash landing. I thought: so this is why they've sent us to Luxor, to burn up discreetly and not clog Cairo airport. We were asked to fasten our seat-belts, take off our shoes and watches, put the cushions from the backs of our seats on our laps and bend double over them with our arms round our heads. I slung my handbag with my passport, tickets and money around my neck and shoulder before I did these things. My Finnish neighbours formally shook each others' hands. On the plane there was perfect silence as we dropped out of the sky. And then a terrible, agonized, protracted screeching of machinery as we hit the tarmac. And in that moment, not only my head, but all of me, my whole being, seemed to tilt into a blank, an empty radiance, but lucid. Then three giant thoughts. One was of him—his name, over and over again. The other was of the children I would never have. The third was that the pattern was now complete: this is what my life amounted to.

When we did not die, that first thought: his name, his name, his name became a talisman, for in extremity, hadn't all that was not him been wiped out of my life? My life, which once again stretched out before me, shimmering with possibilities, was meant to merge with his.

I finished the French plait, and Lucy chose a blue clasp to secure its end. Before I let her run out I smoothed some after-sun lotion on her face. Her skin is nut-brown, except just next to her ears where it fades to a pale cream gleaming with golden down. I put my lips to her neck, 'My Lucy, Lucia, *Lambah*,' I murmured as I kissed her and let her go. My treasure, my trap.

Now, when I walk to the sea, to the edge of this continent where I live, where I almost died, where I wait for my daughter to grow away from me, I see different things from those I saw that summer six years ago. The last of the foam is swallowed bubbling into the sand, to sink down and rejoin the sea at an unseen subterranean level. With each ebb of green water the sand loses part of itself to the sea, with each flow another part is flung back to be reclaimed once again by the beach. That narrow stretch of sand knows nothing in the world better than it does the white waves that whip it, caress it, collapse on to it, vanish into it. The white foam knows nothing better than those sands that wait for it, rise to it and suck it in. But what do the waves know of the massed, hot, still sands of the desert just twenty, no, ten feet beyond the scalloped edge? And what does the beach know of the depths, the cold, the currents just there, there—do you see it?—where the water turns a deeper blue.

GRANTA

Abraham Verghese
A Child's Book of Death and Dying

A fine morning mist had rolled down over Addis Ababa from the Entoto mountains, leaving a sheen on the lawn between the apartment buildings. I was six years old, my brother Reji was eight; for some reason we were being kept home from school. Excited by this unexpected reprieve, we gobbled down breakfast, grabbed our soccer ball and ran outside.

The lawn was the centre of our out-of-school existence. It gave off the scent of earthworms and snails, and was bordered by tall rose bushes, their thorns shaped like the sharp teeth of Koochooloo, the communal bitch. Reji and I balled up our sweaters and planted them as goalposts. We kicked the soccer ball back and forth, and soon I had a deep green stripe on my shorts from sliding along on my rear in my efforts to keep the ball within bounds. We were shortly joined by other kids from the apartments who had been kept home from the French School, the German School, the American School, the English School and the Italian School. All our parents worked as expatriate teachers at Haile Selassie The First University.

After a while, my father's black Volkswagen pulled up alongside the lawn. The gardener, who also functioned as a kind of guard, ran over to the car. He was wearing shit-coloured jodhpurs and his feet, with their horny, opaque toenails, were bare. He fawned over my mother as he helped her select a yellow rosebud to put in her hair. But no sooner had my parents driven off than the gardener-guard started shouting at us in Amharic: Had we seen how he decapitated the chickens for the cook every morning? (We had: the headless chicken would take to the air, spraying blood from its neck stump until it collapsed in a heap some way off.) Well, he said, that was what would happen to us should we dare even to touch his roses. And if we were thinking of running to our parents . . . He stuck out his tongue and chopped the air in front of his mouth with the sickle he had been using to cut the grass.

Our game was barely underway when we spotted the first plane. We froze, letting the ball smash into a rosebush,

Opposite: the hanging of Chief Colonel Gebreheyou Worqineh, one of the leaders of the abortive coup against Haile Selassie.

Photo: Associated Press

which then showered petals. There were distant thuds. There was, I think, some smoke.

Within minutes a car was at the compound gate: someone had rushed home from work. But the gardener-guard, instead of standing by to open the gate, had run off down the road, the soles of his bare feet flashing. We were left to man the heavy metal gates, saluting, playing at soldiers, as our parents returned home and one by one shepherded us indoors. Rubin's father, an Israeli physics teacher, emerged from his house, rifle in hand. He was carrying a heavy chain and padlock and proceeded to lock the gate.

The hallway had no windows and offered the best shelter. We helped drag the mattresses out of the bedrooms. My father, who has never been near a tent in his life, made us believe we were camping. We huddled around the radio as though it were a *kangri* stove, listening to the BBC, waiting for the sound of Big Ben and that calm voice which would tell us what was really happening. My mother made quick forays into the kitchen for bread and jam and milk.

She explained to Reji and me that the shooting outside was a '*coup d'état*'. We repeated this new word. It sounded like the staccato firing: *coo-dey-ta, coo-dey-ta*. 'The Emperor is out of the country on a state visit,' my mother said. 'And now that he is gone, the Bodyguard has taken over the government.'

The Bodyguard was a special wing of the armed forces, barracked a few blocks from us, near the airport. We had seen them on Coronation Day, sitting astride their horses in their white and red parade uniforms, their pith helmets sitting low over their eyes. The Bodyguard was, to us, the epitome of bravery and loyalty to the crown. It was unthinkable that the Bodyguard should be behind this mutiny. 'Why, Mummy? Why are the Bodyguard doing this?'

'They want a new Emperor.' There was a great sadness in my mother's voice. 'Or rather, a new government.'

My brother and I were silent. We had seen the Emperor only two weeks earlier. As we were driving out of town, the sentinel Land-Rover came at us, sirens blaring, blue lights flashing. The men inside—the Bodyguard—stuck their hands out of the window and gestured to us to pull over: the Emperor was coming. My father stopped the car; we piled out and stood respectfully at the roadside. Soon a phalanx of Bugati motorcycles came chugging into view, followed by the Emperor's favourite maroon Rolls-Royce. The yellow, green and red tricolour fluttered on the hood. We saw the Emperor distinctly behind the tinted glass. He was short man but had had the seat built up so that he appeared much taller and could see better.

There we stood beside our Beetle: my father in a dark suit, my mother in a sari, my brother and I in shorts. My father bowed. My brother and I saluted. My mother brought her hands together in a *namaste*. We saw the bearded face smile at us. We saw him bring *his* hands together in a *namaste* and incline his head. My mother has talked about that *namaste* ever since; although she denies it, the incident sealed her loyalty to the Emperor. Twenty years later, during the famines of the early seventies, it made her blind to his shortcomings, just as the Emperor himself was blind to the destruction around him.

The background chatter of gunfire that sounded like nails rattling in a tin can carried on for the whole day and into the evening. Every now and then, my father opened the door to the dining-room and looked out. Reji and I peered between his legs. The sky through the window was lit by fireworks, but they never blossomed into starbursts at the end of their trajectory. Nor did they change colour. As we lay on our mattresses, the thuds were soothing. Snuggled between my parents, I went to sleep.

In the morning, my mother told us that the Emperor had returned and, with the help of the Army and Air Force, had put down the *coup*. Later, we heard the Emperor speak on the radio, assuring his citizens that he was still in charge.

My mother was ecstatic. She wanted to go to St George's church, to give thanks. Our maids had not returned, and as my parents did not feel safe leaving us at home, we were taken along.

My brother and I knelt up on the back seat, looking out through the little port-hole of a back window. There were cars on the road, people on the street, *garis*—horse-drawn taxis—plying their trade. Everything was back to normal. But, as we approached the square outside St George's, we saw that a huge crowd had gathered. People were spilling off the sidewalks into the streets. There were more cars than I had ever seen in my life.

And then, on the crest of the hill, I saw why: three bodies hanging from a large scaffold, swaying slightly, although there was no breeze. Beneath the dead men, directly under their feet, was a dancing horde, leaping into the air in unison, chanting and ululating. My parents said nothing; they had seen the bodies before we had. This was the reason we had come here.

'But where are their shoes?' I asked. The men were dressed in their olive-green uniforms, with epaulettes and ribbons, but their feet were bare. Their cocked heads looked down quizzically. The sad, sloping shoulders, the resignation in the hands fastened behind the back, the gentle, pendular swaying—it was as if they had discovered a greater peace than the mob would ever know. The only element of violation—of savagery—was in the naked feet, stripped of their precious leather shoes.

Foofoo was the oldest of the faculty children. His execution of the puppies might have been a few months after the hangings, but in the compression of memory it seems to me that it happened the next day.

There were too many dogs in the compound, and when Koochooloo gave birth, all the adults agreed that the puppies would have to go. Foofoo offered to dispose of the new arrivals humanely. He was probably only about fourteen, but to us he seemed even older than our parents. Clearly, as an adult in training, he was the man for the job.

Foofoo's plan was to use carbon monoxide to kill the pups. Carbon monoxide was the first organic chemistry term I ever learned. It stayed on my tongue for months. Carbon monoxide, as Foofoo explained repeatedly, was colourless, odourless and tasteless. It was, we thought, a brilliant choice.

But in the end, what was meant to be a humane killing, a 'putting to sleep', turned into a circus. All eighteen children in the compound found a reason to be out on the lawn. And many adults, ostensibly there to ensure the humanity of the process, stood gawking just like the rest of us. My parents, in my rosy memory of these events, did not try to stop Reji and me from attending. After all, it was they who had given us an appetite for this sort of spectacle.

Foofoo put the pups into a large, transparent plastic bag. (I wonder now why he did not just leave it at that and forget the carbon monoxide. Clearly he knew less about death than he thought.) The puppies slid to the bottom of the bag in a writhing, wriggling mass of fur. Foofoo then adroitly tied the top to the exhaust pipe of his parents' car, securing it with wire.

When Foofoo started the car (it was an Opel Cadet—a car I can never pass without thinking of carnage), there were cries for him to stop. The mouth of the plastic bag had blown off the end of the exhaust pipe. The colourless, odourless, tasteless gas now hung as a grey, smelly cloud around the back of the car, bringing a metallic taste to my mouth. Two of the puppies had rolled out of the bag, and Koochooloo was busy licking them.

Foofoo returned the puppies to the bag, retied it to the exhaust and started the car. This time he cut the engine on a hand signal from one of the adults as soon as the bag ballooned up. The distended bag was now a magnifying glass: the brown and black puppies crawled in different directions around the transparent globe, slipping down the walls, bumping into each other, tumbling, applying their tongues and noses to the plastic as if trying to suck air through it. Koochooloo raced around frantically, alternately barking and whining, wagging her tail, then thrusting it between her legs, crawling over to the bag that held her puppies as well as the colourless, odourless gas.

Suddenly it was over. An inert mass of black and brown fur lay at the base of the bag. Koochooloo hid for two days, dropped all pretence of friendship with us and slunk around the compound, brooding and plotting revolution.

By the age of nine, I had finally become aware that I was of a different race from the people around me. I had little idea of where exactly I did belong, but the taunt *ferengi*, foreigner, made it clear that it was not here. The geographical explanation my parents offered—that we were Christian Indians from the south of India—still didn't answer the question of where *home* was. I lacked the inclination, the size and the courage to retaliate when insults were hurled at me: *ferengi*, go home! And by now I had an acute and exaggerated fear of death or dismemberment.

Fighting at school was dangerous. The first time my brother got into an altercation, even before he was aware that he was in one, the other kid's head had come at him like a hammer, striking him on the bridge of his nose, temporarily blinding him. This manoeuvre was known as a *testa*: perhaps it was an Italian legacy, a vestige of Mussolini's brief occupation of Abyssinia. On the battlefields of school and street, at least once a year I would see two combatants laid out cold, their *testa*s having been so timed as to have brought the two crania together with concussive force. We onlookers hung around, waiting to see who would regain consciousness first and claim victory.

And if, as a combatant, you were out of *testa* range—arm's length—when the fight erupted, the next step was to find a rock. The prospect of a *testa* or a rock rendered any fight potentially lethal; it was dangerous even to watch. Years later, as a medical student in the casualty room of an Ethiopian hospital, I became accustomed to wounds inflicted by rocks: a raised, robin's-egg swelling, or else an almost surgical linear incision with puffed-up margins. That is, if the patient was not brought in with a broken nose from a *testa*. Or brought in dead.

My family used to spend summers in a lake-side town called Debre Zeit, about fifty kilometres from Addis Ababa. As a bored and surly teenager, I used to hang out in a little Arab *souk*, drinking Coke and killing time. I would chat with the shopkeeper, nibble on the leaves of *chath* he offered me (which produced a speed-like high), sometimes smoke a cigarette. It was the highlight of my day.

One afternoon, on my way down the dusty rural road to the *souk*, I sensed the approach of what felt like a herd of cattle, their hooves thudding on the brown earth. I turned: a bearded, barefoot young man came into view, running slowly, his shirt torn and hanging out of his trousers. He must have been about twenty. I had never seen anyone so exhausted, so terrified, so determined to escape—or so malevolent. He was being chased by an old man, bald, shirtless, with a grey beard. Blood was running from a linear wound across the bridge of the old man's nose; he looked just as tired as his quarry. But age and fatigue were subsumed by the furnace of his rage and his evident desire for revenge. Both men seemed to be running in slow motion; the chase must have been going on for a mile or more. And behind the old man were others, fresher, stronger, younger, who had joined in.

The air was filled with cries from the old man and his friends: '*Leba! Leba!*'—'Thief! Thief!' The alleged thief was bearing down on me, running so slowly that it would have been easy for me to stick out a foot and trip him up.

When he ran past, he bent down without breaking his stride and scooped up a stone. As he did, the old man, fifty yards behind, also bent over for a stone. The mob was gaining now, and as they thundered past they all reached for stones. The thief rounded a corner, followed by the old man and the rest; the tail end of the crowd was made up of young children and even some women who had tagged along to see how this would end.

I turned and ran the other way, back to our cottage, abandoning my trip to the *souk*. I had witnessed no violence, only the prospect of it. Judging by the number of stones that had been gathered, I had little doubt that when the mob caught up with the thief, he would be stoned, perhaps stoned to death. I felt as if I lacked some inner resolve when it came to violence and brutality, even though I had seen so much of it. To this day, when I am in the hospital, I have no qualms about examining the grisliest gunshot or knife wound—the *results* of violence. But should I inadvertently witness a violent *act*, I am affected viscerally. It is as if I am the victim; as if in the throes of my physical pain I am asking my attacker, 'How can you possibly do this to me?'

Now I am a doctor, working in a different arena of death: I take care of people with Aids. My practice is in the United States in a city on the Mexican border. It has gradually extended out of the clinic to the homes of my patients, for we have decided—patients and physician—that it is far better to die at home than in the hospital.

I am now in the house of Harry, a patient who is dying.

After two years of seeing him in the clinic, this is my first glimpse of his house, a tidy cottage full of sculptures by Xavier, his Hispanic lover. Xavier died in the hospital under my care, a long-drawn-out death with many stops in the intensive care unit because Harry would not let go.

I find Harry asleep in a recliner near his bed, naked but for a thin sheet, a little bell by his side along with his medications and a pitcher of water. He breathes rapidly, his whole head moving up and down with each breath. In the shadows between his ribs, I see a rhythmic sucking in and out of the flesh, as if it is straining against the bones, as if this wicker-basket chest will implode at any moment. Watching his laboured breathing makes me acutely aware of my own breath.

Harry's skin, stretched thin as paper, is covered with a pattern of purple splashes—Kaposi's sarcoma. These lesions, his bald pate with its fringe, the Rudolf-the-red-nosed-reindeer tuberose swelling of his nose, give him the appearance of a sleeping clown, exhausted after a performance, too lazy to remove his make-up. Nasal prongs deliver oxygen, and the sound of it bubbling through a water reservoir is not soothing. Two months ago, I looked into Harry's lungs with a bronchoscope: in his trachea and in the bronchi were discrete currant-jelly-like patches that had a stuck-on appearance. It was as if there had been a food fight in the bronchial lumen. These patches were lesions of visceral Kaposi's.

In a minute, Harry opens his eyes; he comes to consciousness as if surfacing from a well of slow treacle. I can see each idea as it forms in his mind: *I am alive, I am in my room, Abraham is here, my breath comes hard, it is daylight . . .*

He gives me a wonderful smile. After a few minutes he says, 'I have been thinking about this Kervorkian guy—you know, "Doctor Death"?'

I don't let him finish. 'Carbon monoxide—it's awful. Don't even think about it.'

'But,' he says after a bit, having registered my strong and clearly less than scientific response, 'it's odourless, painless—'

'No!' I say. 'Maybe it's none of those things. Maybe it's awful, maybe it's painful, maybe it's too sudden . . . '

Harry looks at me strangely. What is it I want for him? A slow death?

'Speaking hypothetically,' Harry says, taking two breaths to say 'hypothetically', and I know what is coming because he has asked me this same question every day for the past week and I have yet to answer, 'Speaking hypothetically, what would you suggest? How would you want to die?'

I look at the ceiling.

'For yourself,' Harry adds, as if this will help. 'If you were in my boat.' He is giving me all the time in the world to formulate an answer, but is determined not to close his eyes till I respond. 'Just picture yourself in my boat.' He settles back, tired from the effort of speaking.

I picture his boat. I am terrified, as always. Images fly through my mind: stones flung at my head, bullets flying towards me, a fatal head butt, being trapped in a laundry bag.

Strangely, despite being a physician (or because of it), I think I would want no drugs. I would want perfect clarity of sound and sight. I have a vision of three men, of how, as they stood on the truck platform with the nooses around their necks, they must have had that perfect clarity. They would have seen the mob not as a mob but as individual faces: young men, old men, bearded men, a few women. They would have felt fingers tugging and pulling at their shoelaces like naughty puppies do. They felt the rope resting slack on their necks, its implied contract, a symbolic boundary between body and mind. They heard the truck's engine idling, felt the vibration transmitted through their proprioreceptors and up the spinal cord and to their sensory cortex even as they sensed their bladder and bowels give way. They heard the rise in the pitch of the truck engine, felt the jolt of the gear engaging, saw the crowd's excitement peak, felt the absolute clarity of sight and sound that precedes the maelstrom.

REEF

ROMESH GUNESEKERA

A love story set in the spoiled paradise of modern Sri Lanka

'This is a book which touches powerfully and deeply, a book to be slowly savoured, page by page.'
The Times

'Grace and barbarism haunt Sri Lanka in a delectable first novel about growing up.'
Guardian

'Gunesekera has written a book of the deepest human interest and moral poise ... Very few contemporary novels combine at so high but natural a pitch qualities of epic strength and luminous intimacy.'
Independent on Sunday

£13.99

GRANTA

William Finnegan

The Silent Majority of Cape Town

NP

By mid-April, the smiling face of Nelson Mandela, framed by the green, black and gold of the African National Congress flag, seemed to decorate the majority of South Africa's lampposts, and the country's historic transition to democracy had become all but unimaginable without his steely, unifying leadership. There were powerful forces, notably the white ultra-right, sworn to resist or abort that transition, however, and so it was strange and alarming to arrive, as an unidentified white male, at a jammed-full Dutch Reformed Church in the Coloured township of Belhar, near Cape Town, on a Sunday morning nine days before the election, make my way to a seat near the pulpit—never being asked for any credentials—and then turn, a minute later, as the congregation sang 'Great is Thy faithfulness', to find Mandela himself filing into the pew behind mine, silently shaking the hands of the people he passed. He shook my hand, too, and then sat down, less than a yard away. No bodyguards were in evidence. Next to Mandela sat Allan Boesak, the ANC candidate for premier of the Western Cape province. Great is thy faithfulness, indeed, I thought.

People crept from their seats, beaming sheepishly, and took snapshots of the great man. Towards the end of the service, we all stood and sang *'Nkosi Sikelel iAfrika'*, the slow, sweet, pan-African liberation anthem, and I found myself studying, out of the corner of my eye, Mandela's fist, which was round and raised—not high but at chest level, held close to his side. He sang gently, almost sadly, and the thousand voices around us seemed to rise beneath his reedy tenor like an immense swell lifting a small boat towards the sky.

At that moment, in that powder-blue, cinder-block church, the South African transition seemed less a political campaign than a transcendent process, some inexorable, Hegelian movement of history, African destiny made manifest. Certainly, Mandela was the quiet, courtly, crucial figure at the eye of an international storm of revolutionary hope, reactionary fear and millennialist fantasy. Perhaps the casual arrangements for his security reflected a chiliastic belief among his entourage that nothing could now stop his ascension to the presidency. In any case, the idea that Mandela and

Opposite: a National Party meeting in the Coloured township of Ennerdale in the Cape Flats.

Photo: Ian Berry (Magnum)

his comrades should rightfully lead the country into the post-apartheid promised land seemed, by now, effectively beyond dispute.

Of course, it was nothing of the kind. The political competition included regional contenders such as Chief Buthelezi's Inkatha Freedom Party, the traditional white liberal opposition, an assortment of special-interest parties, white segregationists and black ultra-leftists, as well as the still-formidable National Party which had ruled the country since 1948 and was now trying to shed the stigma of having invented apartheid. Nowhere, as it happened, were the Nationalists stronger than in the Western Cape. Indeed, that was why Mandela was here, singing with a Cape Coloured congregation. He was trying to help the ANC pull a crucial provincial election out of an unforeseen fire.

It was an absurd proposition: that Coloureds, who form the majority in the Western Cape (outnumbering whites by two-to-one and Africans by three-to-one), should be supporting the National Party. Under apartheid, they had suffered extraordinary indignities at the hands of the Nationalists. Some of the most atrocious apartheid legislation—such as the Prohibition of Mixed Marriages Act, which destroyed an untold number of 'mixed' families, and the Immorality Act, which forbade interracial sex (and, it was often said, had made the very existence of the Coloured people a crime)—had been directed primarily at Coloureds. In Cape Town, thousands of Coloured families had been forced from their homes by the ethnic engineers of apartheid, consigned to bleak clumps of row housing out on a vast, sandy expanse known as the Cape Flats, many miles east of the city. For Coloureds to vote for the National Party now would be, as the common analogy had it, a bit like Jews voting for the Nazis.

And yet, according to the opinion polls, huge numbers were planning to do so.

I found the situation particularly flabbergasting because I thought I knew Cape Town. In the early eighties, I had taught at a Coloured high school on the Cape Flats and had seen the Coloured townships rise up against the Nationalist regime. The Cape Flats had remained in the forefront of protest throughout the repressive eighties, and I still thought of the Flats as a resistance stronghold. But something, obviously, had changed.

The Silent Majority of Cape Town

On the last Sunday before the election, I was on my way out of Manenberg, a Coloured township twelve miles east of Cape Town, when Maqbool Moos, a local ANC organizer, tapped on my car window as I was stopped in a driveway, suddenly jumped in the passenger seat and asked: 'How are your skills?'

He meant, I assumed, my evasive-driving-under-hostile-fire skills. I lied that they were fine—in fact, I had no idea what they were like—and we set off, following a small white Ford at a frightening speed. The Ford was being driven by another ANC organizer, Irvin Kinnes, and carried a band of young supporters known as 'comrades'. Our destination, Moos said, was the headquarters of a gang called the Schoolboys. It seemed that an ANC-brokered gang truce had broken down.

Moos, in his early twenties, was a lapsed law student and a familiar South African hybrid: part left-wing intellectual idealist, part street-tough. He had spent time in prison, detained without trial as a high-school activist in the eighties, and was still scuffling in the mean streets of Manenberg, yet could argue all night about the true relationship between western imperialism and racial capitalism in South Africa. He was dark-skinned, heavily bearded and had the sort of liquid physical poise that made it unsurprising to learn that he had once been a figure-skating champion.

'Here,' Moos said. Kinnes had swerved to a stop in front of a long row of two-storey brick flats. The comrades guarded the cars while we followed Kinnes into a ground-floor apartment. At least twenty-five people were jammed into the tiny front room—babies, grandmothers, with perhaps a dozen young gangsters. There were a lot of earrings, a few tattoos, but none of the heavy facial tattooing seen on those who have passed through the Cape's ancient and infamous prison gangs. People seemed calm, and all eyes were on Kinnes, who made a short speech in Afrikaans, while Moos and I squeezed along a wall. Kinnes was crisp but polite and, according to Moos's translation, apolitical. He was here to help stop the violence. In his white shirt and dark tie, he looked like a hard-charging junior executive. He whipped out a pen, opened a black Filofax, knelt next to a couch and began asking questions. His main informant was a thin boy of about eighteen, whose hand was wrapped in a rough bandage, blood seeping through it.

He had been stabbed, the boy explained, in a fight between his gang and the Dixie Boys.

Kinnes rose abruptly, shut his Filofax, gestured to Moos and me, and we left. As the door shut behind us, Moos glanced at an upstairs window in the flat. I followed his gaze and saw that the window had three bullet holes in its frame and a National Party campaign sticker plastered on the glass.

We drove through a maze of alleys into Dixie Boys territory. Again, while the comrades guarded the cars, we followed Kinnes into a warren of dark, noisy, stinking passages between lines of washing and blocks of flats, and finally into a small compound and a tiny, immaculate, low-roofed room where a rangy, raw-boned teenager seemed to be waiting for us. This was the leader of the Dixie Boys. He was wearing, I noticed, eight gold rings. In a soft, sober voice, he gave his version of the fight, while Kinnes took notes. When the gangster finished his story, Kinnes shut his notebook and asked him to stay out of the Schoolboys' territory for a while. The young man studied Kinnes for a long moment and then nodded. 'Yeah, no, OK, fine,' he said.

Our next stop was the police station. Sentries recognized Kinnes and Moos and allowed us in. The acting commander showed us into a meeting-room, where Kinnes explained the state of play between the Schoolboys and the Dixie Boys, and the commander responded by describing the weapons they had confiscated from the gangs—the cache included AK-47s, which everyone seemed to find significant. As we left the station, Kinnes said exultantly, 'Did you see how nice those cops were being? They are *never* like that. I think that is a very good sign. They must think we're going to win this election. Just like the HLs do.'

The HLs were the Hardliving Kids, Manenberg's most powerful gang. Its leaders were publicly backing the ANC—an awkward situation for the local activists. 'We can't dance with them, man, we *can't*,' said Moos, as we headed off again. 'They're a negative force. *Everybody's* against the HLs. They're just bloody evil.'

Becoming identified with any gang would ultimately be damaging for any political party. But keeping the peace—and letting the voting public see that the ANC was doing so—was important, and that required building relationships with the gangs, including those, like the Schoolboys and the Dixie Boys, who did not support the ANC. The people of Manenberg, asked about the township's problems, invariably put gang violence at the top of the list.

ANC officials gave various reasons for the National Party's popularity among the Coloureds. One was 'racism'. Many Coloureds told me they had simply never met an educated African, and could neither believe—nor accept—that Africans were going to start running the country. Such people were receptive to the National Party's repeated reminders that black rule had been a disaster in much of sub-Saharan Africa. Coloureds, it was said, simply refused to make common cause with the black African majority. While this view clearly contained some truth, it was also profoundly ahistorical, for brown and black Africans had fought together many times over the long, twisting course of the South African liberation struggle.

But since 1990, when Nelson Mandela was released and the ANC unbanned, the Western Cape had been politically marginalized, as the fierce local struggles that characterized the anti-apartheid period gave way to constitutional negotiations. The ANC had largely failed to make poor and working-class Coloureds feel included among the winners of the liberation struggle, and the National Party had adroitly filled the political vacuum, with President De Klerk pleading publicly for 'forgiveness' for the sin of apartheid ('Our church teaches us that we must forgive,' an elderly Coloured flower-seller told me, and it was clear from her expression, I thought, just what a knotty, delicious pleasure it was to consider this powerful white man's humble plea), and then, in the heat of the election campaign, pandering shamelessly to Coloured fears of African rule.

Ironically, these fears had been stirred already in Cape Town by the repeal of the apartheid-era pass laws, which had unleashed a flood of new African arrivals who were now competing for housing and jobs with long-time Coloured residents. The result was a great political paradox: in the Western Cape, at least among the Coloured majority, the ANC, the historic movement of the poor and oppressed, could apparently count on support only from the small, educated élite, while the National Party, the infamous citadel of white-minority rule, had captured the illiterate masses.

The National Party's political infrastructure in the Coloured townships is strikingly thin. It contains no prominent political figures and has no history to speak of. In Manenberg, Alawia Traut, the local National Party chairwoman, informed me proudly that she had been appointed chairwoman the day after she attended her first National Party meeting, shortly after the party began admitting Coloured members less than two years ago. Mrs Traut, her massive bulk swathed entirely in white, sat in the front room of her small, asbestos-roofed row cottage, surrounded by some of the other ladies of the neighbourhood, and recalled how the residents had chased Nelson Mandela out of Manenberg. 'He doesn't belong in this Coloured area,' she said. 'He got up there and started promising people washing-machines and fridges, and they just laughed in his face. They don't want to hear that from *him*. Everybody knows that he can't even control his own people.'

I asked about the sources of National Party support in Manenberg. 'The disabled and the pensioners are our staunchest supporters,' she said. 'They believe that De Klerk personally is giving them the money. And the families of prisoners, they get disability grants, too. And they all believe that Mandela will take away their pensions and their houses.'

Did she believe that?

'Definitely not.' Mrs Traut laughed at the absurdity of the thought. She was not unsophisticated. 'But these Coloured people are fantastic,' she continued. 'Once they believe something, they won't change. So I don't argue with them. They can believe what they want.'

Yusuf Sampson, Mrs Traut's second-in-command, was an older man whose allegiance to the National Party seemed to stem primarily from its leadership's willingness to allow his Cape Flats Royal Pipe Band to play on ceremonial occasions. President De Klerk himself had heard the band in 1991. 'We got the honour of blowing him the South African national anthem,' Mr Sampson told me. Then, noting my nationality, he observed, 'The Coloured nation was born in slavery, just like the Negroes in

America. Over there they accept the white system of government. So why can't we accept it?'

Voting lasted three days in the Western Cape. Each morning, I awoke to shouts of joy. My hotel window overlooked the back door of a polling station in a lower-middle-class Coloured neighbourhood on the Cape Flats, and the voters emerged from the booths crying, hollering, whooping and ululating. Nearly all of them were voting for the first time in their lives.

In Manenberg, there were some scuffles. The Dixie Boys would not allow ANC taxis—vans covered in Mandela posters—to travel down Crayfish Road, and an older gang called the Jesters threatened the ANC activists at the polling stations. The Hardliving Kids continued to embarrass the ANC, driving up and down the streets in a noisy convoy that included BMWs, Mercedes-Benzes (the Hardlivings' income derives mostly from drug-dealing) and a big, white van plastered with ANC posters. Moos was beside himself. 'We just can't stop them,' he said. 'They want to be part of things. We asked them to stop canvassing. I don't think they're consciously trying to destroy us. I mean, they have the firepower to blow us apart any time they like. But they're really putting us in a bad spot with the voters.'

Unlike Kinnes, who still believed that no one who had been victimized by apartheid could possibly vote for the National Party, Moos was pessimistic. 'Boesak and Trevor Manuel [a national ANC leader with roots in Manenberg] were here last night,' he said. 'And they're still optimistic. They say they're counting on the rural areas.' He shook his head. We were in his flat, which the ANC was using as a 'command centre', for it overlooked the high school which was being used as a polling station. Outside, an amplifier was blasting '*Nkosi Sikelel iAfrika*', and a line of at least a thousand voters snaked around the playing fields below Moos's window.

Moos's flat was tiny and spare and cheaply furnished. In the kitchen, young women made sandwiches and coffee, while a stream of activists poured through the door. The phone rang constantly. Between calls, Moos and I talked. 'I just think the ANC is making a major mistake,' he said. 'It wants to believe the Coloureds are going to vote ANC. But the Coloured people here really don't understand politics properly. Most of them believe in the Bantustans, that the Africans have their places and shouldn't come out of them. And that the Africans are the colonialists now.'

I moved to the window. It was raining now, but hundreds of people were still queuing to vote. The activists at the ANC table were trying to keep their Mandela posters from blowing away. As their wet, giddy comrades moved about Moos's kitchen, joking together in Afrikaans, I caught the English phrase 'silent majority', despairingly spoken. I wondered if they knew the term's origin. I was sure I knew why they feared it.

And that was when the unlikely pathos of this transition to democracy among the Manenberg resistance struck me. This apartment had been a nerve centre of local resistance for years—cells within cells of the anti-apartheid movement meeting and planning strategy here; revolutionary zeal, debate, idealism; courage, romance, naïvety; police raids, violence, fear. A few days earlier, Moos had told me about the friend from his schooldays, Ashley Kriel, who had first interested him in politics. Ashley had joined Umkhonto We Sizwe, the ANC's armed underground, and had been killed by the police on the Cape Flats in 1987. Moos had survived the 'struggle years', but his apartment, his world—while still buzzing with the same core of bright-eyed militants—had been transformed. This flat, I thought, was suddenly like any party precinct office anywhere—banal, full of ward-heelers hustling to get out the vote on election day.

The next afternoon, Moos and I stood outside the high school, watching that day's voters file past. The line was shorter, the sun was shining, the mood relaxed. But there was the same hapless mismatch between high-intensity South African militancy and dull bourgeois democracy. Moos was keeping one eye on the voters while talking with me, and every now and then he would call out to someone—a weathered-looking woman in work boots, say, with a baby on her hip—to 'vote the right way'. And she would smile knowingly, nod and reply, 'My vote is my secret.' These exchanges were wonderful, heartbreaking, ironic. 'The people' were finally getting to speak, and the radicals, who had been speaking and acting in their names all these years, could do nothing but listen.

As things turned out, the National Party won easily in the Western Cape, taking an absolute majority of votes and crushing the ANC by more than twenty per cent. The ANC won nationally, of course, defeating the National Party by an even greater margin.

It is still not clear how much power the provincial parliaments will have; but it is certain that in the Western Cape, the only one of the nine new provinces that the National Party won, the old party of apartheid will be able to slow the major reforms—in health, education, welfare and local government—that the ANC plans to institute in most of the country.

While South Africa as a whole had had its election, its grand apotheosis of hope and dignity, the Western Cape had done something far more ordinary; its voters had been preoccupied with personal fears and perceived sectional interests. Perhaps future South African elections will be more like this one. In the end, the Western Cape campaign had been less about great themes than about regional-minority politics—and a newly restricted sense of the possible.

The day after it became obvious that the ANC was going to lose in the Western Cape, I found Maqbool Moos in his apartment, watching television. 'Although I was pessimistic, I still feel a bit shit,' he said.

I asked about his plans.

'I could go into politics full-time,' he said. 'But that would nullify the whole question of fighting for the people. I'm a member of the ANC, but if the ANC steps out of line, I want to be the first to counter it. I think that I will stay outside and just give the ANC a massive headache.' He laughed ruefully.

Then he brought out a stack of photographs—black-and-white enlargements of scenes of street fighting with the police. 'Here's the time they arrested me by helicopter,' he said. 'That was 1989. And here's the march on Pollsmoor Prison in 1985. That was the start of the uprising that led to the state of emergency. Boesak got arrested that day. I got shot.' He lifted his shirt and showed me a scar. 'Just grazed.' Another rueful laugh. 'The good old days.'

GRANTA

Nelson Mandela
African Renaissance

In the distant days of antiquity, a Roman sentenced this African city of Tunis to death: *Carthago delenda est*; 'Carthage must be destroyed.' And Carthage was destroyed. Today we wander among its ruins. Only our imagination and historical records enable us to experience its magnificence; only our African being makes it possible for us to hear the piteous cries of the victims of the vengeance of the Roman Empire.

And yet we can say this: that all human civilization rests on foundations such as the ruins of the African city of Carthage. These architectural remains—like the pyramids of Egypt, the sculptures of the ancient kingdoms of Ghana and Mali and Benin, like the temples of Ethiopia, the ruins of Zimbabwe and the rock paintings of the Kgalagadi and Namib deserts—speak of Africa's contribution to the formation of civilization.

Carthage was destroyed. During the long interregnum, the children of Africa were carted away as slaves. Our lands became the property of other nations; our resources, a source of enrichment for other peoples; our kings and queens, mere servants of foreign powers.

In the end, we were held up as the outstanding example of the beneficiaries of charity, because we became the permanent victims of famine, destructive conflicts and the pestilences of the natural world. On our knees because history, society and nature had defeated us, we could be nothing but beggars. What the Romans sought with the destruction of Carthage had been achieved.

But the ancient pride of the peoples of our continent asserted itself and gave us hope in the form of giants such as Queen Regent Labotsibeni of Swaziland, Mohamed V of Morocco, Abdul Gamal Nasser of Egypt, Kwame Nkrumah of Ghana, Murtala Mohamed of Nigeria, Patrice Lumumba of Zaire, Amilcar Cabral of Guinea Bissau, Aghostino Neto of Angola, Eduardo Mondlane and Samora Machel of Mozambique, Seretse Khama of Botswana, W.E.B. Du Bois and Martin Luther King of America, Marcus Garvey of Jamaica, Albert Luthuli and Oliver Tambo of South Africa. By their deeds, by the struggles they led, these and many other patriots said to us that neither

This is adapted from a speech given at the Organization of African Unity meeting of heads of state on 13 June 1994.

Photo: Ian Berry (Magnum)

Carthage nor Africa had been destroyed. They conveyed the message that the long reign of humiliation was over.

The titanic effort that has brought liberation to South Africa and ensured the total liberation of Africa constitutes an act of redemption for the black people of the world. It is a gift of emancipation also to those who, because they are white, imposed on themselves the heavy burden of assuming the mantle of rulers of all humanity. It says to all who will listen that, by ending the apartheid barbarity that was the offspring of European colonization, Africa has, once more, contributed to the advance of human civilization and expanded the frontiers of liberty everywhere.

When the history of our struggle is written, it will be a glorious tale of African solidarity, of Africa's adherence to principle, of the sacrifices that the people of our continent made to ensure that the intolerable insult to human dignity, the apartheid crime against humanity, became a thing of the past. It will speak of the contribution to freedom—whose value is as immeasurable as the gold beneath the soil of our country—a contribution which all Africa made, from the shores of the Mediterranean in the north to the confluence of the Indian and Atlantic Oceans in the south.

Africa shed her blood and surrendered the lives of her children so that all her children could be free. She gave of her limited wealth and resources so that all of Africa should be liberated. She opened her heart of hospitality and her head so full of wise counsel so that we should emerge victorious. A million times she put her hand to the plough that has now dug up the encrusted burden of oppression, accumulated for centuries. The total liberation of Africa has now been achieved.

One epoch with its historic tasks has come to an end. Surely another must commence. Africa cries out for a new birth; Carthage awaits the restoration of its glory. If freedom was the crown which the fighters of liberation sought to place on the head of mother Africa, let the upliftment, the happiness, prosperity and comfort of her children be the jewel of the crown.

The fundamentals are known to all of us: Africa continues to be a net exporter of capital and suffers from deteriorating terms of trade. Our capacity for self-reliance, to find the resources to generate sustained development, remains very limited. Equally complex questions that bear on the nature and quality of government are also central to our capacity to produce the better life which our people demand and deserve. We must face the matter squarely that where there is something wrong in how we govern ourselves, it must be said that the fault is not in our stars, but in ourselves that we are ill governed.

Rwanda stands as a stern and severe rebuke to all of us for having failed to address these matters. As a result, a terrible slaughter of the innocent is taking place in front of our very eyes. Thus do we give reason to the peoples of the world to say of Africa that she will never know stability and peace, that she will forever experience poverty and dehumanization and that we shall be forever knocking on somebody's door pleading for a slice of bread. We know that we have it in ourselves, as Africans, to change all this. We must assert our will to do so. We must say that there is no obstacle big enough to stop us from bringing about an African renaissance.

It will never happen again that our country should seek to dominate another through force of arms, economic might or subversion. We are determined to remain true to the vision of a non-racial society, which asserts the ancient African values of respect for every person and commitment to human dignity, regardless of colour or race.

The objective we all pursued was the creation of a South Africa that would be a good neighbour and an equal partner with all the countries of our continent, one that would use its abilities and potential to advance the common struggle to secure Africa's rightful place within the world economic and political system. Thus must we build on the common victory of the total emancipation of Africa to obtain new successes for our continent as a whole and prevail over the currents that originate from the past, and ensure that the interregnum of humiliation symbolized by, among other things, the destruction of Carthage, is indeed consigned to the past, never to return.

God bless Africa.

Notes on Contributors

William Boyd's most recent novel was *The Blue Afternoon*. His screenplays include *Aunt Julia and the Scripwriter*, based on the novel by Mario Vargas Llosa; Richard Attenborough's *Chaplin*; and, most recently, *A Good Man in Africa*, based on his own novel. **Lynda Schuster**, a journalist, has reported from Central and South America, the Middle East and Africa for the *Wall Street Journal*. She is currently working on a book about a South African family. She lives in Mozambique. **Mark Doyle** reports for BBC. He has covered the crisis in Rwanda since before the war, and for a time was the only foreign journalist in Kigali. **Gilles Peress**'s *Farewell to Bosnia*, a book of photographs of the war in the former Yugoslavia, has just been published. He is a regular contributor to *Granta*. **Paul Theroux** was stationed in Malawi as a member of the Peace Corps from 1963 to 1965. In 1988, he returned to Ntakataka, but the Leper Mission—now that the 'last disease in Africa' has been eradicated—had been closed. He lives in Hawaii. **Sousa Jamba**'s novel *A Lonely Devil* was published last year. He is currently working on a third novel. **Ryszard Kapuściński**'s most recent book, *Imperium*, has just been published by Granta Books. During the sixties, he was the Polish Press Agency's sole representative in Africa. *The Emperor*, Kapuściński's first book published in English, is based on his experiences in Ethiopia, especially at the court of Haile Selassie. **Ahdaf Soueif** was born in Cairo and now lives in London. Her latest novel, *In the Eye of the Sun*, will be published in January. **Abraham Verghese** is professor of medicine at Texas Tech University, El Paso. His book *Soundings: A Doctor's Life in the Age of Aids* has just been published by Phoenix House in Britain and, under the title *My Own Country*, by Simon and Schuster in the United States. His previous contribution to *Granta* was in *Granta* 39, 'The Body'. **William Finnegan** is the author of *Crossing the Line: a Year in the Land of Apartheid* and *Dateline Soweto: Travels with Black South African Reporters*, both of which will be reissued by the University of California Press this year. His next book will be about race, poverty and the drug trade. **Nelson Mandela** is president of the Republic of South Africa.